A Garland Series

OUTSTANDING DISSERTATIONS IN THE

FINE ARTS

The Image of George Washington
Studies in Mid-Nineteenth-Century American History Painting

Mark Edward Thistlethwaite

Garland Publishing, Inc., New York & London

1979

All volumes in this series are printed
on acid-free, 250-year-life paper.

Library of Congress Cataloging in Publication Data

Thistlethwaite, Mark Edward, 1948-
    The image of George Washington.

    (Outstanding dissertations in the fine arts)
    Originally presented as the author's thesis,
University of Pennsylvania, 1977.
    Bibliography: p.
    Includes index.
    1. Painting, American. 2. Painting, Modern--19th
century--United States. 3. History in art.
4. Washington, George, Pres. U.S., 1732-1799--
Portraits, caricatures, etc. I. Title. II. Series
ND1441.5.T55 1979   757'.3'0973   78-74384
ISBN 0-8240-3970-X

Printed in the United States of America

This publication revises the author's 1977 dissertation by updating credit lines for reproductions, by changing the sizes of some reproductions and by correcting typographical errors. The author wishes to thank Frances Hard for her generous assistance.

THE IMAGE OF GEORGE WASHINGTON: STUDIES IN MID-NINETEENTH-CENTURY

AMERICAN HISTORY PAINTING

Mark Edward Thistlethwaite

A DISSERTATION

in

HISTORY OF ART

Presented to the Graduate Faculty of the University of Pennsylvania
in Partial Fulfillment of the Requirements for the
Degree of Doctor of Philosophy
1977

ACKNOWLEDGEMENTS

During the course of this dissertation a number of people significantly contributed to its progress and conclusion. I gratefully
acknowledge their aid.

My interest in history painting was generated by Professor John
W. McCoubrey, University of Pennsylvania. I am grateful for Professor
McCoubrey's constant support and his insightful comments and suggestions. In the early stages of research, Professor Arthur S. Marks,
University of North Carolina, greatly aided in giving direction to my
work. I gained much from correspondence and conversation with
Professor William H. Gerdts, City University of New York, who graciously
shared his vast knowledge of nineteenth-century American art. Professor Paul F. Watson, University of Pennsylvania kindly read my dissertation and offered numerous helpful suggestions. Several University
of Pennsylvania graduate students patiently listened to my ideas and
made thoughtful comments; especially helpful were Ms. Teri J.
Edelstein and Mr. Thomas P. Bruhn.

My research was made easier, and pleasurable, by: Ms. Elizabeth
R. Albro, Edison National Historic Site, Orange, New Jersey; Ms. Anne
Ricard Cassidy, Division for Historic Preservation, Waterford, New
York; Ms. Elizabeth H. Culler, Virginia Museum of Fine Arts, Richmond;
Mr. Thomas J. Dunnings, Jr., and Mr. William Asadorian, Manuscripts,

iii

The New-York Historical Society, New York; Mr. Frank H. Goodyear, Jr.,
The Pennsylvania Academy of the Fine Arts, Philadelphia; Mr. Philip
Harris, Sherburne, New York; Ms. Deborah Matlack, The Cooper Union for
the Advancement of Science and Art, New York; Mr. John C. Milley,
Independence National Historical Park, Philadelphia; Mr. Peter J.
Parker and Ms. Lucy Hrivnak, Manuscripts, The Historical Society of
Pennsylvania, Philadelphia; Mr. L. Corwin Sharp, Senate House State
Historical Site, Kingston, New York; Mrs. Lorraine Seay, The Henry Clay
Memorial Foundation, Lexington, Kentucky; Dr. Roberta Waddell, Prints
Division, The New York Public Library, New York; and Mr. M. M. Well-
brook, Secretary to Mr. Clarence Dillon, Far Hills, New Jersey.

Throughout this endeavor my family encouraged my efforts. I
owe a special debt of gratitude to Randi Thistlethwaite for reading
and listening to various drafts of this dissertation and for offering
valuable suggestions and observations.

TABLE OF CONTENTS

LIST OF ILLUSTRATIONS

xv

xvi

xvii

CHAPTER I

INTRODUCTION

Before beginning his verbal account of George Washington,
Uncle Juvinell, in Morrison Heady's 1864 book <u>The Farmer Boy, and
How He Became Commander-In-Chief</u>, removes from the wall a dusty old
picture of the hero, announcing to his young friends gathered about:
"This my cherubs is the portrait of the good and great George Washington, who is called the Father of our Country." After silently
studying the picture for some moments, the children speak:

"That scroll he holds in his left hand must be his farewell
address to his army," said Daniel, the young historian, looking
very wise.
"What a fine long sword he carries at his side!" said Bryce,
a war-like youngster . . . .
"How tall and grand and handsome he looks!" said Laura, a
prim and demure little miss of thirteen, "in his presence, I
am sure I could never speak above a whisper."
"That, yonder, among the trees and evergreens on the hill,
must be the house where he lived," said Ellen, a modest, sweet-
mannered little lady of twelve. "What a beautiful place it is!
and what a happy home it must have been when he lived in it! . .
"And such a pretty play-house as I see there among the
bushes in the hillside!" said Fannie, a stout little matron of
five, the mother of a large and still increasing family of
dolls.
"That is not a play-house, Fannie, but the tomb where
Washington lies buried," said Dannie with an air of superior
wisdom.
"What a splendid white horse that black man is holding for
him! How he bows his neck, and champs his bit, and paws the
ground!" said Willie, a harum-scarum, neck-or-nothing young
blade of fourteen . . .
"How kind and good he looks out of his eyes, just like

1

father!" said Mary, an affectionate and timid little creature of seven.

Finally, after all have commented upon it, the picture is returned to its "accustomed place."[1]

Heady's usage of the Washington picture (which cannot be identified) and the various reactions it causes delightfully illustrates the role art played in perpetuating the real and the mythic image of the hero. The consideration of that role forms the topic of my dissertation.

Extensive scholarly thought has been given to landscape and genre painting as embodying an American spirit. However, the most obviously national form--visual images of American history--has received relatively little attention.[2] This situation is somewhat surprising considering the extent to which such art has shaped our image of the past. American history painting of the nineteenth century has occupied a sort of "ugly duckling" position compared to the other art forms of the time. A certain disdain for narrative, especially patriotic, works has, in large part, caused historical art to be shunned. Quantitatively, history paintings are less numerous than portrait, genre and landscape paintings. And, admittedly, the quality of much American history painting is low. I will not attempt to argue these points (except to indicate how many more history paintings exist than is generally realized and how the quality, if not first-rate, is often quite solid), nor to apotheosize history painting. Rather I shall consider the nature of and rationale for such art in America. Works of both a popular and a "high art" level will be discussed, as both contributed to the visual concretization of American history. Since the subject is vast certain limitations have been imposed: the study is primarily concerned with images (paintings and prints) of George Washington; the period to be investigated is the middle decades of the nineteenth century, 1840-70. Washington is studied because he is the Great American Hero. The history of America is the history of Washington. The period 1840-70 is emphasized because it is during these years that the greatest number of nineteenth-century paintings of American history were executed. The seventy-fifth anniversary of the Declaration of Independence and various Revolutionary events helped sustain a concern for the past. The era is also characterized by a great interest in Washington. His image appears on the first adhesive postage stamp in 1847; the cornerstone of his Monument is laid in 1848; in 1850, the Senate passed a well-publicized motion to purchase the manuscript of his Farewell Address; February 22 officially became a national holiday in 1857; Mount Vernon was finally saved for restoration purposes in 1858 after five years of intense campaigning and fund-raising; and throughout the age Washington was continually invoked as a symbol of Union. As an 1853 journal succinctly states: "Eventthing that concerns the great Virginia chief must be forever interesting."[3]

In returning to the account of Uncle Juvinell and the picture of Washington, it becomes apparent that at least five interrelated aspects common to Washington imagery are acknowledged in the author's

handling of the scene: accessibility; legibility; didacticism; appropriateness of past for present; the multi-sided quality of the hero's
life. By discussing each of these traits, an understanding of the
visual representations of George Washington, and of American history,
can be gained.

In the context of mid-nineteenth century America, Uncle Juvenill's
picture of Washington hanging on the walls of his home "somewhere in
green Kentucky" is not at all surprising, and indicates the popularity
and physical accessibility of such images.

The high visibility of pictures and prints of Washington impressed
the Russian observer Pavel Svinin who commented long before mid-
century (1811): "It is noteworthy that every American considers it
his sacred duty to have a likeness of Washington in his house, just
as we have images of God's Saints."[4] An article in the American
Magazine of March, 1836, proudly claimed that "prints of Washington,
dark with smoke are pasted over the hearths of so many American houses.
And long may he be there!"[5] Paintings and prints provide visual
documentation of the validity of these statements: the hero appears
in the center of the composition above the fireplace in John Lewis
Krimmel's Quilting Frolic of 1813, Francis William Edmonds's 1854
Taking the Census and the 1866 lithograph Home Again (figs. 1-3).
Cheap prints and paintings executed by itinerant artists made Washington's image accessible to all households. Further, such non-
domestic institutions as taverns, put the hero's countenance before

the people (figs.4, 5).

Of all the representations of Washington, the most familiar is, undoubtedly, Gilbert Stuart's "Athenaeum" portrait of 1796 (fig. 6). Reproduced scores of times by the artist himself and in hundreds of prints, the "Athenaeum" type assumed such elevated status that as early as 1823, a character in John Neal's novel Randolph remarked: "If George Washington should appear on earth, just as he sat to Stuart, I am sure that he would be treated as an impostor, when compared with Stuart's likeness of him, unless he produced his credentials."[6] While numerous paintings of Washington had relied on the delineations of Stuart's image, no better indication of the celebrity and mythic level attained by that icon exists than C. H. Schmolze's 1858 Washington Sitting for His Portrait to Gilbert Stuart (fig. 7).

Schmolze, who came to the United States from Germany in 1854,[7] portrays Stuart commencing a portrait of the president. The small ensemble, circularly arranged, shows the artist at his easel, Mrs. Washington, a young woman (probably Jane Custis, Mrs. Washington's daughter), an army officer (Henry Knox?) and Washington, who sits at the apex of the composition. Scrutinized by the thoughtful officer, the president appears nobly aloof and, in his physical and "spiritual" presence, above the situation. Behind and over Washington's head hangs richly brocaded drapes, functioning as a Baroque canopy. Busts and paintings belonging to the artist occupy the upper reaches of the chamber. Casting Stuart in the role of official court painter, Schmolze renders a well-dressed, almost aristocratic, group in a

sumptuous studio space. Stuart, rather condenscendingly, speaks with
Mrs. Washington. She commissioned the portrait later known as the
"Athenaeum" version. Barely visible to the viewer, a rudimentary
delineation of the portrait appears on the artist's canvas. Schmolze's
painting then re-creates the birth of Stuart's icon.[8]

In depicting an event from American art history, Schmolze's
painting shows several levels of interest. The work reflects the mid-
century's veneration of George Washington. The "domestic "nature of
the scene undoubtedly pleased contemporary taste. The painting also
functions as a homage to Gilbert Stuart as the creator of an image
destined to perpetuate in an iconic fashion the fame of the hero.
Schmolze's apotheosis echoes a popular journal's 1853 remarks on the
"Athenaeum" portrait: "The noble head, that hand that traced the lineaments, have long ago crumbled into dust; but the genius of both is
enshrined on the canvass."[9] By honoring Stuart as the originator of
such a celebrated and influential masterpiece, Schmolze, in essence,
elevated his own profession.[10] At a time when the importance of the
artist as a recorder of history was being emphasized, the appearance
of Washington Sitting for His Portrait to Gilbert Stuart seems hardly
fortuitous.

In the inaugural address before the Washington Art Association
in February, 1858, Horatio Stone proclaimed: "The commemorative
period of the nation's history has arrived . . . ."[11] Four months later,
a Congressional committee, responding to an artists's petition, stated:
"Painting and sculpture are the handmaidens of history . . . ."[12] The
middle decades of the century witnessed great interest in paintings

of American history, with this phenomenon intensifying in the years
1857 to 1860. In 1857, the Federal Government offered the renown
French artist Horace Vernet a commission for a historical work to
be placed in the Capitol. This upset   American artists who were
already disenchanted with the Capitol extension decoration then being
carried out by the Italian fresco painter Constantino Brumidi.[13]
Criticism of Brumidi's work focussed on its "foreign-ness;" the Cosmopolitan Art Journal said his frescoes of the battles of Lexington
and Bunker Hill show "at a glance that they are the work of foreigners,
to whom the countenances, costumes, and character of the men of the
Revolution were not familiar. They have no nationality about them;
whereas, nationality is, above all things, to be desired in decorating
the National Capitol."[14] The resentment of foreigners receiving
patronage American artists regarded as their just due peaked in 1858,
with artists meeting in Washington, D.C., and formally memorializing
Congress of their grievances.[15] Much debate, duly reported by the
various art journals, ensued over the validity of employing non-native
artists for the depiction of national scenes. Given this situation,
an underlying content, very personal in nature, may be comprehended
in Schmolze's work. In selecting such a scene from American history,
the European-born artist may have intended his painting to show his
respect for American art accomplishments as well as his ability, even
though a foreigner, to render a national subject successfully. Whatever the strength of this interpretation, it is certainly secondary

to the more obvious and important meaning of Schmolze's work as an expression and reflection of the potency of Gilbert Stuart's image of Washington.

Aside from the popular print or painting depicting the hero which the typical household might possess, his visual image was also accessible through large numbers of illustrated books. James Thomas Flexner has noted how history painting, although the "high style," was, because of its narrative quality (and, one must add, its patriotic, moral didacticism), admirably suited to popular illustration.[16] Contemporaries often put it more bluntly; Godey's Lady's Book of September 1846, for instance, noted that no facilities for art existed for art in this country, therefore, art "necessarily takes on a popular form."[17] The magazine continued:

> . . . those who in Europe would have been engaged for years on a philosophical work or an historical painting, become in America writers of newspaper paragraphs and magazine articles and portrait painters or illustrators of annuals.[18]

Often the illustrations in books were after paintings by well-known artists: Thomas Sully's Washington at the Passage of the Delaware of 1819 (fig. 73) was regularly reproduced, being replaced in 1851, by Emanuel Leutze's version of the subject (fig. 72). Other times, the embellishments were the work of such prolific and popular illustrators as Alonzo Chappel and Felix O. C. Darley. Biographies of Washington were commonly illustrated; J. T. Headley, John Frost and Benson J. Lossing all produced books (in 1859, 1857, and 1870, respectively) which offered the "pictorial life of Washington." General histories of the United States which included drawings, contained illustrations of the hero: the history of Washington was the history of the new nation. Similarly, school readers as well as the hundreds of books aimed at children, such as Horatio Hastings Weld's Life of Washington (1845) and Entertaining Anecdotes of Washington (1846), reinforced their texts with illustrations. In addition to books, journals provided another avenue for the dissemination of the image of Washington. As with books, illustrations in periodicals were often after celebrated works of art. Godey's Lady's Book, the Columbian Magazine, Graham's Magazine, and Sartain's Magazine are only a few among the scores of journals which made readily available to large numbers of people visual representations of Washington.

Scenes of Washington's life and of American history reached a broad audience through the medium of inexpensive prints published by firms like Currier and Ives, and as premiums offered by the many art-unions in existence in the 1840s and 1850s. These art-unions were particularly important because they tended to stress and encourage the depiction of national subjects and their influence pervaded the country. Their wide dissemination of art effectively democraticized art, as well as aiding in the securing of an American identity.

Regular exhibitions of art at the National Academy of Design, the Pennsylvania Academy of the Fine Arts, and the American-Art Union further allowed accessibility to images of Washington. Although proportionately small in numbers at such annual exhibitions, historical art generally received, because of its subject, much coverage in reviews and newspaper accounts of the shows. Besides the annual affairs, the artist might undertake to exhibit a single painting on his own. The showing of individual works was usually well-publicized (the artist, after all, was engaging in a commercial venture). Paintings shown in this manner included Thomas Sully's Washington's Passage of the Delaware, John Trumbull's The Resignation of Washington, Emanuel Leutze's Washington Crossing the Delaware and Thomas P. Rossiter's Washington and Lafayette at Mount Vernon.

The visual form of Washington also entered into the mainstream of American society by way of stamps and currency. These items often appropriated images of the hero for their embellishment. The 1847 ten-cent postage stamp (the first adhesive stamp issued in this country), featured a Stuart portrait of Washington. In the pre-Civil War years, state, municipal and private banks provided their own notes. These regularly depicted Washington. The practice of picturing the hero on money continued when the United States Government began to issue currency in 1861.

Exhibitions, books, prints and stamps made the "Father of his Country" overwhelmingly accessible during the middle decades of the nineteenth century. As an 1854 writer noted: "In all branches of Art and in all shapes of Literature, WASHINGTON is now the leading subject--dwelt upon in essay, oratory and poetry, and represented in er.graving, painting and marble."[19]

Images of George Washington reached a wide audience not only because of their physical accessibility, but also their legibility.

"Legibility" here means an image's readily comprehensible formal and content. The youngsters looking at Uncle Juvinell's picture could easily comment on the work because of its legibility.

Paralleling, and, in fact, partially influenced by popular European writers and artists like John Ruskin and Paul Delaroche, American history paintings of the middle decades achieved their formal legibility through a realistic style. Emphasis was placed on the "truthfulness" of the form. The roots of this aesthetic traced back to the Death of Wolfe (1770; fig. 8) by Benjamin West, the first American artist to achieve international fame. Although the so-called "revolution" in history painting occasioned by this work has been questioned and discussed extensively,[20] no doubt existed in the minds of nineteenth-century Americans that West had radically altered the nature of the art. American literature perpetuated the 1820 account of West's biographer, John Galt, of how the American, much to the critical consternation of Sir Joshua Reynolds, "the" arbiter of taste, painted his contemporary figures in modern costume, eschewing the traditional and universal garb of antiquity. Despite the dramatic decline in West's reputation after his death (with writers scornfully reproaching his art as where "badness may be estimated by the acre"[21]) Americans proudly acknowledged his role as the originator of the modern history piece. Repeatedly, West's "revolution" was interpreted as evidence of the bold spirit of American pragmatism: the American artist paints what he knows to be real. West, as has often been pointed out, tempered his realism by arranging the dying Wolfe and

attendants into a Pietà and was historically unfaithful in other
details. However, thanks to this combination of the real and the
ideal, this much-publicized painting can be seen as a first step in
the direction of increased realism in history painting. John Singleton Copley, in works like his Death of Chatham (1781), contributed
even more to the appearance of reportage in historical art, although
Copley never received the recognition West did in the nineteenth century. These two Americans, West and Copley, laid the foundations for
the devaluation of the ideal form of history painting, accomplished
in the nineteenth century. Neither of the two artists would, however,
have probably approved the genre-like quality of many mid-century
paintings. But the issue of truthfulness to reality, which became
so important for the nineteenth-century painter, was incipient in the
works of Copley and West. Truthfulness became doctrinal in the nineteenth century. For West and Copley, it had been ancillary to the
universal ideals of their painting; for later artists, ideals were
only expressible through the truthfulness of the forms.

Adherence to reality became a major, if not the most significant, criterion of mid-century history painting. Despite the oft-
repeated American penchant for factuality, realism in art was not a
local phenonmenon. European art also stressed the concrete reality
of the event.[22] This desire for truthfulness can be, and was then,
understood as indicative of the materialist bent of the era; an age,
noted the Austrian traveler Francis J. Grund in 1837, of "reason, not
belief."[23] In America and Europe, art (not just history paintings,

but other forms as well) was conditioned by and aimed to attain a sense
of the real, the actual. Hence, the continuing popularity of portraiture in the United States throughout the nineteenth century. As an
epoch of increasing democratization, the early and mid-century's
artistic bias toward truthfulness can be interpreted as an extension
and reflection of the society's democratic spirit. In America, Jack-
sonian democracy, as well as the interest in genre painting, helped
create a climate favorable for anecdotal history painting. Thus, in
1831, Jacob Eichholtz, a major portraitist of the Philadelphia area,
could paint a work like An Incident of the Revolution (fig. 9), which
presents, in genre-like fashion, an insignificant historical event.
One of the earliest, if not the first, to cast the hero in a less than
heroic role, Eichholtz's painting shows George Washington in an amusing
situation. The incident depicted involves the mistaking of General
Charles Lee, wearing a tattered and unkempt uniform, for a common
vagrant. A servant-girl puts him to work for his victuals, and while
he is acting as a scullion, Washington and other officers come upon the
scene. Lee explains his station by showing Washington his disheveled
outfit. The humorous intentions of of Eichholtz's work clearly outweigh
its moral quality. Since the painting involves known historical
participants, it renders history as genre, rather than as
historical genre (a depiction of anonymous people of the past).
As shall be discussed further in Chapters II and IV, this representation of history came to mark mid-century historical art. This realistic,
even genre, treatment of history appeared not only in the United
States, but also in Europe, particularly in France as part of the

Bourbon restoration.

The realist bias propagated by the Death of Wolfe was implicit in an 1827 writer's definition of history painting:

> The Historic . . . portrays a fact, not an event; Its characters may be ideal, provided truth is observed in time, place, and custom, and that it reveals an event which has happened . . .[24]

This emphasis on truthfulness opposed the traditional ideal of history painting, and, despite a mid-century respect for Reynolds ("the best works on art that were ever written are Sir Joshua Reynolds"s desultory Notes and Discourses"),[25] the concern for factuality was fundamentally anti-Reynoldsian. An 1847 article reproved the English artist and taste-maker for his injunction "to avoid details and individual character;" the writer arguing that truth in details was as necessary as general effect in making a painting successful.[26] John Gadsby Chapman, a well-known history painter of the middle decades, received praise for the faithful representation in his painting The Retreat to Fort Necessity (1843):

> The general colour of the picture may be remarked as cool; but, it will be remembered, that the occurrence took place in early spring, and the artist has preferred to sacrifice what advantages he might have obtained by the introduction of the full tints to the truth of history: a practice worthy of all limitation.[27]

A quest for historical fidelity, even at the expense of aesthetic form, distinguished his art. Describing Chapman's painting for the United States Capitol Rotunda, Baptism of Pocahontas (fig. 10), a critic noted:

> In the execution of the picture, the artist has been governed

by the best authorities as to facts and details, and has made all the research within his power, in England as well as in our country, for information with regard to the subject; and in some points he may have sacrificed the picturesque for the sake of historical truth, to which he has endeavored to adhere.[28]

Robert W. Weir's Rotunda painting drew similar praise. Countering a criticism of the work being too cold and repulsive, Charles Lanman, landscapist and sometime-critic, lauded Weir's Embarkation of the Pilgrims (fig. 11) for successfully conveying the Puritan ambience.[29] An artist, then, may have to "sacrifice" an eye-pleasing composition for a historically honest rendering, but, in the end, he would have created a more significant work.

Painters who disregarded factual details drew suitable reprimand for their negligence. Asher B. Durand's The Capture of Major André (fig. 12) received negative notice because one of the captors appeared:

an affected fine gentleman, instead of what he really was, a rough and not particularly sensitive, but honest yeoman-ranger, who would be more likely to answer a bribe with a flow, than to throw himself into a stage position about it.[30]

Writers directed numerous devastating comments at William Powell's Rotunda painting Discovery of the Mississippi by DeSoto (1853; fig. 13) for its lack of veracity. A "fanciful creation," looking "like a triumphful entry into Madrid of the conquerors of an El Dorado--not the end of the exploration of a homesick and wretched band," an 1860 article described the composition.[31] The Albion of 1853, liked the subject of Powell's work, but faulted the painting because: "A great artist would have adhered to the strict facts of the case."[32]

Achieving truthfulness, "the alpha and omega of art," claimed an 1850
journal,[33] became an aim history painters shared with historical
writers.

A longstanding connection between history painters and writers
of history existed prior to mid-century. Jonathan Richardson had
observed that a history painter most possess the traits of a historian.[34] Similar remarks, perhaps influenced by the eighteenth-century
Richardson, frequently appeared in mid-nineteenth century commentaries
on art. Graham's Magazine of 1843, asserted that: "To falsify the
truth of history in painting is no less a crime, if willful, no less
proof of total incapacity, if accidental, in an artist, than the same
defects would be in a writer . . . "[35] Commenting a decade later on
Powell's much-maligned Discovery of the Mississippi by DeSoto, a
Putnam's Magazine writer protested the work's "falsification of history"
by stating:

> What if Mr. Headley, or any other of our popular writers, should
> be employed to write a description of the landing of the Pilgrims,
> for instance, and should for the sake of making an agreeable
> thing of it, make the Pilgrim rock a sapphire, and line the
> coast of Massachusetts bay with groves of palm and olive trees,
> while Miles Standish and his companions were described as dressed
> in the costume of Charles the Second's court at masquerade. It
> would be very absurd, to be sure, and every body would condemn
> it as a libel upon truth and nature; but it would be no greater
> departure from fact than Mr. Powell's representation of DeSoto and
> his companions.[36]

If the painter strived to resemble a historian, then the historian
aimed to be "a limner, a painter, a creator," with "the picture [glow-
ing] beneath his hand."[37] David Levin has treated this issue,[38] noting how romantic historians, like George Bancroft and William Prescott

(from whom artists often drew), considered themselves painters. James

Hubard so felt the correlation between historical writing and history

painting, and the burden of truth, that he felt obliged to admit to

taking a risk in painting Philip of Mt. Hope Rescuing the Body of One

of His Chiefs, an incident not found in a book "and perhaps therefore

not esteemed legitimate."[39] Hubard's remark implies that the apprecia-

tion of a history painting depended upon the familiarity of the subject

to his audience. The public was generally well-read in history, and

contemporary accounts indicate that historical art was commonly com-

pared to the relevant historical text. In discussing John Gadsby

Chapman's The Desertion of Sergeant Champe (fig. 14), the New York

Mirror of 1837, remarked that the artist had "represented this incident

with great truth and spirit, and the spectator who has read Lee's

Memoirs (that is, the American Lee), will derive great pleasure from

contemplating the picture."[40] The Crayon correspondent "D. E." des-

cribed, in 1855, how, as a boy, he had marveled at John Trumbull's

Rotunda paintings, noting:

> . . . 'Washington Resigning his Commission' completely absorbed
> me, and I fancied I could hear his touching words fall in solemn
> accents from his lips. I was then fresh from school, and the
> account of the whole scene, as related in 'Grimshaw's History'
> was familiar to me.[41]

Exhibition catalogues usually included the relevant passage from a

history to describe the painting's subject. In applying for a com-

mission from the American Art-Union in 1847, Junius Brutus Stearns,

a prominent mid-century history painter then beginning his career, sent

a sketch of the proposed work (Washington in the Indian Council), as

well as an extract from a related historical document (Washington's
journal) which elucidated the subject. Robert W. Weir, in an 1837
letter to the New York art patron Gulian Verplanck, mentioned that, in
seeking our subjects he had just finished the second volume of Ramsey's
History.[42] While artists commonly relied on history books in their
search for appropriate subjects and historical veracity, and although
art and literature were viewed as kindred spirits, basic differences
existed between the two media.

Compared to literature, painting possessed little "latitude";
painting lacked "the advantage of repeated and progressive impressions."[43]
Washington Allston claimed that in the rendering of a battle "the poet
and the historian have the advantage of the painter," for they can
represent the sustained action and noise inherent in warfare.[44] However, not all critics and artists accepted these views, and often turned
them around to the benefit of the painter. An 1807 writer asserted:
"By a single Coup d'aeil [sic], may be seen and comprehended what
wolumns [sic] vould [sic] be unable to effect."[45] Mid-century Americans
often voiced variations of this sentiment. Citing Emanuel Leutze's
Washington Crossing the Delaware, an 1851 article "proved" the superiority of art over literature because of art's power to present in
one view, the multitude of associations which made up the event.[46]
The writer calls John Marshall's famous early nineteenth-century
biography of the hero "tame" compared to the painting and asserts
that a half-hour study of the painting will teach more than years of
reading.[47] Reverend Henry Bacon, writing in the popular mid-century

journal <u>Gleason's Pictorial Drawing-Room Companion</u>, essentially, agrees

with these ideas, stating:

> The same circle of friends who could endure history read but a
> brief while, can be held together for hours by the conversations
> which arise from pictures of the same facts and scenes . . . And
> how the craving for pictures abounds is evident from the fact
> that those historians <u>will be</u> preferred, who are the most suc-
> cessful in making word-pictures . . . [48]

Despite a lack of accord concerning the relative merits of history

painting and historical writing, ultimately an unresolvable issue,

contemporary documents indicate the close and supportive relationship

between the two. A quest for truth and a desire to visualize the

past linked history painters and writers of history.

The emphasis placed on truthfulness in history painting

is further witnessed by the American admiration for the French artist

Paul Delaroche. During the late 1840s and through the 1850s, American

writings on art roundly praised Delaroche for his works's factuality.

The purchase of a version of his <u>Napoleon Crossing the Alps</u> (fig. 15)

by Woodbury Langdon of New York in 1849, merited much favorable press.

Compared to Jacques-Louis David's famous earlier painting of the same

historical moment (fig. 16), Delaroche's exhibited "literal

realities."[49] An 1853 writer claimed: "Painters in dealing with

history have no more right to take such liberties with facts than

writers have. But they will, excepting those of a higher class, like

Delaroche."[50] In an 1856 review of a Delaroche painting at Goupil

and Company in New York, a journalist observed: "At present, the mere

mention of Delaroche will draw a crowd."[51] Although Americans admired

other artists of the French School, such as Ary Scheffer and Horace
Vernet, Delaroche captured the most acclaim, largely due to his
adherence to facts. The popularity of this painter reflected the
American belief in veracity as a key factor in history painting;
his art reinforced American notions.

Exhibitions, engravings and regluar art journal coverage
made the work of the French artists known. Their art, like that of
the celebrated Düsseldorf School, served as models for American
artists. For example, at least twice in the career of respected
illustrator Alonzo Chappel (who always strived for historical
authenticity), two compositions appear which are after well-known
works by Vernet and Delaroche(figs. 17-20).

Artists achieved legibility not only through the formal
means of realism, but also by their choice of subject. The history
painter, to be successful, had to select a scene comprehensible to
his public; hence, paintings of American history were deemed most
appropriate, and during the middle decades such representations
reached their zenith in American art history. By 1840, Americans
had developed a sense of history sufficient to claim: " . . . we
now have a glorious past, and it is time for us to value and venerate
it."[52] No doubt existed in the minds of Americans concerning their
history's uniqueness; America was conceived of as the New World, the
New Eden, and the beginning of a new history. While this stress
of "newness" caused many Americans, particularly in the spirit of
Manifest Destiny, to look forward rather than back, the assertive

nationalism of the age moved one speaker to announce that the United
States "is the richest country in the world . . . in historical events
for the pencil of the painter."[53] Given such beliefs, it became easy
to place subject matter over form: " . . . faults in execution will
be more readily pardoned, when the subject selected is colonial or
national, than when it is foreign or classical;" remarked a writer in
1849.[54] Of John Trumbull it was said: "He was gifted with no powers
of lofty conception, nor beauty of disposition. His subjects dignified
his performances."[55] This elevated status of subjects from American
history characterized an 1851 Bulletin of American Art-Union article,
where the writer indicated the national appeal of such paintings:

> . . . we find Vanderlyn painting Marius on the ruins of Carthage,
> when with the same feeling and power, he might have painted a
> Washington in his reverses, and thus rendered a vital page in
> our history that would have borne the artist's name, and endeared
> him to the people, forever. The fact that third-rate painters
> have been so eager to seize such subjects, deters many of the
> better ones from taking them--they seek to establish an aristoc-
> racy of art, forgetting that it is by its very nature democratic.
> The success of these third-raters, owing entirely to their choice
> of subjects, should have taught them the power of the popular
> theme.[56]

Despite erring in his claim that first-rate artists were not depicting
American historical events, the writer does correctly evince the
popularity of such representations at mid-century, a prevalency owed
to their psycholgical accessibility.

While nationalistic sentiment called for the extolment of
uniqueness, the lack of a material basis to substantiate the claim of
American superiority vexed early nineteenth-century Americans. An

interpretation then developed, originating in American Puritanism, which comprehended the history of the United States as Providentially-blessed and, consequently, exemplary of the highest moralism.[57] George Bancroft, for example, held this point of view, and his immensely popular history of the United States was followed by school textbooks as "the" authority on American history.[58]

The moral exemplar quality of American history allowed the artist to overcome charges that the brevity of the American past rendered history painting impossible. Some felt that a patina had not yet formed on American history--"Her history has scarcely outlived her oldest inhabitant . . . ," stated the Literary World of 1848.[59] Gulian Verplanck noted that America "has not, like the history of the old world, the charm of classical or romantic associations, and it bends itself with difficulty and without grace, to the purpose of poetry and fiction [and he might well have added the visual arts]."[60] Verplanck, however, justifies its representation in terms which characterized the American image of history--"But in ethical instruction, in moral dignity it has no equal."[61] Similarly, Francis F. Marbury, rhetorically asked the audience of the American Art-Union in 1845: "Are not our annals, breif though they may be, pregnant with deeds of highest heroism, sublimest import, and true historic dignity?"[62] The virtuous nature of American history nullified deficiencies like lack of "classical or romantic associations." Seba Smith, in 1843, claimed:

Talk as you will of the heroic days of Greece and Rome, you may

look in vain for brighter examples of human sympathy of sublime
self-devotion, than are to be found in the annals of the rude
aborigines of our own country.[63]

Addressing the American Art-Union in 1844, John Jay chauvinistically

asserted that:

. . . if the painters and sculptors of Greece, found no difficulty
in selecting subjects for this end [moral elevation and patriot-
ism], subjects for their easels and their chisels, the painters
and sculptors of America need not be at a loss in choosing from
our brief history, scenes of moral grandeur and heroism, unsur-
passed by any that have lent such imperishable lustre to the
Athenian name.[64]

Albert G. Remington triumphantly stated in 1851: "Though we have no

Marathon, Thermopylae, Agincourt of Cressy, we have Saratoga, Bunker

Hill and Monmouth."[65] Indeed, an earlier writer, speaking of the

Revolution, had proclaimed: "It is doubtful if any other event in

the history of the nations called forth so many heroic deeds, so many

noble virtues, and so many sublime sentiments . . . "[66] Scholarly

and popular literature successfully mythologized the truncated past

into a history superior to that of any other nation.[67] Works of

art integrally figured in this process with double potency, as they

not only visualized the exemplary nature of American history, but

they also represented the most elevated branch of art.

The exalted status of history painting, derived from Leon

Battista Alberti and filtered through Joshua Reynolds, continually

resounded during the middle period of the nineteenth century. The

New York Mirror of 1841, confirmed history painting as the standard

of exellence by which the state of the arts was to be judged.[68] The

widespread proliferation of this idea is witnessed by an article in

the Pittsburg Chronicle, which matter-of-factly notes that historical

painting "is recognized as the highest department of art."[69] Little
doubt existed in mid-century America that: "Historical painting, to
which common comment allots the first position in the various depart-
ments of art, is justly first . . . "[70]

History painting enjoyed exalted status because of its form
and content. The history painter aimed: "Nobly to conceive a great
event or a touching scene of history."[71] Miss Ludlow summarized the
traditional conception and requirements of history painting in her
1851 book on art:

> Historical painting is the noblest and most comprehensive
> branch of the art, as it embraces man, the head of the visible
> creation. The historical painter, therefore, must study man,
> from the anatomy of his figure, to the most rapid and slightest
> gesture expressive of feeling, or the display of deep and subtle
> passions. He must have technical skill, a practised eye and hand,
> and must understand so to group his skilfully executed parts as
> to produce a beautiful whole. And all this is insufficient with-
> out a poetic spirit, which can form a striking conception of his-
> torical events, or create imaginary scenes of beauty. Long and
> patient cultivation both of the taste and the mechanical means
> of execution, are indispensable; for though a lively imagination
> may easily invent interesting scenes, how difficult is it for
> the inexperienced artist to present in visible forms that which
> he had thought perfectly distance in his own mind. To obtain
> this skill, requires long practice, both in designing and colour-
> ing; the artist must have executed numerous studies, be familiar
> with the best models of art, and above all with the Protean
> forms of Nature.[72]

Few paintings in mid-century America, however, attained the grand
manner. Aware of this condition, apologists cited the lack of museums
to provide proper examples, the lack of academies to teach the requisite
study of the figure, and the lack of institutional patronage as factors
that impeded the development of "High Art." Writers also ascribed the
large size associated with history painting as a hindrance in a society

predominantly middle class. A contemporary of Miss Ludlow cynically,
yet accurately, accounted for the failure of the grand style in
America:

> The acquisition of the necessary knowledge for historical paint-
> ing is both troublesome and unproductive, and but very few men
> of sound mind willingly embrace so much labour and anxiety, when
> the events of each hour prove that he is most successful who
> is most ignorant, and that he is most honoured who is most suc-
> cessful.[73]

Of course, the realist inclination of the age generally, and American
conceptions of history specifically, argued against the ideal form
of history painting. Even in a heroic image like Emanuel Leutze's Washington Crossing the Delaware, realism conditions idealism. By mid-
century, the "revolution" initiated by Benjamin West was complete:
realism was tempered by idealism, rather than the reverse. Yet,
despite this lack of the grand manner, paintings of American history,
because of the subject itself, remained exempla virtutis, a quality
of the "highest branch of the art." This especially described
visualizations of George Washington, for as Charles Burroughs, a
Portsmouth rector, claimed in 1832: "It pleased the Supreme Being
to favour this nation with his [Washington's] valor, virtue and bright
example . . . "[74] The Bulletin of the American Art-Union reflected
the mid-century regard for Washington when it remarked in an 1851
article:

> Is the heart of our people stirred by no deep, universal, gen-
> uine impulse, noble enough to be embodied in Art? Is there
> no ideal of unsullied patriotism, inflexible justice, the high-
> est wisdom blended with the rarest modesty, and the most unequaled
> courage and perseverance, to which thousands and tens of thousands
> of our people are striving to give adequate expression? We

believe there is, and that it is afforded by the Character of
Washington. The reverential love of Americans for that character
is so deep and so widespread, that the artist who can respond to
it and interpret it--who can show us the lineaments of our
hero in such a way as to satisfy our conceptions of the grandeur
of this nature and his position--will receive honors equal to
those which attended the greatest of the ancient masters.[75]

Washington was the great exemplum virtutis for America, and any work

of art in which he figured, whether grand or anecdotal, possessed a

morally didactic possibility.

Invoking his didactability, writers often spoke of the hero

in artistic terms. Authors described his "symmetry" or character

and likened his simple grandeur and stability to a Greek temple.

Washington as a divine work of art was expressed by James K. Paulding:

"He is a great work of the almighty Artist, which none can study

without receiving purer ideas and more lofty conceptions of the grace

and beauty of the human character."[76]

When Uncle Juvinell placed the picture of the hero before the

children, his motives were primarily didactic. Insight was to be

gained into the Washington's character and history by means of the

visual image. Such a usage of art is doubly expressed (once for the

compositional figures and once for the viewer) in Francis William

Edmonds's The Image Peddler (1844; fig. 21), where a man points to

a cheap plaster bust of Washington for the edification of a child.

As the educational system and school textbooks of the era indicate,

the moulding of children into responsible and patriotic citizens was

a primary goal of the middle decades, and no finer model for the child

to follow existed than that of Washington. In the preface of the

1845 Life of George Washington (from the "Young American Library Series"), the author declared: "The first word of infancy should be mother, the second father, and the third WASHINGTON. Through life, his glorious example should be constantly before the citizen to animate and encourage him in the performance of duty."[77] This attitude is superbly embodied in an illustration in John Frost's Pictorial Life of George Washington (1857; fig. 22). Here the child pays homage to his moral model by reverently hugging a bust of the "Father of his Country." That the illustration reflected cultural values is witnessed by two contemporary photographs by Southworth and Hawes (fig. 23) and Gabriel Harrison (fig. 24). Originally published in 1844, Frost's book very likely provided the source for the Harrison photograph. All three evince the same feeling of ancester/hero-worship as well as recording Washington as the New World exemplum virtutis.

One of the risks in depicting American history involved chauvinistic, didactic overkill. An 1846 article warned that:

> . . . the partiotic artist will sometimes err in his design
> through an excess of patriotism, and present us the revered
> image of our Washington in undignified and affected attitudes.
> He will be engaged, like a symbolical figure of some Hindoo
> Diety, in doing one thing with one hand and something else
> with the other; he will point to heaven with one finger, and to
> his sword or the earth with the other; so that we wish him
> provided with several more of those graceful organs, to perform
> as many symbolical actions . . .[78]

The artist of the mid-century intended then to visualize in a readily comprehensible fashion, realism, a familiar subject, American history, which by its very nature, expressed a high morality, creating a work imbued with an elevated didactic sensibility.

It is axiomatic that each generation interprets history in terms of its own needs and expectations (just as Uncle Juvinell's children regard Washington in respect to their own personalities). Thus, the paintings of historical events will necessarily be appropriate to that era's concerns. Further, owing to the moralistic bent American history had assumed by mid-century, the exemplum virtutis such works offered could not be ignored. Although characterized by assertive nationalism, the middle period also exhibited an intense sectionalism which ultimately, of course, led to disunion. That great numbers of history paintings should appear at this time is, then, hardly surprising. The Columbian Magazine remarked in July 1844, that the name of George Washington appears frequently in "these troubled times."[79] The journal could have easily substituted "painting" for "name." In Richard Caton Woodville's Old '76 and Young '48 (fig. 25) and John L. Magee's Reading of an Official Dispatch (Mexican War News)(fig. 26), prints of John Trumbull's Declaration of Independence and a bust and portrait of Washington hang in the interiors, evoking past patriotism and moral grandeur for present trials. During the Civil War years, depictions of the Revolution and the "Father of his Country" related the past to the current situation. Tompkins H. Matteson's The Spirit of '76 (fig. 27) served as a frontspiece to the Ladies' Repository of July 1862. The editor of the periodical wrote:

> Nearly a century has passed away, yet the present is in wonderful harmony with the past. The same sacrifices are now made by the fathers, mothers, wives, and children, to sustain the Republic, which were then made to establish it. The very

> atmosphere is electric with the same spirit among the great
> mass of people, a self-sacrifice for the public weal. The pic-
> ture of the former time, which we here reproduce, is also a
> picture of to-day. Its lessons are in every respect appro-
> priate to the hour.[80]

In the Artist and the Tyro (c. 1863; fig. 28) by David Claypool

Johnston, a portrait of Washington lends patriotic support to the

scene. Interestingly, the composition, which emphasizes militancy,

casts the hero as "Father of his Country." This is appropriate in

regard to his two young "sons," but it also signifies Union. John-

ston's usage of Washington is not unlike that intended by Morrison

Heady:

> In this period of mighty struggles and issues, when our nation
> is groaning and travailing in pain to bring forth a future of
> surpassing renown and grandeur, it is important to inspire the
> hearts of American youth by the noblest examples of patriotism
> and virtue. And such is WASHINGTON, the "Father of his Country."
> It is best that the young of this battling age should study his
> character and emulate his deeds.[81]

This important issue of the relationship between past and

present is fundamental to my study of Washington imagery. It is only

mentioned here as it will be discussed throughout the following

chapters.

It is particularly striking how the young folks to whom

Uncle Juvinell showed the picture of Washington were able to comment

on numerous aspects of the hero's life--his status as soldier, as

statesman (the farewell address he holds), as pater patriae, as

paterfamilias, and even in death (the "pretty play-house," i.e.,

the summer house, erroneously understood as his tomb). As interpreted

by the children, the picture becomes a compilation of the many depictions of Washington executed during the middle decades. While the
numerous paintings and prints of this period chronicle all facets of
the hero's life and career, only one painter, Junius Brutus Stearns,
attemped to cyclical presentation.[82]

Stearns (1810-85), a New York artist, painted works of history
as well as portraiture, genre and a number of fishing subjects. Well-
known in the New York art world, he served as Recording Secretary of
the National Academy of Design from 1851 to 1865. The Home Journal
evaluated his status as a history painter in 1851: "Mr. Stearns has
now upon his easel another of those picturesque extracts form our
national history which have deservedly won for him his distinguished
position among American historical painters."[83] Prior to undertaking
his series on the life of Washington in 1848, Stearns had painted
scenes from American history which included: Ethan Allen Demanding
the Surrender of Ticonderoga (1846), Perils of the Colonists in 1697
(1847 National Academy of Design exhibition), Washington in the Indian
Council (1847), Death of Pocahontas (1848 American Art-Union exhibition), Trial of André (1848) and Scene from the Battle of the Brandywine (1848). The artist had, then, twice rendered incidents from the
life of Washington before commencing his series: Washington in the
Indian Council (fig. 29) and Scene from the Battle of the Brandywine
(fig. 30).

Stearns informed the American Art-Union of his intended cycle
in a letter dated November 15, 1849. He wrote that the idea of painting

four pictures from Washington's history came to him while executing

his Marriage of Washington (1848; fig. 31). The four compositions

were to be: The Marriage, The Death, The Farmer, The Soldier. Stearns

mentioned that such a series had never been painted and "would be most

popular with that class throughout the country."[84] The artist then

explained his writing to the American Art-Union:

> This series I am confident would form a most interesting
> and attractive feature in any collection of American pictures.
> My present circumstances will not admit of my undertaking these
> pictures as a Series unless I can get such aid as will meet my
> expenses during the time I should be engaged upon them. I there-
> fore solicit of you a commission, at a reasonable price, receiv-
> ing half the amount of each picture when finished and the
> balance when all completed.[85]

Stearns probably held high hopes that the Art-Union would favor him

with a commission as it had in 1847, when its order for Washington in

the Indian Council enabled the artist to travel to Europe for several

month's study. However, no evidence exists indicating the Art-Union's

interest in the series,[86] even though the artist did, in fact, carry

out his cycle.

The four paintings were published by Goupil-Knoedler of New York

in 1853 and 1854, as lithographs by [Claude?] Regnier. These prints

carried subtitles which left no question as to the role Washington

assumed in each scene. In marriage, he represents "The Citizen,"

while in death he exemplifies "The Christian." The didacticism of the

set is further evidenced by the prints bearing appropriate quotations

from Jared Sparks's popular Life of George Washington (1839). A

fifth painting, executed in 1856, portraying the hero as statesman,

never appeared as a print. Yet, it, like the others, became known through reproduction in later nineteenth- and twentieth-century history books. In fact, this later work attained the greatest visibility of any of the compositions, as it served as the basis of the special United States three-cent stamp issued on September 17, 1937, in com- memoration of the 150th anniversary of the signing of the Constitution. While Stearns himself has faded into obscurity, his visual interpre- tations of American history have achieved familiarity and have helped condition the way we perceive our history. Such is the case with many, if not most, of the artists discussed in this study.

Stearns's decision to execute a series based on the life of Washington indicates the probable influence of Thomas Cole's cycles: The Course of Empire (1836) and The Voyage of Life (1840). Treating man's passage through time, The Voyage of Life is the closer of the Cole sets to the Stearns. Like Cole, Stearns depicts the hero at different stages of his life, encountering different circumstances. The moralism which inbues the Cole series is, likewise, integral to the Stearns, for the artist is rendering that most moral of men, George Washington.

Junius Brutus Stearns's series serves as the benchmark for the following chapters. In discussing the imagery of the "Father of his Country," each chapter will first consider a Stearns painting, then proceed to examine other ways that that particular facet of Washington's life was treated by the visual arts during the middle decades of the nineteenth century.

Notes--Chapter I

1. [M, Heady], The Farmer Boy, and How He Became Commander-In-Chief, by Uncle Juvinell (W. M. Thayer, ed.), Boston, 1864, 28-31. Heady was known as the "blind bard of Kentucky," and this book was subsequently published in embossed print for the blind (W. A. Bryan, George Washington in American Literature, 1775-1865, New York, 1952, 110).

2. Notable exceptions are: V. Barker, American Painting, New York, 1950; J. T. Flexner, That Wilder Image, New York, 1962; L. B. Miller, Patrons and Patriotism, Chicago, 1966; J. K. Howat, "Washington Crossing the Delaware," The Metropolitan Museum of Art Bulletin, 26, March, 1968, 289-299; B. S. Groseclose, "Emanuel Letuze, 1816-1868: A German-American History Painter" (Ph.D. dissertation, University of Wisconsin, 1973); I. S. Fort, "High Art and the American Experience: The Career of Thomas Pritchard Rossiter" (M.A. Thesis, Queens College, New York, 1975).

3. W. Dowe, "George Washington," Graham's Magazine, 43, July, 1853, 34.

4. Quoted in B. I. Strauss, "The Memorial Iconography of George Washington" (M.A. Thesis, University of Delaware, 1966), 15.

5. "Washington," The American Magazine of Useful and Entertaining Knowledge, 2, March, 1836, 266.

6. Quoted in Observations on American Art, Selections from the Writings of John Neal (1793-1876) (H. Dickson, ed.), State College, Pa., 1943, 3.

7. Carl Hermann/Heinrich Schmolze (c.1823-1861) executed several designs of American history for engravings in Graham's Magazine. He also painted the ceiling of the Academy of Music, Philadelphia.

8. In rendering an incident from art history, Schmolze was working in a genre which became popular in Europe in the early nineteenth century, and in America by mid-century (see F. Haskell, "The Old Masters in Nineteenth Century French Painting," The Art Quarterly, 34, Spring, 1971, 55-85). Interest in this area was much in evidence in Philadelphia, Schmolze's adopted home. The Pennsylvania Academy of the Fine Arts exhibition of 1847, included Daniel Maclise's Salvator Rosa Painting Massaniello, owned by the Philadelphia art patron, E. L. Carey. The following year, the Pennsylvania Academy exhibition catalogue listed a Death of Raphael by [Frederick?] Fink and Henry Grégoir's Vandyke and the Miller's Daughter (both, again, owned by Philadelphians). Joseph Sill, prominent Philadelphia businessman, amateur artist, and art

patron, received a commissioned work, Cimabue discovering the Genius of Giotto, from the English artist Edward Matthew Ward in 1851. After his arrival in 1854, Schmolze had the opportunity of seeing Augusti Ratti's Guido Painting the Portrait of Beatrice Cenci (1856 Pennsylvania Academy exhibition) and, in the Pennsylvania Academy Annual of 1857, H. F. C. Tenkate's Rembrandt Painting the Wife of Burgomaster Six and Hendrick F. Schaefels's Rubens in his Studio. Plenty of stimuli then existed for painting of a scene like that of Stuart and Washington. In addition, Schmolze may have seen a work of a decade earlier, Joseph Kyle's Washington in Stuart's Studio. Unlocated today, Kyle's painting was exhibited at the American Art-Union in 1847 and 1848. In 1848, it was awarded to Robert Lay of Albany, N.Y. "The Fine Arts--The Art Union Pictures," The Literary World, 2, October 23, 1847, 277, said of the painting:

"No. 93 is neatly painted, but there is as little made out of the subject as well could be. We advise the artist to paint it again and make a composition of it; as it is he only gives us full length portraits of the two personages."

Perhaps Kyle took the reviewer's advice, for an untitled, 1848(?) newspaper clipping mentions that the artist is hard at work on The Levee of Gilbert Stuart, the Portrait Painter, and that the subject affords the means of including portraits of distinguished men of that day (American Art-Union Newspaper Cuttings Collection, The New-York Historical Society, New York).

9. "The Fine Arts," Gleason's Pictorial Drawing-Room Companion, 5, August 27, 1853, 141.

10. Schmolze had been active in the art world in Germany, where he was a lieutenant in the Artist Free Corps, and in Philadelphia, where he founded a German art association called "The Nameless" and edited an art journal (K. Mott, "Forgotten Painter," The Philadelphia Inquirer Magazine, May 5, 1957, 12-13).

11. H. Stone, Inaugural Address, Delivered February 24, 1857, and An Address on National Art, before Art Association, February 10, 1858, Washington, 1858, 31.

12. "American Artists," House Reports, 35 Cong., 2 sess. (March 3, 1859), No. 198, 1.

13. For support of Vernet, see J. R. Tyson, Address Delivered Before the Washington Art Association, Philadelphia, 1858. Brumidi (1805-1880) came to America in 1852, and began work at the Capitol in 1855, where he was employed until his death. For a survey of his art, see M. C. Murdock, Constantino Brumidi, Michelangelo of the United States Capitol, Washington, 1950.

14. "Art-Desecration of the Capitol," Cosmopolitan Art Journal, 2, March-June, 1858, 136.

15. See Miller, Patrons and Patriotism, 79-84. Schmolze, in fact, signed this petition, demonstrating both his involvement in art politics and his assimilation into the "American" art world.

16. Flexner, That Wilder Image, 152.

17. Our Artists--No. II, "Godey's Lady's Book, 33, September, 1846, 118.

18. Ibid.

19. "Mere Mention--George Washington at Home," The Home Journal, no. 720, November 26, 1859, 2, col. 4.

20. E. Wind, "The Revolution of History Painting," Journal of the Warburg Institute, 2, October, 1938, 116-127; C. Mitchell, "Benjamin West's 'Death of General Wolfe' and the Popular History Piece," Journal of the Warburg and Courtauld Institutes, 7, 1944, 20-33; A. Addison, "The Legend of West's Death of Wolfe," College Art Journal, 5, November, 1945, 23-26; E. Wind, "Penny, West, and the 'Death of Wolfe'," Journal of the Warburg and Courtauld Institutes, 10, 1947, 159-162; R. Todd, "Benjamin West vs. the History Picture," Magazine of Art, 41, December, 1948, 301-305; G. Evans, Benjamin West and the Taste of His Times, Carbondale, Ill., 1959.

21. "The Fine Arts--The Pennsylvania Academy of the Fine Arts," The Broadway Journal, 1, February 22, 1845, 121.

22. See L. Nochlin, Realism, Harmondsworth, England, 1971, for a full discussion of the issue.

23. F. J. Grund, The Americans, in their Moral, Social and Political Relations, Boston, 1837, 88.

24. D. Fanshaw, "The Exhibition of the National Academy of Design," The United States Review and Literary Gazette, 2, July, 1827, 245.

25. "Review of Modern Painters," The North American Review, 66, January, 1848, 110.

26. "The Fine Arts," The Literary World, 1, March 27, 1847, 182.

27. "National Academy of Design," The New Mirror, 1, May 13, 1843, 94.

28. "The Fine Arts," The American Repertory of Arts, Sciences, and Manufactures, 2, January, 1841, 435.

29. C. Lanman, "Correspondence--Our National Paintings," The Crayon. 1, February 28, 1855, 137.

30. "The Fine Arts," The Knickerbocker, 5, June, 1835, 555-556.

31. "Art at Washington," New-York Daily Times, 20, May 19, 1860, 5.

32. "Fine Arts," The Albion, 12 October 8, 1853, 489, col. 3.

33. "Fine Arts--Lessing's Martyrdom of Huss," The Albion, 9 December 7, 1850, 585, col. 1.

34. The Works of Jonathan Richardson (suppl. Walpole's Anecdotes of Painters and Sculptors), London, 1792, 11-12.

35. "Review of New Books," Graham's Magazine, 22, June, 1843, 367.

36. "Editorial Notes--Fine Arts," Putnam's Magazine, 2, November, 1853, 575.

37. "The Epochs and Events of American History, As Suited to the Purposes of Art in Fiction," The Southern and Western Monthly Magazine and Review, 1, 1845, 114.

38. D. Levin, History as Romantic Art, New York, 1967, 12f.

39. Smith, "The World of Art," The New World, 1, November 2, 1839, n.p. Hubard justified the painting by citing that the incident was based on oral tradition.

40. "The National Academy of Design," The New-York Mirror, 14, June 17, 1837, 407.

41. D. E., "Correspondence," The Crayon, 1, February 7, 1855, 88.

42. Weir to Verplanck, March 15, 1837, Verplanck Papers, The New-York Historical Society, New York.

43. The Literary World, March 27, 1847, 182.

44. J. B. Flagg, The Life and Letters of Washington Allston, New York, 1892, 230-32.

45. Companion to the Historical Paintings, of the ever memorable Battle of Bunker's Hill, By the Americans, and regular British Forces, June 17th, 1775, Boston, 1807, 3.

46. "The Chronicle--Art and Artists in America," Bulletin of the American Art-Union, November, 1851, 131.

47. Ibid.

48. H. Bacon, "Ideas from Pictures," Gleason's Pictorial Drawing-Room Companion, 4, July 9, 1853, 23.

49. "Fine Arts," The Albion, 9, November 30, 1850, 573, col. 3.

50. Putnam's Magazine, November, 1853, 576.

51. "Fine Arts," The Albion, 15, May 17, 1856, 237, col. 2.

52. "Review of the National Portrait Gallery of Distinguished Americans," The New York Review, 7 April, 1839, 353.

53. "Paintings for the Rotundo," Debates in Congress, 23 cong., 2 Sess. (December 15, 1834), 794. The speaker was Henry A. Wise of Virginia.

54. "The Romance of the Colonies," The Nassau Literary Magazine, 9, October, 1849, 40.

55. "American Art; the need and nature of its History," The Illustrated Magazine of Art, 3, 1854, 263.

56. "Development of Nationality in American Art," Bulletin of the American Art-Union, December 1851, 139.

57. See R. P. Hay, "Providence and the American Past," Indiana Magazine of History, 65, June, 1969, 79-101. S. Bercovitch, The Puritan Origins of the American Self, New Haven and London, 1975.

58. A. Goldberg, "School Histories of the Middle Period," Historiography and Urbanization (Eric F. Goldman, ed.), Baltimore, 1941, 175.

59. "The Fine Arts," The Literary World, 2, January 8, 1848, 559. The journal was quoting, in agreement, the London Art-Union Journal of December, 1847.

60. G. C. Verplanck, "An Anniversary Discourse Delivered Before the New York Historical Society," in Discourses and Addresses on Subjects of American History, Arts, and Literature, New York, 1833, 75-76.

61. Ibid.

62. Transactions of the American Art-Union, for the Year 1845, New York, 1845, 21.

63. S. Smith, "Examples of Female Heroism," Godey's Lady's Book, 27, December, 1843, 267.

64. Transactions of the American Art-Union, for the Promotion of the Fine Arts in the United States, for the Year 1844, New York, 1844, 15.

65. A. G. Remington, "The Influence of Art," Sartain's Union Magazine of Literature and Art, 9, December, 1851, 476.

66. H., "Revolutionary Recollections," The New-York Mirror, 7, June 23, 1830, 227.

67. See, for example, S. G. Fisher, "The Legendary and Mythmaking Process in the Histories of the American Revolution," Proceedings of the American Philosophical Society, 51, Philadelphia, 1912.

68. "Review of the National Academy of Design Exhibition," The New-York Mirror, 19, May 22, 1841, 167.

69. Quoted in "Art at Home," Cosmopolitan Art Journal, 1, July, 1856, 15.

70. "The Fine Arts--Exhibition of the National Academy," New-York Daily Tribune, 12, June 7, 1852, 5.

71. "Modern French Painters," The North American Review, 74 January, 1852, 135.

72. Miss Ludlow, A General View of the Fine Arts, Critical and Historical, New York, 1851, 42-43.

73. "Art and Artists," The Home Journal, no. 287, August, 9, 1851, 3, col. 2.

74. C. Burroughs, An Oration on the Moral Grandeur of George Washington on the Centennial Anniversary of his Birth Day, February 22, 1832, at the request of the Citizens of Portsmouth, N.H., Portsmouth, 1832, 15.

75. "Art and Artists in America," Bulletin of the American Art-Union, December, 1851, 149.

76. J. K. Paulding, A Life of Washington, 2, New York, 1836, 231.

77. [H. H. Weld], Life of George Washington, Philadelpnia, 1845, ii-iv.

78. "Hints to Art Union Critics," The American Review: A Whig Journal of Politics, Literature, Art and Science, 4, December, 1846, 608.

79. "Washington," The Columbian Magazine, 2, July, 1844, 23.

80. "Editor's Table," The Ladies' Repository, 22, July, 1862, 447.

81. W. M. Thayer, "Introduction," The Farmer Boy, and How He Became
    Commander-In-Chief by Uncle Juvinell, 4-5.

82. The same idea appeared in M. Willson, Juvenile American History,
    for Primary Schools (revised ed.), New York, 1847, 119: "For
    the purpose of fixing the history of the great and good WASHINGTON
    more permanently in the memory, we give, on the following pages,
    a series of four engravings, illustrative of different periods
    of his eventful life." These showed the boy (cherry tree story),
    the surveyor, the General (after Sully's Passage of the Delaware)
    and the President (taking oath).

83. "Art and Artists," The Home Journal, no. 267, March 22, 1851, 3,
    col. 2.

84. Stearns to Executive Committee of the American Art-Union, November
    15, 1849, American Art-Union Collection: Letters from Artists,
    The New-York Historical Society, New York.

85. Ibid.

86. The Art-Union bought The Marriage of Washington in 1850, after
    much haggling; see p. 66.

CHAPTER II

WASHINGTON HUMANIZED

> But the lovers of Washington could gain from every
> event of his life, whither little or great, only
> fresh evidences of his exalted purity, his ennobling
> sense of right, his disinterested self-sacrafice.
> And how eagerly every little anecdote of his hours of
> boyhood or manly relaxation has been seized upon
> and treasured up.
> Rev. Henry F. Harrington, Godey's Lady's Book,
> June, 1849

The first painting in J. B. Stearns's cycle treating the life
of George Washington, The Marriage of Washington (1848; fig. 31),[1]
impresses the viewer by its seemingly unusual choice of subject.
Depicting an event of moot political significance and lacking the
awe-inspiring actions traditionally associated with history painting,
the work offers, instead, a dignified, yet unheroic, scene of a
nuptial ceremony. As an image of romance for a Romantic age, Stearns's
painting was not, however, unusual. During the 1840s, the home
functioned as the central social institution,[2] with the husband-wife
relationship its foundation. Engravings and illustrations, like
The Wedding (fig. 32.), found in the May, 1845 Columbian Magazine,
reinforced popular conceptions of matrimonial harmony. The era also
witnessed a growing domestication of George Washington in art. Stearns
has rendered not the Hero, but the Citizen (as the title of the
1853 lithograph after the painting made clear). This democratization,
by domestication, of Washington by Stearns, as well as other artists's
efforts to humanize the hero, forms the topic of this chapter.

40

The earliest notice of Stearns's painting of Washington's
marriage appeared in the Alexandrian Gazette of September 30, 1848:

> We learn that Mr. J. B. Stearns, a distinguished artist of New
> York, and lately from Europe, has been for some days at Arling-
> ton House, in this vicinity engaged in making very beautiful and
> successful copies from the original pictures of Colonel and Mrs.
> Washington, the one of the date of 1772, by Peale, and the other
> of 1759, by Woolason [sic], with a view to the painting of a
> large picture of Washington's Marriage, founded upon the relation
> of the interesting event, in the Custis recollections and private
> memoirs of the Life and Character of Washington.[3]

In setting the scene at the Parish Church of St. Peter's, the writer
spoke of foreground and background, as though describing a painting.
Commonly, writers of the day used painting as a metaphor in character-
izing their literary creations; a writer "painted" as much as he wrote
a piece. Thus the Alexandrian Gazette reviewer's usage of painting
terms may simply have been part of his picturesque style. However,
with Stearns's painting dated 1848, it is entirely possible that the
writer may have actually studied the painting. Here circumstances
prevent the reader from knowing if the writer was describing a real
painting, in fact, or painting his own word-picture.

The major significance of the Alexandrian Gazette article lies
in its documenting Stearns's efforts to achieve historical veracity
in his composition. This artist's usual concern for authencity is
supported by a letter he wrote to the American Art-Union, recounting
the execution of his Trial of André, painted the same year as The
Marriage of Washington: "I have been about five months painting it
besides a considerable outlay in cash for Models, Costumes, visiting
New Haven and West Point in search of materials."[4] Stearns's regard

for factuality typified that of mid-century history painters and
indicated the importance of historical fidelity for a successful painting. By travelling to Arlington House for his Marriage of Washington,
the artist not only enjoyed the opportunity of copying the eighteenth-
century portraits of the Washingtons, but also gained the chance of
meeting the master of the house, George Washington Parke Custis. The
grandson of Martha and the adopted son of the General, Custis devoted
himself to maintaining their memory in the public's heart and mind.
To this end, he published a series of newspaper articles on Martha
Washington, between 1825 and 1830, and in 1859 and 1861, the popular
Recollections and Private Memoirs of Washington (largely a compilation
of his many writings) appeared posthumously. Further, Custis was an
amateur artist and painted several works, mainly battle-pieces, high-
lighting the hero's career (figs. 33 and 34).[5] While at Arlington
House, Stearns probably painted the portrait of Custis, dated 1848,
now in the collection of Washington and Lee University, Lexington,
Virginia. This visual documentation testifies to Stearns meeting
Custis, as does an article in The Ladies' Repository of January, 1849,
which stated that the artist had visited Custis for the purpose of
the painting[6] and by the American Art-Union catalogue of 1850, which
noted that Stearns had been assisted in his painting by the Virginian.
Given this information, as well as Custis's deep interest in the
Washington name, the hero's adopted son undoubtedly proved eager to
supply Stearns with pertinent knowledge.

As re-created by Stearns, the wedding scene assumes a tableau vivant-character: figures in dark garb close the composition on either side, focusing the viewer's attention on the centrally-placed bridal couple. With men dressed in velvet coats, women in satin gowns, and the Reverend Dr. Mossom in full canonicals, the depiction manifests elegance and aristocracy. In emphasizing the material splendor of the group, Stearns presaged the courtly atmosphere of Daniel Huntington's The Republican Court (1861; fig.146). In many ways, Stearns's nuptial scene parallels the aims of the nineteenth-century French artists who kept alive a Rococo spirit in order: "to arouse pleasant sensations and associations . . . They represented either human beings engaged in enjoyable activities in subjects which were considered beautiful and desirable in themselves. Amorous themes were, of course, central to their art."[7] G. W. P. Custis was seminal in imbuing the courtship and marriage of his descendants with this pleasurable ambience, writing: "And rare and high was the revelry at that palmy period of Virginia's festal age . . . "[8] Underlying Custis's descriptions, and contemporary accounts of Stearns's painting, is a sense of nostalgia. Custis related an interview with Cully, an aged family servant, who after nearly seventy-five years still remembered how striking the young George Washington and his bride appeared amidst the splendor of the occasion. When asked by the biographer if he recalled when Washington came courting, Cully answered, "Aye, master, that I do, great times, sir, great times-- shall never see the like again!"[9] The description of Stearns's painting which appeared in the American Art-Union catalogue of 1850,

continued in this nostalgic vein, referring to "the beautiful costume
of the period . . . the elite of the old Virginia aristocracy."[10] The
article in The Ladies' Repository of January, 1849, remarked on the
depiction of the ladies in "the gorgeous English costume of that
ancient period."[11] Such revelatory statements indicate that by 1848,
the United States had developed a keen sense of history and even a
longing for the past. Even though Washington's marriage had taken
place less than one hundred years earlier, Americans could speak of
their "ancient period." Though truncated by Europeans standards,
American history served its citizens remarkably well.

     The focal point of Stearns's nuptial representations is the
giving of the ring to the bride. While the minister blesses, the
young, wide-eyed and innocent-looking Washington places the ring on
his demure bride. Numerous figures encircle the couple. Among these
secondary participants are Governor Dinwiddie, between Reverend Mossom
and Washington, and various members of the bridal couple's families.
In rendering correct likenesses of these individuals, the artist
also attempts to create an eighteenth-century ambience through formal
means (e.g., the crispness and sheen of the bride's dress (derivative
from Woolaston) and her pose). The inclusion of the young widow
Martha Custis's two children, looking suitably childlike, adds genre
quality to the scene. Although neither pure genre nor a true conversation piece, the scene does represent a humanizing of Washington.
No longer the heroic soldier, Washington appears as a man engaged
in an activity common to men. By showing him in a familiar situation,

albeit more elegant than most person's weddings, Stearns renders Washington more accessible to the common individual.

By representing Washington in a scene expressive of love, the artist is working not only within an iconographic tradition of Washington, but also painting in general. G. W. P. Custis, through his writings, attempted, of course, to imbue a romantic sensibility to the young officer; Washington cannot help being immediately smitten by the sight and personality of Martha Custis. In James McHenry's 1823 novel, The Wilderness; or, Braddock's Times (a new edition appeared, with much publicity, in 1848), Washington suffers unrequited love. However, even this fate proves favorable, for:

> . . . from the day on which it was forced to abandon the tender hopes of a youthful and enthusiastic love, it would be impossible to find an example of human nature having produced a heart more purely and entirely devoted to all the calls of philanthropy, patriotism and duty, and productive of actions more conducive to the world's benefit, than the heart of WASHINGTON.[12]

The hero meets with disappointment in love in a History of the Early Adventures of Washington among the Indians of the West by Joshiah Priest (1841). The author sets the mood of his novel in the title-page poem, which begins:

> The great have loved as well as the small,
> For love's the power that conquers all.[13]

Priest, in attempting to support the plausibility of his fictional account, reminds the reader that: "Washington, it is well known, when young, was a man of great sensibility of mind, ardor or tempera-ment, exceedingly fond of refined society, and the excitements of social relations . . . "[14] Washington in love was also a theme in

George Lippard's Washington and His Men of 1850. Lippard delineated the young hero in terms that could have been derived from Stearns's painting:

> And you will remember that the young Virginian, in mere personal appearance, was worthy of the proudest woman's love. He was tall-well-proportioned--his face moulded not so much after the "classical style," but moulded--as a face should be, which is intended to express the manhood of a chivalric heart.[15]

Numerous periodical articles, usually based on the writings of Custis, treated Washington's courtship and marriage of Martha. A typical example is "Washington's First Interview with Mrs. Custis," in Godey's Lady's Book of April, 1846, which accompanied an illustration: F. O. C. Darley's drawing of the elegant couple bowing upon their first meeting (fig. 35). Paintings of the courtship are few: John Ehninger's version depicting a refined and opulent world (fig. 36), was exhibited at the National Academy of Design in 1860, and later engraved by George R. Hall in 1863; Edward May's Washington and Miss [sic] Custis was shown at the Second Annual Exhibition of the Yale School of Fine Arts in 1870. Such efforts, including Stearns's, attempt to present another aide of the hero, a more human side, a more emotional facet; however, through all such depictions Washington retains his dignity.

Stearns's painting relates to not only an American interest, but also to a European concern popular in the first half of the nineteenth century: depictions of famous lovers of the past. These include Jean-Auguste-Dominque Ingres's Raphael's betrothal to Cardinal Bibiena's Niece (1812), his Raphael and the Fornarina (c. 1814) and Paolo and Francesca (1819). William Dyce also rendered this

latter couple (1837). In 1822, Paul Delaroche, an artist favored by
Americans, completed his <u>Filippo Lippi Falling in Love</u>. While George
and Martha Washington could hardly rival the romantic legends of
Raphael and the Fornarina or Paolo and Francesca, they do offer, however prosaic, an American counterpart and an opportunity for an
American artist to treat the theme of love in a historical vein.
Stearns's work relates, too, to the domestication of the hero, an
aspect of art particularly visible in Europe and America at mid-century,
and to be discussed in detail in Chapter IV.

Although he mentioned Washington's marriage only in passing
("Their friendship commenced with the first hour of their acquaintance
and was soon nurtured into marriage . . . "[16]), Parson Weems certainly
made a depiction of such scenes possible. By relating anecdotes of
Washington, real and fictive, which aimed at essentially humanizing
the hero, Weems provided a basis for such familiarized visual representations of the "Father of his Country." Undoubtedly, the most
famous tale Weems created in this regard was that of the cherry tree,
first appearing in the fifth edition (1806) of <u>The Life of Washington</u>:

> George, said his father, <u>do you know who killed that beautiful</u>
> <u>little cherry-tree yonder in the garden?</u> This was a <u>tough</u>
> <u>question</u>; and George staggered under it for a moment; but quickly
> recovered himself; and looking at his father, with the sweet face
> of youth brightened with the inexpressible charm of all-conquering
> truth, he bravely cried out, "<u>I can't tell a lie, Pa; you know</u>
> <u>I can't tell a lie. I did cut it with my hatchet.</u>"[17]

The cherry tree incident invented by Weems, perhaps best
represents the combination of humanization and moralism evident in his
work. Weems synthesized the natural Washington (the little boy who
chops the tree) and the cultural Washington (the model lad who is

always truthful). Linking the familiar with the ideal, Weems anticipated, and probably influenced the nature of nineteenth-century
American children's literature; Weems, it should be remembered,
directed his Life of Washington at his "young countrymen." Bernard
Wishy has pointed out in The Child and the Republic (1968) that in
all types of children's stories before the Civil War, a major concern
is the learning of clear moral lessons.[18] In the early nineteenth
century, didactic tales, couched in moralism, replaced the more formal
books of good behaviour of the eighteenth century.[19] Also, beginning
in the 1820s, great quantities of school textbooks and manuals of
American history intended for children emerged. These featured
humanized anecdotes tinged with moralism and partiotism. A passage
from Entertaining Anecdotes of Washington (originally published in
1833) typifies the bias toward Washington:

> No mind can dwell upon such a character as that of Washington,
> without delight; and presented, as it may be, and should be,
> to the children of the land, at their forming period, it is
> eminently calculated to their patriotism, piety, and benevolence;
> and, in truth, to every virtue which can enrich and adorn the
> human mind.[20]

Weems's anecdotes, and children's literature in general, evidenced,
than, a belief in the importance of childhood in the formation of
the adult.

Despite the nineteenth century's familiarity with the "dis-
figuration of the cherry tree by GEORGE WASHINGTON,"[21] the subject
attracted few artists. Engravings, such as Charles Kuchel's of 1839,
and illustrations, like those found in Anna C. Reed's 1842 biography
of the hero and in Entertaining Anecdotes of Washington (figs. 37 and

38), do exist. However, reference to only one painting treating the subject during the middle period has been discovered: The Home Journal of April, 1851, mentioned that "Mr. Wright, an artist of varied attainments and much promise" has chosen to depict the scene.[22] After praising the work's clever form, the Home Journal writer concludes: "There is a moral in this picture which should commend this, his first essay in genre painting, to some publishing house."[23] By calling the work "genre," the journalism indicates the artist's success at humanizing Washington. Depicting a known individual. the painting exemplifies not "genre" or "historical genre"," but history as genre, or "genreized" history. Despite the Home Journal's feeling that the work possessed popular appeal, mid-century painters in general, avoided the cherry tree incident. Perhaps even then the tale was too hackneyed to be represented in "high" art. Yet, while the cherry tree incident failed to attract a major nineteenth-century painter, another episode, less renowned, from Washington's youth did: Early Days of Washington by Henry Inman (1843; fig.39).[24]

The 1846 Inman memorial exhibition catalogue refers to Jared Sparks as the text for Early Days of Washington, although the painting more closely illustrates Weems's passage: "He was never quilty of so brutish a practice as that of fighting . . . nor would he, when able to prevent it, allow [other school boys] to fight one another."[25] Inman's work casts Washington, the boy, in the role of peacemaker, stepping between the well-dressed child on the right and the more rustic lad on the left. That the artist chose a subject

of Washington's boyhood was unusual for American art, and Inman's work
is the earliest painting portraying Washington as a Weemsian child.
Though unique, Early Days of Washington does fit into Inman's work at
that time. The artist, primarily a portraitist, did execute three
genre paintings in the early 1840s: The Newsboy (1841), Mumble the
Peg (1842), and Dismissal of School on an October Afternoon. (1845).
All of the paintings have children as their subject matter and are
genre scenes, qualities shared by Early Days of Washington. Mumble
the Peg is especially close to Early Days of Washington, in that,
both show a rural child pitted against a more urban one. Early Days
of Washington treats history as genre: it represents a more-or-less
ordinary event in the life of a famous historical person. Compositionally, the work appears as if Inman has taken the form of David's
Sabines (1799) and rendered it as a genre scene from American history.
Inman's selection of a little-known episode from Washington's childhood can be partially explained by his interest in genre paintings
involved with children, at the time. It also can be understood as
being part of a broader interest: the increasing nineteenth-century
awareness of children, as well as part of a European art mode of
depicting events from the early life of famous people.

The early nineteenth century in America witnessed a new
attitude with regard to children, that manifested itself as an increasing tendency for adults to look upon children as people and not as
something less.[26] At this time publications tailored to children
came into existence. Further, children now achieved greater

visibility in art forms other than portraiture. Although based on an English engraving, Jeremiah Paul's Four Children Playing in a Court-yard (1795) was an early American painting of children in a genre situation (interestingly, Inman's composition has a reclining child pointing out the action to the viewer as does the Paul). A sample of other American genre paintings featuring children include: John Lewis Krimmel's Fourth of July Celebration in Center Square, Phila-delphia (1819), Charles Bird King, The Itinerant Artist (c.1813-25), Asher B. Durand, The Peddler Displaying his Wares (1836), William Page, The Young Merchants (1836) and Thomas Le Clear, The Young Hunter (c.1840). Children were, then, more and more evident in American art; yet, Inman's representation remained unique because it showed the childhood of a famous adult. Although the type had antecedents in popular engravings and illustrations, Early Days of Washington appears to be the first painting of its kind in this country. The vogue for depictions of celebrated person's childhoods continued, at least, into the 1850s. In the March, 1850 issue of Godey's Lady's Book appears an engraving entitled Benjamin West's First Attempt at Drawing, while in the same journal, two years later, included Watt's First Conception of the Steam Engine (figs. 40 and 41). The precedent for the type of painting Early Days of Washington heralded in this country existed in Europe.

An interest in the youth of a hero or celebrated individual developed in the late eighteenth century. Numbers of paintings displayed this fascination appeared in the early nineteenth century.

Examples include: <u>The Birth of Henry IV</u>[27] by Eugène Devéria (Salon of 1827-28), Pierre-Henri Revoil's <u>Giotto Discovered by Cimabue</u> (1841 Salon) and Paul Delaroche's <u>Childhood of Pico della Mirandola</u> (1842). The Salon of 1842 included works rendering the youths of Henriette d'Angleterre, Henry IV, Saint Genevieve and Rembrandt. The European works thus create the ambience into which the Inman neatly fits.

The content of such painting treating the childhoods of famous people involved the belief that early incidents presaged future greatness. Certainly such is the case of the Inman. <u>Godey's Lady's Book</u> of November, 1843, remarked that in the Inman: "The air of the peacemaker has all the authority in it which so distinctly pronounced the Father of his Country, one who was born to command."[28] <u>The Gift</u> of 1844, eloquently asserted:

> The whole grand result of the American Revolution points back to this very scene, and this scene again points forward to the great public and political position which the man, George Washington, afterwards assumed. The harmony between the great fact and the little one is complete. In the rude garb and air of the boy on the right of the Peacemaker, and backwoodsman, Yankee, North America colonist is visible, while the better dress and bearing and light hair of the other combatant, the Saxon gentleman from the other side of the water is betrayed. And there is the very look of Washington throughout the whole war. He loved his country dearly, but he was no partisan. Justice was his aim and law; and of course he looks neither at the one party or the other, but straight forward, like one who has light in his eye. It is the look of your true mediator, not bent upon passions, but fixed upon principles.[29]

This moral disinterestedness, which marked Washington, was then even present as a youth. The reproduction of Inman's work in this issue of <u>The Gift</u>, raises the possibility of its having been specifically

executed for the gift book market. To be given as presents during
the Christmas season, such books, with their prose, poetry and prints,
reflected the Romantic desire for beauty, refinement and elevation
of the senses. As Benjamin Rowland, Jr., has noted, after 1840,
gift books became increasingly interested in genre subjects.[30] While
the appearance of Inman's image in The Gift is its own proof of the
painting's suitability for such books, the emergence of Inman's work
so soon in this literary form suggests its having been intended for
that medium.

Well-received, Early Days of Washington became widely known
by reproduction in The Gift of 1844, and the Literary Souvenir of
of 1845. The composition also appeared in a modified, but immediately
recognizable, form in Frost's Pictorial Life of George Washington
(1857; fig. 42). Inman's celebrated work probably influenced Washington, The Boy Hero (fig. 43) attributed to Thomas Hope, as well as
renderings of Washington at Cambridge, where he subdued a brawl in
a fashion which fulfilled the "prophecy" of his boyhood. These
include John McNevin's illustration in the March 23, 1861, issue
of Harper's Weekly and F. O. C. Darley's Washington Subduing a Camp
Brawl (fig. 44).

Although the first painting, evidently, to re-create a scene
from the hero's childhood, Inman's Early Days of Washington was not
the earliest to treat Washington before adulthood. That honor belongs
to John Gadsby Chapman and his Washington in His Youth (1841; fig.
45).

A prolific artist, Chapman gained renown for his paintings as well as his numerous illustrations. To be a history painter of the first rank formed Chapman's goal, a desire generally frustrated, but ultimately attained in his mind, by receiving a commission to paint a panel for the United States Capitol Rotunda. The resulting work was the Baptism of Pocahontas (1840; fig. 10). The following year, the artist completed Washington in His Youth.

Minimizing the obvious didacticism of the Inman, Chapman creates a romantic image of the youth standing in the American wilderness, with all its attendant nationalistic and moralistic associations. Chapman's representation shows the young man as a surveyor at rest, and might rightly be deemed a historical portrait d'apparat. From his seventeenth to his twentieth year, Washington was a public surveyor. As might be expected, mid-nineteenth century Americans regarded the youth's time as a surveyor to be integral in the formation of the man. "His soul was shaped by his wilderness experience," wrote George Lippard in 1850, and Henry T. Tuckerman later stated,

> "You have George the Surveyor," said Carlyle, in his quaint way, to an American, when talking of heroes. Never had that vocation greater significance. It drew the young Virginian unconsciously into the best education possible in a new country for a military life. He was thereby practised in topographical observation; inured to habits of keen local study; made familiar with the fatigue, exposure, and expedients, incident to journeys on foot and horseback, through streams and thickets, over mountains and marshes; taught to accommodate himself to limited fare, strained muscles, and bivouac, the woods, the seasons, self-dependence, and effort. This discipline inevitably trained his perceptive faculties , and made him the accurate judge he subsequently became of the capabilities of land, from its position, limits, and quality, for agricultural and warlike purpose.[31]

Like Inman's depiction of the young Peacemaker, Chapman's rendering
of the youthful Surveyor treated the hero's early days not only for
their historical and humanizing value, but also as illustrating the
idea that youthful experiences mark the man.

Washington assumes a relaxed attitude in Chapman's picture.
His tools are set down as he pauses to absorb the panoramic view from
his lofty perch. This splended young man, with his wonderful curls,
is obviously at one with the picturesque Allegheny environment in
which he finds himslef. The highly romantic nature of this painting
struck a writer in the Arcturus of Nomember, 1841, who remarked that
the representation seemed like "a drawing-room picture of the forest;
the landscape is softened, and one thinks it was a very elegant kind
of life in the backwoods."[32] Another contemporary, objecting to the
historical inaccuracy of Washington's costume, felt the dress of the
hero suited more "the boudoir than the backwoods of the west."[33] The
Arcturus writer favorably compared the style of the work to that of
Watteau. Indeed, an air of elegance pervades this painting, an
attitude that relates it to Stearns's Marriage of Washington. Tailor-
ing style to subject both offer an essentially aristocratic view of
Washington, evidencing a sense of nostalgia for the chivalric Old
Dominion of the hero's younger days. Chapman's canvas certainly
counters the then standard view that during his three years as a
surveyor Washington was continually "strengthening his habits and
constitution by hardships and exposures."[34] Interestingly, an
engraving after the Chapman painting served as the frontispiece of

the book from which this quotation was taken; presumably, the celebrity and quality of the Chapman painting outweighed its inappropriateness to the text.

Besides functioning as a historical portrait d'apparat, Chapman's painting relates to the artist's own day. Landscape painting was increasingly becoming the most significant mode in American art. Binding together a conception of God-in-nature and an American manifest destiny, the American landscape took on a decidedly nationalistic cast. By selecting a subject which allowed setting Washington in a landscape space, Chapmen makes an obvious linkage of American history, personified by Washington, and nature. Washington, as a surveyor, had been one of those involved in the opening of western territories. In Chapman's picture, Washington serves as a historical sanction for this type of westward movement, and an appropriate symbol for the great expansion then beginning in the 1840s.

Chapman's placement of the figure in the landscape was, of course, not a new type of painting; colonial portraiture frequently set individuals in an outdoor space, as in Robert Feke's Isaac Winslow (c.1748; fig. 46). The nineteenth century commonly saw figures fully integrated into the environment and in commune with nature, as in Thomas Doughty's In Nature's Wonderland of 1835 (fig. 47). Commencing in the 1840s, a branch of portraiture developed which characteristically featured a pioneer or backwoodsman at rest, surveying the land about him. Chapman's image falls into this category and is, in fact, one of the earliest examples of the type. Works, including

historical scenes, in this mode are exemplified by William Ranney's
Daniel Boone's First View of Kentucky (1849), Ranney's Squire Boone
Crossing the Mountains (1852; fig. 48), and Promised Land by William
S. Jewett (1850). Chapman's Washington in His Youth not only created
a scene from the past, but, like most history paintings, spoke to
its contemporaries; in this case, sanctioning the American involvement with nature as well as Manifest Destiny.

Discussing Horatio Greenough's life-size sculptural group,
The Rescue (fig. 49), an 1851 review made a direct identification
of Washington with the American frontier. Lauding the representation
of the American hunter for its "calm, self-controlled and majestic"
bearing and as "perhaps the noblest type of native manliness that
ever issued from the imagination of the sculptor," the reviewer then
offered his highest praise when he noted of the frontiersman:

> Though the features are not at all a reproduction of Washington's,
> there is a sublime Washingtonianism of sentiment and character
> in the figure. It is just the attitude and the head that the
> youthful Washington would have presented, had he been called
> upon to act in such a scene during one of his wanderings in
> the forests of Virginia. The freedom, firmness, ease, and
> natural grace and inherent force of this magnificent form, are
> those of one conscious of an irrestistible ascendant . . . [35]

As described by the writer, this marmoreal image of an agent of Manifest Destiny, characterizes Emanuel Leutze's painting of the young
Washington.

Shown with the artist's Washington Crossing the Delaware and
Washington at Dorchester Heights at the 1853 Washington Exhibition in
New York, Leutze's Washington as the Young Surveyor (c.1850; fig. 50)
treats the same theme as Chapman's earlier painting. Although less

delicate-appearing than Chapman's Washington, the lad in Leutze's composition is equally as handsome and certainly as romantic.[36] Leutze's Washington seems to be a visualization of J. T. Headley's 1847 description of the surveyor: " . . . the noble young dreamer presents a perfect specimen of what a youth should be--full of enthusiasm, feeling and daring and full, too, of application and serious thought."[37] Pausing as he crosses a log and leaning on his rifle, Washington looks upward, apparently lost in thought. Since the viewer knows of the young surveyor's great destiny, the lad's dreamy attitude takes on the character of an awareness of that future. A sense of the heroic is also achieved in the placement of the figure near the picture plane, filling up most of the vertical space, and rising above both other men (here the black servant)[38] and the land itself. As Washington's thoughts are in the clouds, so is, compositionally, his head. In this romantic image, less emphasis is placed on the land itself and more on the psychological condition of the young man.

Depicting Washington in his younger days offered one manner of humanizing the hero. Placing him in situations of a less-than-heroic nature represented another way. An example of this latter mode is Tompkins H. Matteson's Harvey Birch's Warning to Young Wharton (1846; fig. 51), a tension-filled conversation piece in which Washington appears comfortably reading a book. Matteson, a history painter famous for his engraving designs, provided this composition for a Charles Burt engraving included in the February, 1846 issue

of The Columbian Magazine. The scene derives from James Fenimore
Cooper's The Spy. Published in 1821, this novel was one of the earliest
books to conceive of Washington as human. Although Washington appears
through most of the story as a mysterious Mr. Harper, Cooper's
minimal efforts at making Washington accessible are nevertheless
evident. The success of Cooper's humanization of the hero was apparent
in John Neal's novel Randolph, where a character caustically remarks
on The Spy: " . . . George Washington is profanely introduced; and
always profanely employed in situations totally unworthy of him--
perilous--foolish--and ridiculously mysterious . . . "[39] Fanny
Wharton, the novel's heroine, recognizes that Washington-as-Harper has
" . . . the benevolent expression that characterizes the best feelings
of the human heart," while her brother Henry, a British officer,
remarks: "If ever there was a stamp of truth, simple, honest benevolence, in the countenance of many, it shone on his."[40] This benevolence is brought to test in Matteson's scene. Henry Wharton had
concealed himself behind a curtain while his family entertained the
stranger, Mr. Harper, and purchased goods and gossiped with the
peddler and "Spy" Harvey Birch. Then, to the consternation of his
family, the young Wharton suddenly revealed himself. Mr. Wharton
steals a sidelong glance to check the reactions of Harper, who, in
typically Washingtonian fashion, remains calm in the midst of con-
fusion. Later all worry about Harper's vow to remain silent. However, Caesar, the Wharton's servant, assures Henry: "No, no, no
Massa Henry . . . I been to see-Massa Harper on he knee--pray to God--

no gemman who pray to God tell of good son, come to see old foder--
Skinner rabble-rouser do that--no Christian!"[41] Matteson depicts
Washington-as-Harper in a genre-like scene which treats the hero's
benevolent traits.

The theme of Washington's kindness appears in Peter F.
Rothermel's painting The Benevolence of Washington, sometimes called
Washington Prescribing for the Poor Widow (c.1844; fig. 52). Supposedly based on an actual incident, the subject of the painting is
George Washington helping a young boy and his mother, sick, poor and
widowed. The boy, seeking alms, had approached Washington on the
streets, unaware of whom he was, but recognizing a kindly gentleman when he saw one. Washington took pity, accompanied the lad home
and prescribed a cure: a bank draft. Stressing Washington's innate
kindness and the naive boy's immediate discernment of this trait, the
incident makes real the abstraction "The Father of his Country."

According to Joseph Sill, respected Philadelphia art patron
and amateur artist, Rothermel executed two versions of the scene:

> I went to see Mr. Rothermel's Picture of 'Washington visiting
> the sick woman & child' this morning, in order to form a judg-
> ment on it, whether it would do to be engraved for "the Art
> Union" [of Philadelphia]; he has painted the subject twice;
> and I think a good Picture might be made out of the best parts
> of each.[42]

Although the Art Union of Philadelphia elected not to engrave a
Rothermel work, a version did become known, by way of periodicals.
The frontispieces of Godey's Lady's Book of November 1846, and the
Electic Magazine of January 1855, were engravings after Rothermel.[43]
The painting owned by the Pennsylvania Academy of the Fine Arts,

listed in the 1847 and 1848 Academy catalogues, probably provided the source for these engravings.

John Beaufain Irving's <u>Washington Calling upon Col. Rahl</u> (fig. 53) also casts the hero in a sympathetic role. Irving, a South Carolinian who studied with Leutze, renders the General at the bedside of the dying Hessian officer who had been defeated at the Battle of Trenton. The scene's significance lies less in the General's recognition of a gallant enemy, and more in countering, like the Rothermel, the frequent charge that the hero was too cold emotionally, too unfeeling.

For an artist or writer wishing to humanize George Washington, the most powerful incident available was the account of his last visit to his mother. Prior to journeying to New York to assume the Presidency, the leader stopped at Fredericksburg to pay his respects to her. Fated to be Washington's last encounter with his elderly mother, the incident lent itself to a sentimentalization rarely associated with Washington. At this visit, Mary Ball Washington, who ravaged by bad health and time, realizes she will not again see her son. She tells him this, and then urges him to leave and fulfill the high destinies assigned to him by God:

> Washington overcome by her words, leaned his head on her aged shoulder and wept. The hero and the man sunk before the feelings of the son, and tears that honored him more than the laurels he wore, stood on his care-furrowed cheek. What a scene for a painter do they present as they stand together. That tall and commanding form, which had been the terror of so many battle-fields, bowed over the trembling form of his mother, and that brow before which the nation bent in homage, hid on her neck in silent grief.[44]

An artist's opportunity for rendering Washington experiencing such a basic human emotion as crying was not common; one thinks only of this scene and that of his farewell to his officers. Of these two events, that involving his mother is, unquestionably, the more heart-wrenching: the viewer can readily substitute his own parents and the feeling of parting with them for the last time.[45] Having Washington shed "tears of filial tenderness"[46] opens him up to the viewer, but apparently too much, for depictions of Washington and his mother usually avoid representing actual weeping. Nevertheless, the nineteenth-century spectator was sufficiently familiar with the anecdote to be aware of the emotional level reached.

Repeated in virtually every history of Washington, the incident became the subject of illustrations and engravings. Typical of these popular works of art is one which appeared in the Illustrated Magazine of Art in 1854, and later published by William Pate as an engraving in 1860. Titled Washington Taking Farewell of His Mother (fig. 54), the composition displays a sparse interior in which the hero, fighting back tears, embraces his mother. Mary Washington is not at all idealized, but rendered as a sick, old woman. The realism of the illustration is consistent with the article which the drawing accompanied. The mother was described as "afflicted by a disease the most terrible that can tax the fortitude of humanity--cancer in the breast;" however, although bowed with age and shattered with pain, Mrs. Washington was "sustained by Christian resignation."[47] A dog, adding a sense of genre to the scene, serves a symbolic

function; a traditional emblem of fidelity, the canine has been
placed near Washington, to emphasize the son's filial devotion.

While illustrations and engravings of the episode are
fairly common, paintings are not, in fact, only one significant
painted depiction of the occurrence exists: William Powell's
Washington Receiving his Mother's Last Blessings of 1864 (fig. 55).[48]
Powell, an active history painter, best known for his grand Discovery
of the Mississippi by DeSoto, in the United States Capitol Rotunda
(1853). In Washington Receiving his Mother's Last Blessings, the
hero kneels and bows before his seated parent, who bestows her bene-
diction upon him. Above his head, on the wall, hangs an oval portrait and a sword. The portrait bears a strong resemblance to the
features of Washington himself, and recalls Gilbert Stuart's
"Vaughan" portrait type (1795; fig. 56). It may be a portrait of
Washington, but more likely it is intended to represent his father,
who died when the hero was a boy. (The hanging sword would connote,
then, Washington's distinguished ancestry.) Such being the case,
both parents would then be, in effect, offering their blessings.
In the spatially ill-defined middleground area, a black servant
appears at an open door. Presumably, this woman has unwittingly
come upon the scene. Such a figure is not mentioned in the literature; however, her inclusion by the artist may be a manner of
validating the story. Neither Washington nor his mother recorded
as intimate an account of the incident as that found in mid-century
literature. The story then could not be conclusively substantiated.

Powell solves this problem by implying that the servant observes and
then repeats the occurence. As a validating device, Powell's figure
probably derives from the surreptitious Quaker who witnessed Washington in prayer at Valley Forge. A substitute for the viewer, the
servant is allowed to "spy" upon this touching scene in order that
she may tell others its lessons.

The artist's rendering of Washington and his mother was
engraved by Henry Cousins and published by W. Schaus in 1864. A
pamphlet accompanying this mezzotint provides fundamental material
on the content of Powell's composition. Also the rapid appearance
of print and pamphlet suggests that the painting had been commissioned
for engraving.

Throughout the text of the pamphlet a heavy religious bias
becomes obvious. The painting is deemed "at once instinct with true
human feeling, and a religious significance." The writer calls
George Washington "one of the saviours of mankind," and the "High
Priest in the Temple of Liberty." Mary Ball Washington is similarly
cast;quoting from The Republican Court (1855) by Rufus W. Griswold,
the pamphelt asserts that: "There is no fame in the world more pure
than that of the mother of WASHINGTON and no woman since the Mother
of Christ has left a better claim to the affectionate reverance of
mankind."[49]

Although common to put Washington into a Christian context,
the rationale for the pamphlet writer's particularly strong tone
becomes clear when he notes: "The remarkable scene at Fredericksburg

recalls the better days, in the moral life and growth of the country."
In 1864, the United States was, of course, in the throes of civil
war--"The vandals hurl fire brands into the temple of our liberties,
and political infidels pollute the soil long since consecrated by the
dust of WASHINGTON." For the writer every loyal [i.e., Northern]
citizen must become a "Christian Cursader," to regain the "pure
patriotism and lofty integrity which characterized the better days
of the Republic." Finally, the pamphlet set forth the role to be
played by Powell's work in this moral and national restoration:

> It is hardly necessary to suggest to the loyal American the
> propriety of giving POWELL'S WASHINGTON a place in his household,
> for the sake of its influence on the rising generation. It
> teaches the great lesson of filial affection in language more
> eloquent than words, and with the force of the most illustrious
> example. Moreover, since our free institutions are imperiled
> by cold indifference and political apostacy, and many hearts
> have wandered far from their allegiance to the country of
> WASHINGTON, we do well to recall them from the haunts of a
> misguided and selfish ambition; not only by earnest words and
> a loyal example, but by every suggestive symbol and touching
> memorial that may successfully appeal to the mind and heart.[50]

Appealing to "mind and heart," Powell's painting intentionally
reads as a morally didactic humanizing of Washington. Like Parson
Weems and other paintings of a humanized Washington, the artist
brings the hero closer to his audience, yet preserves his function
as a model of virtue.

Notes--Chapter II

1. Two versions are extant. The Virginia Museum of Fine Art owns one
    signed and dated 1848, measuring 40-by-55-inches. A painting of
    the same dimensions, but dated 1849, is in the Butler Institute of
    American Art collection. Virtually identical, the two paintings
    display only minor compositional differences. The painting
    listed in the 1850 American Art-Union catalogue is the work now
    in the possession of the Butler Institute. Stearns had difficulty
    selling the painting to the Art-Union. Responding to an offer
    of five hundred dollars, the artist asserted that the "offer is
    so far below what I have expended in time and labour upon I
    respectfully decline it" (Stearns to P. M. Wetmore, August 15,
    1849, American Art-Union Collection: Letters from Artists, The
    New-York Historical Society, New York). The price Stearns fixed
    on the work was eight hundred dollars. After deferring, the com-
    mittee voted to purchase the work for five hundred dollars; Stearns
    countered with an offer of eight hundred dollars, and included two
    additional paintings: The Path Across the Lots and Country. This
    was accepted (American Art-Union Management Committee Minutes,
    December 6 and 18, 1849, February 7, 1850, The New-Historical
    Society, New York.

2. American Life in the 1840s (c. Bode, ed.), Garden City, N.Y.,
    1967, 86.

3. "Washington's Marriage in 1759," Alexandrian Gazette, 49, September
    30, 1848, 2, col. 1.

4. Stearns to the Committee of Management, July 5, 1848, American Art-
    Union Collection: Letters Received, The New-York Historical
    Society, New York.

5. Custis (1781-1857) said of himself: "I am an untaught artist, but
    hope to make up by zeal of the heart, what I may want in skill and
    experience" (Custis to Charles Fenton Mercer, July 17, 1832 [?],
    Custis Family Papers, The Library of Congress). His amateur status
    did not deter his attempting large paintings: he also told Mercer
    that he was engaged on a 7-by-5 1/2-foot painting of Washington the
    night before the Battle of Trenton. A writer in 1853, observed
    that Custis was:
    " . . . an amateur painter of no common ability and in a
    recent visit of 'Arlington House',' he showed me a large
    and spirited representation of the 'Surrender of Yorktown,'
    then on the easel. Although possessing some artistic
    defects, the picture interested me far more than many a
    'classical work of art' [a slam at Horatio Greenough's
    Washington]. Familiarly acquainted with the prominent actors
    in the great Revolutionary drama, Mr. Custis, has given

            their features, forms and uniforms with faithful exactness,
            and his groupings is [sic] admirable" (Ben:Perley Poor,
            "Waifs from Washington," Gleason's Pictorial Drawing-Room
            Companion, 4, February 14, 1853, 123).
Eight years later, George Templeton Strong visited Arlington
House and judged the battle paintings on the wall "fearful to
behold" (Diary of George Templeton Strong (A. Nevins and M. H.
Thomas, eds.) 3, New York, 1944, 154-55: June 2, 1861.

6.   "Washington's Marriage," The Ladies' Repository, 9, January,
      1849, 4.

7.   .C. Duncan,The Pursuit of Pleasure: The Rococo Revival in French
      Romantic Art, New York, 1976, 18.

8.   "Courtship and Marriage of Washington," The Rover, 3, 1844, 321.

9.   Ibid.

10.   M. B. Cowdrey, American Academy of Fine Arts and American Art-
      Union, Exhibition Record 1816-1852, New York, 1953, 337. At
      mid-century, Virginia was the one state renowned for its romantic
      past: "In the abundance and quality of her poetical and roman-
      tic reminiscence and suggestion, Virginia is unquestionably the
      laureate of our sisterhood of nations" (T. A. Richards, The
      Romance of American Landscape, New York, 1854, 42).

11.   The Ladies' Repository, January, 1849, 4.

12.   [J. McHenry], The Wilderness; or, Braddock's Times, Pittsburgh,
      1848, 230.

13.   J. Priest, A History of Early Adventures of Washington among the
      Indians of the West, Albany, 1841, title-page.

14.   Ibid.

15.   G. Lippard, Washington and His Men: A New Series of Legends of
      the Revolution, New York, 1850, 59.

16.   M. L. Weems, The Life of George Washington (M. Cunliffe, ed.),
      Cambridge, Mass., 1962, 53.

17.   Ibid., 12.

18.   B. Wishy, The Child and the Republic, Philadelphia, 1968, 54.

19.   M. Kiefer, American Children Through Their Books 1700-1835,
      Philadelphia, 1948, 83.

20. <u>Entertaining Anecdotes of Washington</u> (new ed.), Boston, 1846, vii.

21. "The Great Sanitary Fair," <u>The Philadelphia Inquirer</u>, June 20, 1864, 2.

22. "Art and Artists," <u>The Home Journal</u>, no. 269, April 5, 1851, 3, col. 1. The picture was titled <u>Young Washington and His Father</u>. The artist may be George Frederick Wright (1828-81), who was known for his portraits.

23. Ibid.

24. The work was variously known as: <u>Boyhood of Washington</u> (H. T. Tuckerman, Book of the Artists, New York, 1867, 242); <u>Incident in the Life of Washington</u> (Great Central Fair Art Catalogue, Philadelphia, 1864, no. 384); <u>Washington--An Early Incident in his Life</u> (Catalogue of an Exhibition by the Pennsylvania Academy of the Fine Arts of Choice Paintings, January, 1877, no. 21).

25. <u>Catalogue of Works by the late Henry Inman</u>, New York, 1846, 9. Weems, <u>Life of Washington</u>, 19. Sparks wrote: "It has also been said, that while at school his probity and demeanor were such, as to win the deference of the other boys, who were accustomed to make him arbiter of their disputes, and never failed to be satisfied with his judgment" (J. Sparks, <u>The Life of George Washington</u>, Boston, 1843, 5.

26. Kiefer, <u>American Children Through Their Books</u>, 82.

27. Despite Lord Raglan's comments on the excitement attending a hero's birth, the birth of Washington is a subject found in only a single mid-nineteenth-century painting: <u>Washington's Birthday</u>, executed by an anonymous American primitive. Undoubtedly painted on a Washington's birthday, the work expresses a familiarity and humanization akin to George Templeton Strong's reference to February 22, as the day "the nation celebrates 'Pa's birthday'" (<u>The Diary of George Templeton Strong</u>, 1, 226; February 22, 1844). The painting also humorously counters Washington Irving's facetitious remark: "Did anybody ever see Washington nude? It is inconceivable . . . he was born with his clothes on, and his hair powdered, and made a stately bow on his first appearance in the world" (B. Mayo, <u>Myths and Men: Patrick Henry, George Washington, Thomas Jefferson</u>, Athens, Ga., 1959, 33-34). Irvings witticism, in turn, anticipates Grant Wood's splendid <u>Parson Weems' Fable</u> (1939).

28. "Editors' Book Table," Godey's Lady's Book, 27, November, 1843, 239.

29. "Early Days of Washington," The Gift: A Christmas and New Years Present, Philadelphia, 1844, 140.

30. B. Rowland, Jr., "Popular Romanticism: Art and The Gift Books," The Art Quarterly, 20, Winter, 1957, 374.

31 Lippard, Washington and His Men, 15. H. T. Tuckerman, Essays, Biographical and Critical, Boston, 1857, 5-6. Tuckerman is essentially embellishing remarks made eighteen years earlier by Sparks, in his Life of Washington.

32. "The Fine Arts--The Apollo Association," Arcturus, 2, November, 1841, 374.

33. "The Fine Arts, The New-York Mirror, 19, December 18, 1841, 407.

34. [H. H. Weld], Life of George Washington, Philadelphia, 1845, 15.

35. "Greenough the Sculptor, and His Last Production," Bulletin of the American Art-Union, September, 1851, 971.

36. A contemporary claimed that the face of Washington was taken from a miniature in the possession of G. W. P. Custis ("Fine Arts--The Washington Exhibition," The Albion, 12, March 12, 1853, 129.

37. J. T. Headley, Washington and His Generals, 1, New York, 1847, 29.

38. The black figure here perhaps influenced Darley's illustration Washington's Surveying Expedition in Putnam's Magazine, February, 1854.

39. J. Neal, Randolph, 2, Philadelphia, 1823, 213.

40. J. F. Cooper, The Spy (C. Dahl, foreward), New York, 1946, 29, 269.

41. Ibid., 10. Caesar's remarks are a variation on the prayer at Valley Forge story (see Chapter III).

42. Diary of Joseph Sill, vol. 5, September 19, 1844, The Historical Society of Pennsylvania.

43. The plate in Godey's Lady's Book was engraved by J. Gross, while that in the Electric Magazine was by John Sartain. Each journal also accompanied the plate with an account of the incident.

44. Headley, Washington and His Generals, 81.

45. The sentimentality of the hero's last visit with his mother is
    paralleled by "last meetings" of famous Europeans. Such scenes
    reproduced in American journals, include Charles I Bidding
    His Family Farewell (Godey's Lady's Book, May 1845) and Crom-
    well's Last Interview with his Favorite Daughter (The Ladies'
    Repository, December, 1857). The latter work was praised in
    the magazine for affording a view of Cromwell's domestic life
    as opposed to his more familiar public history. The death of
    Cromwell's mother, also discussed in the same issue, reminds one
    of Washington's visit with his mother, in terms of content. As
    death approaches, "she called the mighty Protector of England
    to her bed side. He had ever entertained for her most sincere
    and respectful affection. Stretching out her feeble hands she
    blessed him . . . " She spoke of his accomplishing great things
    for the glory of God, and expired. Cromwell than burst into
    tears ("Editor's Table," The Ladies' Repository, 17, December,
    1857, 763).

46. [Weld], Life of Washington, 157

47. "Washington Taking Farewell of His Mother," The Illustrated
    Magazine of Art," 4, 1854, 73-74.

48. Tuckerman, Book of the Artists, 407, mentions Washington
    Receiving his Mother's Blessings by George Whiting Flagg
    (1816-97).

49. Washington Receiving his Mother's Blessing. Painted by W. H.
    Powell, engraved by Henry Cousins, New York, 1864, 4-7

50. Ibid., 7-8.

CHAPTER III

WASHINGTON THE MILITARY HERO

In moral elevation, no warrior of ancient or modern times
approached him.

J. T. Headley, Washington and His Generals, 1851

In selecting the subject for his painting exemplifying

Washington the Soldier, J. B. Stearns chose a scene from the French and

Indian War, the Battle of the Monongahela. Battle pictures, the staple

commodities of the history painter, had long been favored because they

represented man at his most heroic, displaying his military skills, his

noble courage and his virtuous judgment under conditions of extreme

duress. Their popularity also owed to their ability to easily arouse

patriotic feelings and associations. Further, with the historiography

of the middle decades of the nineteeth century decidedly militaristic,[1]

battle paintings found a ready audience. Stearns's painting successfully

accomplished the aims of a battle scene as well as effectively embodying

three fundamental traits of Washington the soldier: his leadership, his

fortitude and his divine nature.

' J. B. Stearns's Washington as a Soldier, painted around 1851,

shows the hero as a twenty-three year old Colonel in the French and

Indian War (fig. 57). The painting relates to two other paintings exe-

cuted by the artist about the same time which also evince an interest in the earlier days of Washington: The Marriage of Washington (1848) and Washington in the Indian Council (1847; fig. 29).[2] These works, along with John Gadsby Chapman's Washington in His Youth (1841) and Henry Inman's Early Days of Washington (1843), reflect the popularity, during the 1840s, of representations of the hero's younger life. Scenes related to the French and Indian War also appeared then. Washington's Retreat to Fort Necessity by Chapman was exhibited at the National Academy of Design in 1843.[3] This work received praise in 1850 as being the artist's masterpiece in the "historical landscape" department.[4] At approximately the same time Stearns executed Washington in the Indian Council, William Ranney painted the same theme. Both depict Washington's first public endeavor, his journey to the Ohio Valley on behalf of the British Crown. Unlike Stearns's composition, where Major Washington, in the relative comforts of the long house, urges the Indians to remain peaceful, Ranney's painting shows the young soldier and his group "struggling over the mountains through a blinding snowstorm."[5]

These works of Washington's earlier days reflect a romantic strain of the 1840s (Stearns's Washington as a Soldier was conceived in 1848). Against a picturesque background of Indians, battle and untamed wilderness, the future hero was delineated maturing under the "protecting hand of God."[6] Washington as a Soldier also relates to literature as James McHenry's romantic novel, The Wilderness; or, Braddock's Times (originally published in 1823, but a new edition, widely known, appeared in 1848), in which, as a reviewer observed, Washington played "the double part of Romeo among the ladies, and Alexander the Great among

the Indians, with signal success."[7] George Lippard's <u>Washington and His</u>
<u>Men</u> of 1850, featured three chapters, or "legends," revolving around the
Battle of the Monongahela, with an especially thrilling account of the
battle itself. Stearns's painting fits well into the fabric of contemporary interest in the earlier career of George Washington.

The incident which Stearns depicts is the Battle of the
Monongahela. A representation of this 1755 event appears, perhaps, a
bit odd, considering that the British and colonial forces were
devastatingly routed and that the British commander, General Sir
Edward Braddock, along with a number of his officers, was slain. Out
of this holocaust, however, Washington emerged a hero. After chronicling
the horrors of the conflict, Jared Sparks, concluded:

> Such was the termination of an enterprise, one of the most
> memorable in American history, and almost unparalleled for its
> disasters, and the universal disappointment and consternation it
> occasioned. Notwithstanding its total and even disgraceful failure,
> the bitter invectives everywhere poured out against its principal
> conductors, and the reproaches heaped upon the memory of its ill-
> fated commander, yet the fame and character of Washington were
> greatly enhanced by it. His intrepidity and good conduct were
> lauded by his companions in arms, and proclaimed from province
> to province.[8]

Thus, though retreat and defeat sounded for the British forces at the
Battle of the Monongahela, Washington's reputation as a courageous, and,
as shall be shown, even blessed, leader began to advance.

The disastrous defeat at the Monongahela was generally attributed
to General Braddock's obstinancy. The British leader ignored advice
and warnings given by Washington regarding fighting in the rigid manner
customary in Europe. Old World military tactics proved useless in the
New World wilderness, where the enemy conceal himself behind bush, rock

and tree. Braddock stubbornly ignored the unique colonial circumstances
and continued his traditional European battle decorum. Embroidering on
reality, as usual, Parson Weems presented a hysterical Braddock, "an
epauletted madman"[9] (obviously the prototype for future mad Britons to
be encountered in Weems):

> For General Braddock, who had all along treated the American officers
> with infinite contempt, rejected Washington's counsel, and swelling
> with, most unmanly rage, replied, 'High times, by G-d! when a young
> Buckskin can teach a British General how to fight.'[10]

The inevitable occurred: the Redcoats, in their fixed marching order,
made easy marks for the hidden French and Indians. As one British
officer after another fell, Washington assumed greater authority, until
he virtually took command, leading the remnants of his force in retreat.

In his composition, Stearns conveys a sense of the chaos and
desperation of the British position. At the right, British troops file
past, some conscious of the impending doom. On the left, a heroic band
of "Buckskins," Washington's Virginians, take a stand behind a tree.
Washington, sword held out, commands a dynamic white charger. Typical
of many images of him, Washington's countenance appears virtually ex-
pressionless. Near him two colonials support a wounded British officer,
perhaps Braddock (although the man's age argues against it). The
wounded man's gesture toward the enemy is echoed by Washington's gaze
and sword, and continued by the firing rifles of the men at the left.
This compositional arrangement creates a strong lateral movement towards
the left, that is, toward the unseen enemy. Stearns's picture, without
actually depicting blood, evokes the carnage and noise of battle, by the
strewn bodies and firing, smoking rifles and artillery. Washington

occupies a conspicuous place as the figure of leadership, a representation which, in fact, is accurate.

While Stearns's Washington is mounted, Emanuel Leutze's conception of the same subject (fig. 58) depicts the unhorsed young leader directing cannon fire as the mortally wounded Braddock is carried off the field. A sweeping panorama of the battle, peopled by scores of combatants, characterizes Leutze's 1858 painting. In this work, Washington's leader status is less immediately obvious than in Stearns's. Closer to Stearns than Leutze is a small illustration from the 1846 children's book published in Boston by Otis Clapp, Entertaining Anecdotes of Washington. Obviously derived from Weems's account, this delightful book includes a representation of the Battle of the Monongahela as its frontispiece and as a hand-colored text illustration (fig. 59). Similarities between this primitive graphic form and Stearns's painting abound. In both works the space of the conflict is small in scope. Mounted on a rearing horse, Washington commands with a sword in each. A dead Indian and a wounded officer occupy the ground near the hero in both illustration and painting. Both use trees and smoke to fill the background. Stearns, like other history painters, delved into the literature of his day in the process of creating his art. Although the point cannot be pressed, the affinities between the engraving and Stearns's painting suggest, at least, that the artist encountered this popular work while formulating his scene of Washington at the Battle of the Monongahela.

Washington miraculously escaped the debacle of this battle, and his survival became part of his mythology. The young man himself commented on his good fortune:

"By the all powerful dispensations of Providence," said he, in a letter to his mother, "I have been protected beyond all human probability or expectation; for I had four bullets through my coat, and two horses shot under me, yet I escaped unhurt, although death was levelling my companions on every side of me."[11]

Weems offered, of course, a more florid description of the scene:

Horse after horse had been killed under him. Showers of bullets had lifted his locks or pierced his regimentals. But still protected by Heaven; still supported by a strength not his own, he had continued to fly from quarter to quarter, where his presence was most needed, sometimes animating his rangers; sometimes striving, but in vain, to rally the regulars.[12]

Invariably discussions of the Battle of the Monongahela concluded by relating an incident witnessed by Dr. James Craik, a life-long friend of Washington. Craik's account "proved" that the invisible hand of Providence had protected the hero. The story describes how Washington, surveying land on the former battle-site nearly two decades later, was approached by a group of Indians. Their aged chief addressed the hero of Monongahela:

I came to behold my great father, Washington. I saw my great father on horseback in the hottest of the battle . . . fired my rifle at him many times, for I was in the army of the French, and I bade my young men fire their rifles at him. But the Great Spirit turned away the bullets; and I saw that my great father could not be killed in battle.[13]

This anecdote's widespread celebrity in the literature of the day assures us that the idea of Washington's destiny being guided by Providence formed an integral aspect of Stearns's content. Chronologically, the Battle of the Monongahela was not the first example, either in art or history, of the divine protection accorded Washington. That honor belongs to the story of Washington crossing the Allegheny River.

In 1753, Washington, only twenty-one years old and a Major in the colonial army, volunteered to deliver an ultimatum to the French concerning their encroachments on English claims in the Ohio Valley. The fulfillment of this arduous mission through a wild winter frontier established Washington's reputation as a person of courage and fortitude. Returning after successfully accomplishing his task, Washington and his guide, Christopher Gist, constructed a raft to ford the partially frozen, and extremely hazardous, Allegheny River. During the difficult crossing, the young Major was thrown into the icy water. Later generations understood his rescue to have been divinely fated; Washington was being preserved for greater deeds.

The incident became well-known through history books, where either Washington's or his guide's account of the episode could be incorporated into the text. Its popularity was also due to the event prefiguring, in a typological fashion, the more famous crossing of the Delaware. The crossing of the Allegheny further appealed to the public because of its sublimity: what if Washington had been allowed to drown? Finally, works of art, especially Daniel Huntington's painting of the event, fixed the incident in Washington mythology.

Huntington's painting (fig. 60) first appeared in the 1843 Pennsylvania Academy of the Fine Arts exhibition. The work achieved fame through Richard W. Dodson's engraving for The Gift of 1845, and as an illustration in the Columbian Magazine (1844), Weld's Life of George Washington (1845), T. Addison Richard's The Romance of American Landscape (1854), and Graham's Magazine (1855). Huntington's composition features parallel, reverse images of Gist and Washington dramatically poling across

the river before the fall. The artist delineates Washington as the
handsome, ardent, active young man favored in the mid-nineteenth-century
American mind:

> . . . his whole person was so cast in nature's finest mould, as to
> resemble the classic remains of ancient statuary, where all the
> parts, contribute to the purity and perfection of the whole . . .
> he excelled the hunter and the woodsmen in their athletic habits,
> and in those trials of manhood which distinguished the hardy days
> of his early life . . . [14]

Washington Crossing the Allegheny not only expresses this American
romantic attitude toward the young hero, but also evinces the sublimity
of the event.[15]

An 1844 description of Huntington's work clearly revealed the
sublime associations aroused by the work:

> The raft seems to have been frail--the undertaking dangerous;
> conceive the possibility that the hazard might prove fatal!
> What a change might have been wrought, by the event of a few
> minutes, in the whole destinies of this republic--or rather of the
> colonies from which it sprung, for perhaps they would not have
> become a republic. Under another chief the fortunes of the
> Revolutionary armies might have been different; the red-cross
> flag of strong oppression might have waved in triumph at Saratoga
> and Yorktown, instead of going down before the rising splendor of
> the starry banner; the whole history of North America might have
> assumed another and entirely different character. No wonder,
> then, that the mind rests with deep and suggestive intensity upon
> the representation of an incident involving such mighty possibilities.[16]

Washington weathered, of course, this test of nature; divine interven-
tion saving him and America.

Huntington's work inspired William Sidney Mount's small version
of the same subject (1863; fig. 61).[17] While Mount's scene lacks the
dramatic action and large-scale figures of Huntington's work, a sketch
clearly indicates that Mount used that earlier work as a point of departure (fig. 62). Mount's prosaic rendering fulfilled his patron's

expectations:

> None of your Red Sea with the Israelites crossed over and the
> Egyptians submerged, we want to see the Alleghany [sic] river
> full of ice pouring down those stairs and bearing that raft with
> young Washington and Mr. Gist: no other creature in sight, no
> skulking Indian nor bird, no rain in the bramble.[18]

The painting certainly fails to express the drama Mount himself considered the subject to possess: "Washington's desperate struggle in
crossing the Alleghany [sic] river--is the grand turning point in his
history. Life or death. The future of the country depended upon that
crossing."[19]

Other versions of the scene include one, now unlocated, by Isaac
Craig shown at the 1856 Pennsylvania Academy of the Fine Arts exhibition,
and William Ranney's depiction of Gist pulling the soaking Washington
out of the water (1854; fig. 63).[20] An unidealized image of a man, not
a hero, struggling to save his life. Ranney's drawing is noteworthy
for its attempt at truthfulness. Entertaining Anecdotes of Washington
(1846) anticipated, and perhaps influenced, Ranney's depiction with its
illustration of the event (fig. 64). Ranney's depiction comes much
closer than either Mount's or Huntington's to showing the tragedy that
might have been. The work exhibits the high degree of actuality which
characterizes Paul Delaroche's Napoleon Crossing the Alps (c. 1847), a
work highly praised in America. In effect, Ranney's work relates to
the heroics of the Huntington as Delaroche's does to Jacques-Louis
David's Napoleon Crossing the Alps of 1800.

Implicit in all these representations of Washington crossing
the Allegheny is that "there was a hand unseen that affected his escape".[21]

This belief parallels that which marked Washington at the Battle of the Monongahela. Yet at that later conflict the idea became more fully developed. For at the battle, acting as a leader, George Washington utilized his Providential blessings to affect others, and those serving under him saw him as assuming the mantle of divinity itself. By selecting this battle as his subject, J. B. Stearns could represent not only an exciting event, but also depict an early manifestation of Washington as a godlike leader.

Washington's divine or demigod status became fixed after his death. The hundreds of funeral orations and eulogies performed and published immediately after his passing elevated him to national saint and saviour. Continual usage of stellar metaphors for the hero became common in art and literature as one means of rendering his exalted status (to be discussed later). Another way Washington's divine nature was evinced involved works depicting him in an attitude Walter Fried-laender termed the "Roi Thaumaturge."[22] The leader who possesses the "king's touch" passes on his divinity by touching or being touched.

John McNevin's illustration Settlers Imploring Washington's Protection (fig. 65), appearing in an 1870 Benson J. Lossing book,[23] depicts an event which took place the year following the Battle of the Monongahela. The residents of Winchester, a frontier settlement under fear of attack from the French and the Indians, singled out the young Washington as their deliverer: "The women surrounded him, holding up their children, and imploring him with tears and cries to save them from the savages."[24]

Although Washington does not actually touch any of the pleading women, their beseeching attitudes and their reaching for him indicate their belief in his divinity. As Friedlaender connected Napoleon to the conception of the "Roi Thaumaturge," so can we speak of Washington (although, unlike the French hero, the American did not actively campaign to create such an image in the minds of his countrymen). McNevin's design appears to derive from Baron Gros's famous Napoleon at Eylau (1807-08; fig. 66). While differing in content (Napoleon is honored by the conquered for his clemency, while Washington is begged to act), both works treat the hero as saviour. Formally, the compositions are similar in showing figures supplicating before the mounted leader, other equestrian figures near their commander, and acts of devastation in the background.

A work which relates even more closely to the "Roi Thaumaturge" notion is an undated painting by Tompkins H. Matteson, entitled The Benevolence of Washington (fig. 67). The title links the work to Peter F. Rothermel's composition of the hero prescribing for the poor widow, and, in the Matteson, Washington again aids a woman. Now, however, the two figures touch each other. The young woman appears as a supplicant before the standing General. By his touch, the "king's touch," he bestows his benevolence upon her, in effect, "healing" her. Matteson's painting does not render a specific event in the history of Washington. The work is, in fact, taken from fictional literature, The Spy (1821) by James Fenimore Cooper.[25] The passage Matteson illustrates shows young Frances Wharton receiving aid from Washington (disguised as "Mr. Harper") in obtaining her brother's safe release from enemy troops. Harper tells her she has probably saved her brother's life and that:

> God has denied to me children, young lady; but if it had been his
> blessed will that my marriage should not have been childless, such
> a treasure as yourself would I have asked from his mercy. But you
> are my child: all who dwell in this broad land are my children,
> and my care . . . [26]

The moment Matteson depicts follows immediately:

> As he spoke, with a solemnity that touched Frances to her heart,
> he laid his hand impressively upon her head. The guileless girl
> turned her face towards him, and the hood again falling back, ex-
> posed her lovely features to the moonbeams. A tear was glistening
> on either cheek, and her mild blue eyes were gazing upon him in
> reverence.[27]

The Benevolence of Washington delineates a scene which not only described the hero as "Father of his Country," but which clearly indicated
his divinity, a quality the innocent maiden recognized. That she is
"guileless" reinforces the magnitude of Washington's stature.

The artist faithfully renders Cooper's words, except for placing
the scene indoors rather than in "the moonbeams." Matteson's composition
nearly matches an illustration by F. O. C. Darley in an 1861 edition of
The Spy (fig. 68). The obvious correlation between the painting and the
illustration clearly indicates one artist influencing the other. On
stylistic grounds the Matteson probably preceded the Darley.[28] The
figure of Washington in The Benevolence of Washington closely resembles
that in Matteson's Washington at Valley Forge of 1855 (fig. 81). Also
the painter rendered at least three scenes of Washington's life in the
late 1840s and early 1850s. Further, Darley, in at least one instance,
seems to have borrowed from a history painting. His 1854 illustration
(fig. 69) of Washington as surveyor demonstrates an awareness of Leutze's
earlier painting of the same subject. Despite the "evidence" favoring

Matteson, one feels uncomfortable assigning him precedence over the better known and superior talent of Darley. Also, the illustration was easily accessible to Matteson, whereas, the availability of the painting by Matteson (who, after 1855, was ensconced in the small town of Sherburne, New York) is uncertain. Further, Matteson frequently based his illustrations on those of other artists, a practice he undoubtedly carried over into his painting.[29] The indeterminate relationship between the Matteson and the Darley is similar to one to be countered later (Chapter VI) concerning another Matteson work and an engraving by Nathaniel Currier.

A final work which invokes, and best exemplifies, the "Roi Thaumaturge" theme is a drawing by William Ranney (fig. 70). Although the background is very lightly penciled, the scene appears to be a sort of triumphal entry. The central figural group shows Washington surrounded by three soldiers in various attitudes of touching him and paying homage. One kneels and hugs his leg, another grasps his hand, while the third bows and kisses the hero's other hand. The soldiers touch him to absorb his divinity and his blessings. This little drawing (6 1/8-by-7 1/2-inches) presents one of the most telling American idolizations of George Washington.

Although Stearns's painting of the Battle of the Monongahela does not specifically treat the notion of the "Roi Thaumaturge," the work, in depicting an event famous for demonstrating Washington's divine grace, does relate to this idea. Focussing on the hero as a Providentially protected leader, Stearns renders him taking command of a chaotic situation and guiding it to a reasonable and honorable end. The artist

records Washington displaying the traits of command that marked his
military, as well as his political, career. Paintings like Stearns's,
of a mounted Washington leading his troops, abound. Earlier, in 1848,
Stearns had painted a Scene at the Battle of Brandywine (fig. 30).[30]
The hero's pose is identical to that in Washington as a Soldier, although
the artist reversed it in this later painting. Like Stearns's
Washington as a Soldier, Emanuel Leutze's Washington at the Battle of
Monmouth of 1854 (fig. 71), depicts the officer assuming sudden re-
sponsibility.[31]

Leutze's painting delineates a 1778 event, where, in the only
recorded instance, Washington fell prey to uncontrollable passion,
publicly swore and reprimanded one of his officers. The target of this
unique display of wrath was Major General Charles Lee. At Monmouth,
Lee unaccountably failed to initiate a planned offensive attack and led
his troops in retreat, much to Washington's surprise and chagrin. The
General rushed to the scene, passionately cursing (or, speaking with
"great warmth," as Parson Weems priggishly noted) at Lee and, then, with
equal vigor and emotion, urged the retreating soldiers back into the
fray. His actions proved successful; the battle was ultimately won (or,
at least, not lost) by the Americans. With greater emotion and action
than Stearns, Leutze portrays a charging Washington on horseback, sword
held high, assuming immediate command of his soldiers and goading them
on to victory.[32] Washington at the Battle of Monmouth became embroiled
in controversy, carried on in the pages of the eminent art journal The
Crayon, concerning the nature of history painting. Two articles in the

1855 Crayon, one of January 10, the other of January 31, antipodally
viewed the painting. However, both writers did agree on fundamental
aspects of history painting in general: such art should depict a
worthy and dignified subject; grand and noble emotions and elevated
deeds should be shown; a sympathy between viewer and painting should be
established; and the work should be morally didactic. The articles
disagreed over Leutze's choice of subject. The January 10 Crayon
piece maintained that the subject of Leutze's painting, the angry, pro-
fane Washington, was nonheroic and did not elevate him or the viewer.
The contemporary writings of Henry T. Tuckerman reflected the currency of such an aesthetic and moral position:

> The memory of Washington is the highest and most precious
> of national blessings, and, as such, cannot be approached by
> artist or author without reverence. To pervert the traits or to
> mar the unity of such a character is to wrong, not only his sacred
> memory, but the dearest rights of his countrymen.[33]

The second Crayon article, however, commended the artist for his realistic depiction, which the writer argued, rather than distracting from
Washington's exalted fame, created a bond between him and the spectator
by humanizing the hero. A basic issue of nineteenth-century history
painting, the real versus the ideal, found expression in these con-
flicting Crayon commentaries. The first author presents the traditional
conception of history painting, while the second offered a more modern
interpretation. The artist's inability either to stress clearly the
real or the ideal, or to synthesize them, contributed to the painting's
generally unfavorable reception.[34]

    While the two Crayon articles basically argue over subject

matter, other reviews were more concerned with the form of the painting. The Albion of 1854, thought the subject fine, but faulted the poor composition, which pictured Washington galloping past his men:

> as though he were a Balfour of Burley charging a squadron of the enemy at the head of his own troop. Not only is there no thread of connection between himself and the other principal participators in the scene, one can't help wondering both whence he came and whither he is going.[35]

The National Magazine decried the overemphasis on death in the composition, while, contrarily, German critics (Americans were informed) praised the work for its atypical lack of corpses.[36] Such divergent views characterized this painting's critical reception, unlike the highly favorable welcome which had greeted Leutze's earlier Washington Crossing the Delaware. Indeed, Washington at the Battle of Monmouth suffered from inevitable comparison to its predecessor. In fact, Leutze intended the Monmouth scene as a companion piece to the Crossing picture. As The Albion noted, Americans awaited with great anticipation Leutze's follow-up to Washington Crossing the Delaware.[37] The second work, however, lacked the immediate and cohesive formal and psychological nature of the earlier painting; it did not, as one writer explained, have "the look."[38] While the Monmouth picture may have been more "democratic," i.e., truthful,[39] its confusing composition was a disappointment after the clear, ideality of Washington Crossing the Delaware. It is to this most famous of Leutze's paintings that we now turn our attention, for the work is a superb example of Washington as leader.

Washington Crossing the Delaware (fig. 72), has become, along with Trumbull's Declaration of Independence, the best known American history painting. And, except for Stuart's "Athenaeum" portrait, Leutze's painting is, undoubtedly, the most familiar image of the hero. Washington Crossing the Delaware is an icon of Washington the leader, not just as a commander of troops crossing a frozen river, but as the leader of the emerging nation. The painting, executed in Düsseldorf, has been recently discussed in its relationship to the German political climate in which it was created.[40] While this consideration of the European ambience is well-taken, it does not fully explore the symbolism of the painting, which made it valid for the German as well as the American audience. The painting is a profoundly heroic visual summing up of attitudes toward and attributes of George Washington and America.

Depicting the moment on Christmas Day, 1776, when Washington led his men across the frozen Delaware River to launch a surprise attack on the British and Hessian troops, Leutze's painting shows a determined hero in command. As the crossing of the Delaware represented a turning point in the Revolution, its visualization is associated with the bold and courageous leadership which made it possible. The scene had been rendered before, and in a monumental size (twelve by seventeen feet), by Thomas Sully in 1819.[41] His Washington's Passage of the Delaware (fig. 73) represented the standard image of the event before mid-century, frequently being reproduced in books and periodicals. Discussing the great celebrity of Sully's painting, a writer in the December 1844 Godey's Lady's Book wished that the artist would render this type of grand history painting more often and hoped that other American artists would imitate the noble example set in the picture.[42] However, with its arrival in the United States in 1851, Leutze's version supplanted Sully's work as "the" depiction of the scene. Largely due to the efforts of the American Art-Union, which intended to engrave the work, Leutze's painting received an abundance of good advance press, causing Americans to anxiously await its coming to their shores.

The popularity of Leutze's <u>Washington Crossing the Delaware</u>, and the reason for its becoming so implanted in the American psyche, are because of its tremendous and immediate concentration on the heroic leader. A contemporary critic praised the work, saying that unlike many other good history paintings which must be scrutinized before they can be appreciated, the merits of the Leutze: " . . . immediately strike the eye. You feel embued [<u>sic</u>] with its spirit, animated by its impulse, and flushed with its excitement, ere you have breathing time to break it up into groups or scan its details."[43] Echoing these sentiments, another writer, who though highly critical of the painting, admired the composition's success at "focalizing and centralizing the mind, so that the picture at the first blow upon the eye startles and thrills the spectator."[44] Leutze sets a standing Washington within a triangular figural arrangement. Oarsmen at either end of Washington's boat effectively lock the frieze-like composition in place. Despite depicting the hazards of navigating an ice-choked river, stability characterizes the painting. Oars to the left of the hero lead the viewer's eye toward him, while behind him figures build up to culminate in his form. Washington is rendered as above all others, yet, significantly, below the American flag. Washington's posture and placement convey the stability and steadfastness of his leadership in a manner which grandly confirms and perpetuates his mythic stature.

While the compositional form of Washington Crossing the Delaware displays a classicistic bias, its content is decidedly romantic. A element of danger imbues Washington's stance with the heroic. As Napoleon in David's Napoleon at the Passage of St. Bernard (fig. 16), Leutze's Washington assumes, even more than Sully's, a majestic, courageous posture in a threatening environment (an 1832 etching by John Baker (fig. 74) directly links David's image and the crossing of the Delaware. Baker had also executed an etching after David's work. Significantly (see below), Baker's Washington faces a different direction than that taken by the hero in either David's or Leutze's painting).

Although the oarsmen appear in control of their craft, they are clearly struggling against very difficult nautical conditions, and, in this respect, Leutze's painting enters into the "storm-tossed boat" tradition.[45] Washington Crossing the Delaware is not a disaster image, but a formal comparison with Théodore Géricault's The Raft of the Medusa (1818-19; fig. 75) is illuminating. Both monumental paintings feature masses of bodies (more active in the French work than in the American) leading upward to an elevated figure; fluttering elements (flag and sail) provide dramatic movement in each; the Delaware is calmer than the waters off the North African coast, yet ice floes and freezing weather distress and endanger the Americans as giant swells do the Europeans; and in each the meaning is ultimately embodied in an apex figure, who casts his eyes on a distant goal. Whether or not Géricault's famous

painting inspired or influenced Leutze's cannot be conclusively demonstrated; the comparison between the two is offered to substantiate the
romantic sensibility of the American's work.

The romantic nature of Washington Crossing the Delaware becomes
further evident when one considers the direction to which the composition
is oriented. Close up to the picture plane, Washington's boat is on a
course running right to left in terms of the format. Reading the canvas
as though it were a map, the implied progress of the boat to the left
signifies a westerly movement. The rationale for regarding the canvas
as directional is based on the cultural experience of reading maps and
charts, as well as on the evidence of the numerous American paintings
depicting pioneers moving west. Typically, such scenes show figures
moving toward or surveying the left portion of the composition, it
representing the West (fig. 76). This is also true in Leutze's later
composition Westward the Course of Empire Takes Its Way (1862; fig. 77).
Suggestion is here made that in Leutze's painting Washington is crossing
the Delaware in the "wrong" direction. The boat should be travelling
left to right to convey the sense of crossing east to New Jersey from
Pennsylvania, as in Thomas Eakins's 1893 bronze relief for the Trenton
Battle Monument (fig. 78).[46] Leutze, who grew up in Philadelphia, knew,
of course, that New Jersey lies east of Pennsylvania. It could be
argued that the viewer observes the scene from the "north," yet such a
subtle manipulation of direction seems contrary to the otherwise obvious
character of the composition. When we begin to ask why the artist
should choose to render the event in the manner he has, an answer becomes

apparent: Leutze is not depicting the literal crossing of the river (as the unreal stance of the hero and historical inaccuracies, such as the type of boat and flag, indicate), but rather the larger, and mythical, idea of "Westward the Course of Empire." By reversing the real direction of the crossing, the artist creates a much more sweeping national statement. As a turning point of the Revolution, the crossing allowed, in effect, America to fulfill Bishop Berkeley's 1726 prophecy of the westward course of empire. The painting is then a symbolic depiction of a theme which is an integral part of the American myth.

Besides the directional attitude of the painting, another compositional element, a small star, supports the westward-the-course-of-empire interpretation. The star appears above and to the left of Washington. Although included at the suggestion of Andreas Achenbach (the leading landscapist of the Düsseldorf school),[47] to signify time, the star nevertheless does amplify the manifest destiny concept. Often Berkeley's phrase was worded "Westward the Star of Empire." Washington himself was linked to the metaphor. Daniel Webster, in 1832, on the hundredth anniversary of the hero's birthday, claimed that Washington had stood at the beginning of a new era as the head of the New World, and then quoted from Berkeley's poem.[48] The subject matter of Leutze's painting, its implied directional flow, and the star within the composition, all reinforce this interpretation of the painting's content as embodying America as the epitome of the westward course of civilization.

The star also relates specifically to Washington, who was

often regarded in stellar terms: "Thy brightest star--our Washington!"[49] John Morin Scott proclaimed in 1815 that during both the bright and dark days of revolution "the star of Washington shone with unclouded lustre."[50] Equating Washington with the polar star began in the late eighteenth century and continued during the next.[51] In a poem accompanying Daniel Huntington's representation of Washington crossing the Allegheny (an event typologically relating to the Delaware incident), Anne C. Lynch considered the hero not only a "star of victory," but also "a fixed polar star."[52] The star visible in the Leutze composition may, in fact, be the pole star. By mid-nineteenth century, a long established celestial imagery was affixed to Washington, and the star's placement in the Leutze painting certainly appears part of this tradition. Drawing upon the stellar iconography and combining it with another image, Washington as Deliverer, L. Carroll Judson asserted in 1851, that Washington "was designed by his Creator to be a star of the first magnitude on the great theatre of action--the Moses of America."[53]

In depicting the heroic Washington leading his troops across the Delaware, Leutze indeed rendered him as Deliverer. The eulogies and sermons after his death repeatedly cast Washington as a modern day Moses, leading his people out of bondage.[54] Judson remarked in 1851:

> Like Moses, Washington led his countrymen through the dreary wilderness of the Revolution and when the journey terminated he planted them upon the promised land of Freedom and Independence. Like Moses he placed his trust in the God of Hosts and relied upon his special aid and direction under all circumstances.[55]

American tradition allowed, even expected, the viewer of Leutze's painting to associate the crossing of the Delaware with Moses's passage of the Red Sea.[56]

Nevertheless, no reference has been discovered which directly connects the 1776 event with Moses. Rather, the crossing has been linked to another past hero. The Literary World of 1851, referred to Leutze's painting as depicting the boat "bearing our Caesar and his fortunes," and on the Senate floor, on April 8, 1852, Senator James Cooper claimed: "The event of the crossing the Delaware was an event more justly remarkable than the Crossing of the Rubicon."[57] As so often happened in nineteenth-century Washington iconography, the hero became a synthesis of ancient heroes. In regard to Leutze's work, Washington the Deliverer can be seen as explicitly related to Caesar and implicitly to Moses.

Thanks to its heroic form and content, and its technical viruosity, Washington Crossing the Delaware became an American icon. A measure of the painting's popularity is the number of copies and reproductions it spawned. The image became so fixed in the American mind as "the" depiction of that Revolutionary event, that only one nineteenth-century painter attempted to compete with the scene, George Caleb Bingham.[58] Bingham conceived his composition in 1855 (fig. 79), when he announced he intended to "rival the far-famed picture of Leutze."[59] Not completed until 1871, the work never achieved the renown the artist expected. Like Leutze, Bingham fixes Washington within a pyramidal arrangement, which is, however, oriented frontally rather than laterally. In its depiction of advancing leadership, the work recalls Bingham's Daniel Boone Leading the Settlers (1851; fig. 80); certainly, the contents of these two paintings are analogous. Compared to Leutze's work,

Bingham's Washington scene contains too many superfluous elements, distracting the viewer's concentration from the hero. Further, Bingham's General, a portly, mounted figure, lacks the majesty of Leutze's. The focussed and heroic drama attained in Leutze is lost in Bingham, rendering it an impotent competitor.

Although Washington Crossing the Delaware by Emanuel Leutze received popular and critical acclaim, negative criticism, inevitably, appeared. The American Whig Review of August 1852, charged:

> That the whole picture is too melodramatic in its character; too much of costume and accessories, as if it were a tableau vivant; too much dependence upon the background as an opposing force in the principle of effect; and too little reliance upon the expression of countenance which the manly souls and patriotic hearts of those brave men must have carried into that hour of might import.[60]

These remarks anticipated much of the criticism directed at the painting in the following decade. At that time comments reflected the critical disenchantment with the Düsseldorf style in general. The Tribune [New York] critic of 1864 called the work "a drop scene, with the mythical Washington striking an attitude."[61] Similarly, James Jackson Jarves dubbed Leutze "the Forrest [Edwin Forrest the actor] of our painters," explaining that "both men are popular from their bias to the exaggerated and sensational, cultivating the forcible, common, and striking, at the expense of the higher qualities of art."[62] Shown at the well-attended New York Sanitary Fair of 1864, Leutze's painting received reviews which took issue with the composition as well as German art in general:

> The famous painting by LEUTZE, of Washington crossing the Delaware, hangs at the end of the hall in a splendid position-- WASHINGTON with the head and air of a dancing-master, stands upon the prow of the boat ready to teter ashore and dance a pirouet on the snow. It is not the patriot WASHINGTON of the American people.

> And as for the rest, in such a subject, who cares for the boat or
> the ice, how really they are painted, how picturesque and how
> romantically they are arranged. They are well done--but the hero
> is a dreadful failure. It is a very fine specimen of the art of
> picture making as practised in Germany.[63]

Most Americans would not have agreed with this writer's remarks, and
would have been, indeed, quite inspired by the painting (" . . . a
good picture for faint hearts in these times."[64]), which occupied the
place of honor at this 1864 exhibition for the benefit of Union troops.
Leutze did create a viable image of noble, majestic determination and
the painting's celebrity in its day, as well as our own, demonstrates
Leutze's success in interpreting American history and values, and in
adding to the myth of America.

Washington's career as a soldier was marked by and known for
the hardships the hero had to endure. These included his fall into
the freezing Allegheny, the disaster of the Battle of the Monongahela,
and the bitterly cold and dangerous crossing of the Delaware. Yet of
all the deprivations and Herculean tasks faced by Washington, the best
known, perhaps, is the winter passed at Valley Forge in 1777-78.

By all accounts, including Washington's own, the Valley Forge
experience, particularly in late December and early January, was extremely
arduous and cruel. In 1854, J. T. Headley wrote in the popular Graham's
Magazine:

> Valley Forge! What thoughts and emotions are awakened at the
> mention of that name. Sympathy and admiration, pity and love, tears
> and smiles chase each other in rapid succession, as one in
> imagination goes over the history of that wintry encampment. Never
> before was there such an exhibition of the triumph of patriotism
> over neglect and want; of principle over sufferings; of virtue
> over the pangs of starvation. These tattered, half-clad, and
> barefoot soldiers, wan with want, taking up their slow march for
> the wintry forest, leaving their bloody testimonials on every foot

of the frozen ground they traversed, furnished one of the sublimest scenes in history.[65]

Tompkins H. Matteson's Washington at Valley Forge (1855; fig.
81) portrays the harsh conditions endured by the American troops during
the winter of 1777-78. In a composition reminiscent of the often
reproduced Penn's Treaty with the Indians by Benjamin West, Washington
is depicted directing the distribution of provisions. Soldiers in
various states of deprivation, fill the canvas. Martha Washington, aided
by her servant, is seen on the right bandaging an afflicted soldier.
On the left are seen more miserable figures, including one personifying
despair (and recalling a similarly placed figure in Baron Gros's 1804
Pest House at Jaffa, a work which Matteson's composition resembles in
general). The background presents camp activity and soldiers' huts.
Recent archaelogical investigations have revealed that such orderliness
of housing did not actually exist at Valley Forge.[66] Nevertheless,
Matteson's depiction agrees with the historical literature of his day,
which indicated that Washington had ordered uniformity in the location
and construction of the huts. Washington at Valley Forge presents a
generally accurate depiction of the wretched conditions then faced by
the Americans.

Matteson's work is particularly interesting for the degree of
"eye contact" between figures in the composition. Except for the group
around Mrs. Washington, which focuses on her, nearly all of the other
figures concentrate their vision on Washington. Tense psychological
interaction results. The crouching men in the central classicistic
group appear to be anticipating Washington's orders, while the very

dynamic, wind-blown figure behind them, by his countenance and his gesture toward the men on the left, seems to be admonishing the General. Behind Washington stand three officers: one is benign, another stares reproach- fully at the third who glares at the General. Reading facial expressions and gestures, the viewer finds unfolding a narrative of Washington being urged by his miserable men to provide them with supplies, which he does, much to the chagrin of the officer directly behind him.[67] Matteson con- veys a sense of the tension that existed during that hard winter, when men vied for foraged provisions. Officers, in fact, suffered almost as much as the enlisted men, since they were, in European fashion, to pro- vide for their own food and shelter. The artist has chosen a non- specific historical episode to relate the sense of Valley Forge and to cast Washington in the role of provider for the commonweal.

The concern for his men which characterizes Matteson's paint- ing is evident also in Christian Schuessele's Encampment at Valley Forge, Washington and His Wife Visiting the Troops (1854; fig. 83),[68] and Washington and the Committee of Congress at Valley Forge painted by William Powell (1866; fig. 84). Schuessele renders a well-dressed Martha and George Washington surveying a scene of destitution, while the soldiers still manage a "huzzah" for the couple.[69] Mrs. Washington came to the winter camp in February. Headley provided the source for Schuessele's conception, writing in 1854, the biographer noted of the Washingtons that "as the two walked through the wretched camp, even the half-starved and mutinous soldier raised his head to bless them . . . "[70] While Schuessele delineates a melancholic Washington,

Powell offers the viewer an angry General. Due to congressional mis-
management, the American troops were without provisions during the first
weeks of their winter encampment. At Washington's urging, and in an
attempt to rectify the situation, Congress sent a six-man committee to
observe the conditions of the army and to make recommendations. Powell's
symmetrical composition depicts a centrally-located Commander sternly
pointing out to the well-dressed politicos his unclothed, starving men.
Here Washington functions rather like that gesturing form in Matteson's
Washington at Valley Forge. One member of the congressional committee
takes notes while sitting on a dead horse, while the others consider the
miserable, but spirited soldiers. Powell delineates a Washington concerned for his men, stressing the humanity of the hero. As rendered by
the artist, Washington's benevolence is expressed in anger towards the
Congress which created the deprivatory conditions. The hero is then seen
in an atypical emotional attitude, rather like in Leutze's Washington
at the Battle of Monmouth.

Undoubtedly, the most familiar episode associated with the
winter spent at Valley Forge is Washington's prayer in the snow. Weems
included this tale in the ninth edition (1809) of his life of Washington:

> In the winter of '77, while Washington, with the American army
> lay encamped at Valley Forge, a certain good old FRIEND, of the
> respectable family and name of Potts, if I mistake not, had occasion
> to pass through the woods near head-quarters. Treading his way
> along the venerable grove, suddenly he heard the sound of a human
> voice, which as he advanced increased on his ear, and at length be-
> came like the voice of one speaking much in earnest. As he approached
> the spot with a cautious step, whom should he behold, in a dark
> natural bower of ancient oaks, but the commander in chief of the
> American armies on his knees in prayer! Motionless with surprise,
> friend Potts continued on the place till the general, having ended
> his devotions, arose, and, with a countenance of angel serenity,

retired to headquarters: friend Potts then went home, and on
entering his parlour called out to his wife, "Sarah, my dear!
Sarah! All's well! all's well! George Washington will yet
prevail!"

"What's the matter, Isaac?" replied she; "thee seems moved."

"Well, if I seem moved, 'tis no more than what I am. I have
this day seen what I never expected. Thee knows that I always
thought the sword and the gospel utterly inconsistent; and that
no man could be a soldier and a christian at the same time. But
George Washington has this day convinced me of my mistake."

He then related what he had seen, and concluded with this
prophetical remark--"If George Washington be not a man of God, I
am greatly deceived--and still more shall I be deceived if God
do not through him, work out a great salvation for America."[71]

This account, and variations of it, repeatedly appeared in
popular histories of the hero.[72] As one might expect, the veracity of
Weems's narrative is open to question. E. C. McGuire, in his Religious
Opinions and Character of Washington (1836), included a letter supporting
the story, though adding embellishment by having the Quaker also be a
Tory.[73] McGuire also contended that General Knox witnessed Washington's
private devotions, too. In an oration on Washington as a Christian
delivered in 1862, the Philadelphia minister T. W. J. Wylie claimed to
possess a letter which essentially confirmed Weems's tale.[74] Although
the story's plausibility has been assessed more recently by Rupert
Hughes and Marcus Cunliffe, its historical authenticity remains moot.[75]
Regardless of the incident's relationship to the reality of the past,
through art and literature the prayer at Valley Forge, like the crossing
of the Delaware and the cherry tale fable, has become a standard fix-
ture in Washington mythology.

In the visual arts, the subject most frequently appears in a
graphic medium. Two of the most popular versions, both published as
prints, were by Lambert Sachs and Henry Brueckner. Sachs, a portraitist

and history painter, exhibited General Washington at Prayer at Valley Forge at the Pennsylvania Academy in 1854 (fig. 85).[76] The work appeared as a lithograph by Peter Kramer, published by P. S. Duval of Philadelphia, in the same year (fig. 86). In his composition, the artist renders a spotlighted General kneeling in the midst of a lush forest, while an observer stands behind a bush. With his sword and hat lying on the ground, Washington communes, rather beseechingly, with his God. While the overall composition, in its non-winter greenness, recalls an illustration of the scene found in Weld's 1845 Life of Washington (fig. 87), the supplicant attitude Sachs gives the hero is obviously taken from an engraving after Rembrandt Peale's Apotheosis of Washington (1800; fig. 88). This earlier work features an airborne Washington in a pose which Sachs reverses. Further, the concealed Quaker in Sachs compositionally echoes the celestial figures of Martha Washington and her son John in Peale. The artist's content justifies his formal borrowings from Peale; as Washington is ascendant in the earlier work, so he is spiritually uplifted in the later scene of prayer.

Of special interest in Sachs's representation is his rendering of the landscape. The verdant grove the hero prays in is not that of Valley Forge in the harsh winter of 1777-78. Rather, the artist emphasizes the spiritual moment by its "religious" environment: the American wilderness. By the time of Sachs's painting the notion of God-in-nature was an established fact of the American conception of the national landscape.[77] Sachs's reflects this sensibility by rendering Washington's natural "temple" not as it was, leafless and dead, but as it should be, overgrown and wild. This wilderness further relates to the common American notion of the frontier as a place of escape. Here this attitude conceives the frontier not as a safety-valve for overpopulation, but rather as a place of psychological escape, as Thoreau at Walden Pond or Hester Prynne and Arthur Dimmesdale's meeting in the forest in Hawthorne's The Scarlett Letter. Washington may have sought a grove for a very practical reason, as E. C. McGuire explained, he needed this "private oratory" because of camp distractions.[78] However, in the more non-pragmatic and mythical, and hence "truer" sense, the hero sought the wilderness (really an Eden, as created by the artist) for there was to be found God.

Another popular representation of the prayer at Valley Forge was a mixed media engraving by John C. McRae after Henry Brueckner, published in 1866 (fig. 89). Brueckner, a New York lithographer, creates an image much different than Sachs. The work is "real," compared to the "ideal" quality of the Sachs. Washington is now smaller in scale and the environment is convincingly that of winter. The General looks as though he has just walked a few paces from his troops. The spatial composition resembles a "V"-shape, with Washington at the junction of the arms, the observing Quaker along one, and the soldiers placed on the other. Unlike the immediacy of the Lambert Sachs, the Brueckner displays an additive character and a more narrative sense. Compared to the earlier work, however, the Brueckner presents a more convincing representation of the realities, such as they were, of the situation.

While such scenes of the hero in prayer visualize his piety, they, at the same time, depict him as human. Another military episode which furthered this humanization of Washington was his farewell to his officers. For the artist, this historical moment afforded the opportunity, as with his last visit to his mother, of rendering the hero in an extremely touching and emotional state.

Jared Sparks describes the parting between Washington and his officers as a "trial of feeling more severe and painful, then any he had been called to bear":

> This affecting interview took place on the 4th of December 1783. At noon, the principal officers of the army assembled at Frances's [sic] tavern, soon after which their beloved commander entered the room. His emotions were too strong to be concealed. Filling a glass, he turned to them and said, 'With a heart full of love and gratitude, I now take leave of you; I most devoutly wish, that your latter days may be as prosperous and happy, as your former ones have been glorious and honorable.' Having drunk, he added, 'I cannot come to each of you to take my leave, but shall be obliged if each of you will come and take me by the hand.' General Knox, being nearest, turned to him. Washington, incapable of utterance, grasped his hand, and embraced him. In the same affectionate manner he took leave of each succeeding officer. The tear of manly sensibility was in every eye; and not a word was articulated to interrupt the dignified silence, and the tenderness of the scene.[79]

More than Sparks, J. T. Headley stresses the farewell as being too great even for the hero's outstanding self-control, noting the General's voice choked with emotion and his "noble countenance which had moved so calm and fearless through seven years of gloom and carnage, and been the only star of hope to the troubled nation in the night of distress, was now convulsed with feeling."[80] Two paintings by different artists render this scene.

Tompkins H. Matteson's Washington's Farewell to His Officers,

depicts the General toasting his men in Fraunces Tavern (1855; fig. 90).
While the artist's figural arrangement resembles that in his Washington
at Valley Forge of the previous year, Washington's Farewell evinces the
influence of an 1848 Nathaniel Currier print of the same scene (fig. 91).
The placement of the General before an oval architectural motif, a
majority of figures at the left, the officer leaning on the chair, and
the drum on the right, all appear to derive from this earlier lithograph.
That Matteson knew this print is demonstrated by a drawing (now in the
collection of the New York State Historical Association, Cooperstown)
he executed after the Currier.[81]   In Matteson's version of the farewell
scene, Washington toasts his men.   While the emotional countenance ascribed to the hero in the literature is lacking, the officers do display
various attitudes of melancholy.   However, the intensity of feelings of
the Matteson composition is much less than Alonzo Chappel's contemporary
rendering of the same theme.

Chappel was a prolific illustrator whose many "original paintings" were, as engravings of his works habitually stated, in the possession of his publishers.   Washington Taking Leave of His Officers
(1865?; fig. 92) served as an illustration in J. F. Schroeder's 1857
The Life and Times of George Washington.[82]   Rendering the General after
he offers his toast, the artist shows the emotional parting at its most
intense.   As Washington and an officer, probably Henry Knox, embrace,
others watch and some weep.   Sanctioned by history, Chappel paints one
of the few moments when an impassioned response is allowed to surface
from the depths of a personality famed for emotional austerity and

restraint.

After Washington left his officers, he journeyed to Annapolis, where Congress was then in session, in order to tender his resignation as Commander-In-Chief of the American troops. General Washington Resigning His Commission (1824; fig. 93) was one of four Rotunda paintings executed by John Trumbull, consequently becoming famous. Like his other Rotunda works, the scene of the resignation toured the country before its installation in the Capitol, adding to its celebrity. Like his Declaration of Independence, Trumbull's Resignation of General Washington was intended to exhibit moral, rather than military power: " . . . this picture is a record of the loftiest degree of the moral sublime."[83] At least one writer, Samuel L. Knapp, believed, in 1829, that of all the Rotunda pictures, the Resignation of Washington was " . . . perhaps, to most spectators, the most interesting of the whole, rather, however from it moral than natural sublimity."[84] This common nineteenth-century bias of content over form was reinterated in C. Edwards Lester's 1846 account of Trumbull's painting, where he treats less the form and more the implications of the historical event, calling the scene: "one of the highest moral lessons ever given to the world."[85] The 1864 Yale catalogue of Trumbull's work, repeating claims earlier found in such catalogues, asserted:

> The Caesars, the Cromwells, the Napoleons, yielded to the charm of earthly ambition, and betrayed their country; but Washington aspired to loftier, imperishable glory,--to that glory which virtue alone can give, and which no power, no effort, no time, can ever take away or diminish.[86]

A work which never received the fame of Trumbull's, although much publicized in its day, was Edwin White's version of the resignation (fig. 94). Several art journals, especially The Crayon, chronicled the painting's progress from its commissioning by the State of Maryland in 1856,[87] to its completion in 1859. The sustained interest in the work owed to the artist's stature, the governmental commission, and its subject matter.

A well-respected artist, White possessed, in James Jackson Jarves's words, "good taste, pure sentiment, industry and a correct intellectual appreciation of his historical subjects."[88] Regarded as a solid, if not a great artist, White executed numerous history paintings, including Washington Reading the Burial Services Over the Body of Braddock, a study exhibited at the Washington Art Association's fourth annual show in 1860. Artists, history painters in particular, must have been heartened when Maryland commissioned Washington Resigning His Commission for the room where the ceremony had taken place. Public patronage, a traditional source of livelihood for history painters, had, in America, been minimal and sporadic. The Maryland commission, coming in 1856, must have seemed auspicious, for, a year earlier, the last of the Rotunda paintings had been installed and talk among artists concerned the future of government patronage. Additionally, the completion of White's work in 1859, coincided with the widespread interest in the recently established Art Commission and federal support for the arts. The Crayon of October 1859, praised the order for the large (nine by fourteen feet) painting, noting that "Mr. White receives $6,000 for the picture, under circumstances that show the house of assembly of

Maryland to be not only a considerate patron of Art, but a very generous one."[89] Despite its obvious appropriateness for the Maryland State House,[90] the subject of the work was eminently national, assuring its success: "The interest of the work depends upon the event which it commemorates, and the individuals who [sic] it represents."[91]

In praising White's painting, writers lauded not only the content, which was, as Rufus Griswold described the episode, "among the most sublime in human history,"[92] but also the artist's successful handling of form. The Crayon wrote: "Having no energetic posture or dramatic action to express, he has yet contrived to render a formal assembly interesting."[93] The critic writing for The Albion also felt White managed well, considering that "the subject is incapable of very picturesque treat . . . There is, there could have been, no grouping, no action."[94] The artist succeeded through a creative figural arrangement, his varied use of costumes and accessories, by his handling of light and by focussing the participants's, as well as the viewer's, attention on the resigning Washington. The work ranked "with the best efforts of its class" and was felt to be as highly esteemed as "any in which the person of Washington has ever been the prominent figure."[95] Reviewers clearly acknowledged the importance of White's subject and its moral value, but also remarked upon the widespread difficulty of artistically rendering such group scenes. A further discussion of this issue will appear in Chapter V.

Battle scenes and depictions of the military history of America enjoyed high visibility during the middle decades. The form and content

of such works displayed visual excitement and aroused patriotic fervor.
In addition, as interpretations of American history, these representations inherently possessed an exemplum virtutis quality, this being
particularly true of those images involving George Washington. The
military history of the country became, in fact, logically identified
with Washington. Thus, when John McNevin showed, in 1859, his series
of twenty-four paintings chronicling the Revolutionary War, the title
given them was "The Washington Pictures."[96] Likewise, a travelling 1860
panorama featuring thirty scenes (with life-size figures) of American
military history, including Parade of the Stamp Act, Destruction of Tea,
Boston, and Murder of Jane McCrea, was called "The Washington Tableaux."[97]

While the numerous mid-century depictions of American military
history received praise for "kindling that holy patriotism which lies
at the root of national improvement,"[98] their popularity was often
rivalled by compositions of a more domestic nature. Stearns's Marriage
of Washington attests to this interest. In the following chapter, the
issue of "genreization" will be continued, by focussing on the
domesticated hero.

1. R. M. Elson, Guardians of Tradition, American Schoolbooks of the Nineteenth Century, Lincoln, Neb., 1964, 328.

2. Also known as Washington and the Indians, this painting, now in a private collection, was commissioned by the American Art-Union. Stearns had applied for the commission in order to have funds to go to Europe. He provided the Art-Union with a sketch of the composition and the pertinent extract from Washington's published journal, and he received an order in April, 1847, for a painting not exceeding 250 dollars (American Art-Union Management Committee Minutes, April 19, 1847, The New-York Historical Society, New York). The work was praised for its treatment of the Indians; the artist had, in fact, visited tribes in Canada and western New York for the purpose of attaining authenticity. Deeming the principal figures a bit stiff and statuesque, a writer in 1847, nevertheless, considered the painting: " . . . a long stride in advance of anything he has ever before painted . . . and we think it the best Indian picture we ever saw . . . " ("The Fine Arts," The Literary World, 2, December 25, 1847, 510).

3. The painting was shown at the American Art-Union in 1848, and awarded to Edward M. Perine, Cahaba, Ala. The work is unlocated today.

4. Lanman, "Our Landscape Painters," The Southern Literary Messenger, 16, May, 1850, 277. This and other references to the picture as a historical landscape lead one to wonder if the painting resembled the artist's The Desertion of Sergeant Champe (c. 1836: fig. 14), in depicting small-scale figures in a panoramic landscape.

5. "The Fine Arts," The Literary World, 1, March 27, 1847, 182. Ranney's work, entitled Washington's Mission to the Indians in 1753, was painted around 1847, being in both the National Academy of Design and American Art-Union exhibitions of that year. The work is unlocated today. The description of the composition, appearing in The Literary World, sounds somewhat like Alonzo Chappel's later illustration of the same event (fig. 20). While Chappel's work may have borrowed from Ranney, it certainly was inspired by a version of Paul Delaroche's well-publicized Napoleon Crossing the Alps (c. 1847; fig. 19).

6. Entertaining Anecdotes of Washington, Boston, 1846, 42.

7. "The Wilderness," North American Review, 19, July, 1824, 210.

8. J. Sparks, The Life of George Washington, Boston, 1843, 65.

9. M. L. Weems, The Life of George Washington (M. Cunliffe, ed.), Cambridge, Mass., 1962, 39.

10. Ibid.

11. Sparks, Life of Washington, 64.

12. Weems, Life of Washington, 41.

13. "Battle of the Monongahela," Baltimore Monument, 2, November 11, 1837, 344.

14. Entertaining Anecdotes of Washington, 69.

15. The work generally relates to the notion of the "storm-tossed boat," a significant aspect of Romantic painting. See L. Eitner, "The Open Window and the Storm-Tossed Boat: An Essay in the Iconography of Romanticism," The Art Bulletin, 37, December, 1955, 281-290.

16. "Washington Crossing the Allegheny," The Columbian Magazine, 2, November, 1844, 233.

17. See A. Frankenstein, William Sidney Mount, New York, 1975, 375-377.

18. Ibid., 376. "Patron" is not quite the correct word to describe John M. Gardner. Gardner, a Congressman, had approached the artist concerning a commission to fill the east stairway of the United States Senate Chamber (this explains "ice pouring down those stairs"). The commission came to naught.

19. Ibid.

20. The Richard King Mellon Foundation of Pittsburgh owns Ranney's 1854 painting of the episode. I have not been able to see this painting or its reproduction; however, Robert B. Burr, Jr., informs me that the Mellon painting is unlike the sketch in that both figures stand on the raft (Robert B. Burr, Jr., to author, letter, March 31, 1977). The sketch may have been a preliminary study for the painting, with the artist deciding this unheroic representation of Washington inappropriate for a painting.

21. Weems, Life of Washington, 30.

22. W. Friedlaender, "Napoleon as 'Roi Thaumaturge', " The Journal of the Warburg and Courtauld Institutes, 1940-1941, 139-141.

23. An earlier version of the work by the artist had appeared in Mrs. C. M. Kirkland's Memoirs of Washington of 1857, and in Lossing's Life of Washington, 1, New York, 1860.

24. W. Irving, Life of George Washington, 1, New York, 1856, 215. The artist's illustration closely adheres to this text. Coincidentally, a celebrated anecdote of the nineteenth century was that of Irving as a child being introduced to his namesake: "Washington laid his hand upon the child's head, and from that day to this, the blessing of the 'Father of his Country' has rested upon it" ("Irving's Life of Washington," North American Review, 86, April, 1858, 330).

25. This popular novel also provided the subject for Asher B. Durand's Last Interview Between Washington and Harvey Birch. The work was exhibited at the National Academy of Design in 1843, and appeared as a J. I. Pease engraving in The Gift for 1847.

26. J. F. Cooper, The Spy: A Tale of the Neutral Ground, New York, 1861, 412. Cooper draws upon that oft-repeated saw: "Providence denied him children, so that a nation might call him Father."

27. Ibid.

28. Donald Keyes of Smith College, in an unpublished list of Matteson's works, tentatively dates the painting as 1855, also on the basis of style.

29. See B. J. Slavin, "Thompkins Harrison Matteson: Illustrator of Mid-Nineteenth Century America" (M.A. Thesis, State University of New York College at Oneonta), 1969.

30. This painting was exhibited in the National Academy of Design show of 1848. The oil was noticed in "The Fine Arts," The Literary World, 3, March 11, 1848, 107, and reviewed and unfavorably compared to Washington's Mission to the Indians (of the same year) in "The Fine Arts," The Literary World, 3, June 3, 1848, 350.

31. Another version, smaller in size (51 1/2-by-85-inches compared to 156-by-261-inches) and dated 1857, is found in the collection of the Monmouth County Historical Association, Freehold, N.J.

32. Although the content is nearly the opposite, Antoine-Jean Gros's 1810 The Battle of the Pyramids offers a possible compositional source for the Leutze.

33. H. T. Tuckerman, Essays, Biographical and Critical, Boston, 1857, 5. This passage had appeared in an essay published in the North American Review, July, 1856.

34. See B. S. Groseclose, "Emanuel Leutze, 1816-1868: A German-American History Painter (Ph.D. dissertation, University of Wisconsin, 1973), 123-128.

35. "The Fine Arts," The Albion, 13, November 11, 1854, 537.

36. "Fine Arts," The National Magazine, 5, August, 1854, 191. The German critics were cited in Washington at the Battle of Monmouth. A Historical Painting, by E. Leutze, New York, 1854, 15.

37. The Albion, November 11, 1854, 537.

38. Washington at the Battle of Monmouth, 11.

39. Ibid.

40. For a discussion of the work's execution and different versions, see R. Stehle, "Washington Crossing the Delaware," Pennsylvania History, 31, July, 1964, 269-294; J. Howat, "Washington Crossing the Delaware," Metropolitan Museum of Art Bulletin, 26, March, 1969, 289-299; Groseclose, "Emanuel Leutze," 98-144. For the relationship of the painting to German politics, see B. S. Groseclose, "Washington Crossing the Delaware: The Political Context," The American Art Journal, 7, November, 1975, 70-78.

41. For a detailed account of the work, particularly its commission, see P. P. Fehl, "Thomas Sully's Washington's Passage of the Delaware: The History of a Commission," The Art Bulletin, 55, December, 1973, 584-599.

42. "Visits to the Painters by an Amateur," Godey's Lady's Book, 29, December, 1844, 277.

43. "Fine Arts--Washington Crossing the Delaware: By Leutze," The Albion, 10, November 1, 1851, 525.

44. "The American School of Art," The American Whig Review, 16, August, 1852, 143-144.

45. Arthur Marks made the same point in a lecture on Leutze's painting given at a Temple University symposium on nineteenth-century art, April 2, 1974.

46. As far as I know, the only other consideration of this "wrong way" idea occurs in the treasurer's report of December 26, 1893, in the Minute Book of the Trenton Battle Monument Association. The treasurer observes that the Leutze painting is, among other defects " . . . so faulty in its delineation of the direction of the passage . . ." (Quoted in The Trenton Battle Monument Eakins Bronzes (ed. by Z. Buki and S. Corlette), Trenton, 1973, 72, n. 10.

47. Howat, "Washington Crossing the Delaware," 292. Howat quotes Worthington Whittredge's eyewitness account of the painting's progress.

48. The Works of Daniel Webster, 1, Boston, 1872, 221.

49. W. McCarty, _Songs, Odes, and Other Poems on National Subjects_, 3, Philadelphia, 1842, 424.

50. J. S. Morin, _An Oration Delivered Before the Washington Benevolent Society of Pennsylvania_, Philadelphia, 1815, 16.

51. See the 1789 poem, "Columbia's Favourite Son," quoted in McCarty, _Songs, Odes, and Other Poems_, 1, 320.

52. A. C. Lynch, "Washington Crossing the Alleghany," _The Gift_, Philadelphia, 1845, 277-278.

53. L. C. Judson, _The Sages and Heroes of the American Revolution_, Philadelphia, 1851; Port Washington, N.Y., 1970 reprint, 369. It was, perhaps, not entirely fortuitous that a poem entitled "To the North Star" followed (and actually faced) an anecdote of Washington in B. D. Emerson's _The First Class Reader: A Selection for Exercises in Reading, from Standard British and American Authors, in Prose and Verse_, Claremont, N.H., 1845, 204-206.

54. See R. P. Hay, "George Washington: American Moses," _American Quarterly_, 21, Winter, 1969, 780-791.

55. Judson, _Sages and Heroes of the Revolution_, 368.

56. To my knowledge, Marks, "Leutze's _Washington Crossing the Delaware_," was the first to discuss the work specifically in relation to Moses.

57. "Leutze's Washington Crossing the Delaware," _The Literary World_, 9, October 18, 1851, 311. Cooper is quoted in C. Fairman, _Art and Artists of the Capitol of the United States of America_, Washington, D.C., 1927, 136.

58. Thomas Eakins rendered the work in sculptural form in 1893. In the twentieth century, Larry Rivers, Roy Lichtenstein, John Clem Clarke and Peter Saul are among the artists who have reacted to the Leutze painting.

59. E. M. Bloch, _George Caleb Bingham_, 1, Berkeley and Los Angeles, 1967, 233.

60. _The American Whig Review_, August, 1852, 143-144.

61. Quoted in "Our Artists and Their Critics," _The New Path_, 2, May, 1864, 5.

62. J. J. Jarves, _The Art-Idea_, New York, 1864, 178.

63. "Art Notes--The Art Gallery of the Sanitary Fair," The New-York Times, 13, April 11, 1864, 2.

64. A Wounded Soldier, "Recollections of the Fair in New York.--No. 2," Our Daily Fare, June 10, 1864, 18.

65. J. T. Headley, "George Washington," Graham's Magazine, 45, November, 1854, 419.

66. John B. B. Trussell, Jr., Epic on the Schuylkill, The Valley Forge Encampment, 1777-1778, Harrisburg, 1974, 7.

67. In the artist's preparatory oil sketch (fig. 82), the dynamic, pleading figure is more prominent, while Washington's gesture is much more forceful. Here Washington seems almost to be ordering the provisions to be put away. Tension between officers and enlisted men is symbolized by the rude shelter on the left, compared to the more solid hut, with fireplace, on the right.

68. A. B. Walter's engraving of Schuessele's painting appeared in Graham's Magazine of August, 1854, and in J. T. Headley, The Illustrated Life of George Washington, New York, 1859.

69. Schuessele also painted Washington at Valley Forge, which was exhibited at the third annual show of the Washington Art Association in 1859. This work may or may not be the same as the artist's painting of Washington and the Duché letter. The Reverend Jacob Duché, formerly a supporter of the Revolution (he had given the first prayer in Congress), urged Washington to surrender to the British. In Schuessele's painting, a tense, thoughtful hero crumbles the letter. This event was erroneously thought to have occurred during the Valley Forge period. In fact, the episode took place two months earlier.

70. Headley, Graham's Magazine, November, 1854, 422.

71. Weems, Life of Washington, 181-182.

72. Scholarly books, like Sparks and Irving, omit the tale.

73. E. C. McGuire, Religious Opinions and Character of Washington, New York, 1836, 158-159.

74. [T. W. J. Wylie], Washington. A Discourse Preached Feb. 23, 1862, in the First Reformed Presbyterian Church, Philadelphia, by the Pastor, Philadelphia, 1862, 29.

75. R. Hughes, George Washington, 3, New York, 1930, 270-298; Weems, Life of Washington, xxxvi.
    One of the most fantastic variations on this theme is George

Lippard's account of the "temptation of Washington" in his <u>Washington and His Generals</u> of 1847. As the hero prays in the snow, reminiscent offers Lippard, of "that dark night in Gethesmane," his arch-enemy Sir William Howe materializes, offering the colonist a Dukedom and the Viceroyship of America. Washington is suitably shocked, telling Howe, in no uncertain terms, what he thinks of the proposal. All the while, an aged Tory has been surreptiously watching. So moved is this witness, that he later volunteers for the American army (G. Lippard, <u>Washington and His Generals: Or. Legends of the Revolution</u>, Philadelphia, 1847, 108-109).

76. The Valley Forge Historical Society, Valley Forge, Pa., owns, apparently, the painting auctioned by Sotheby Parke Bernet in early 1976. In the sale catalogue, it is stated that the painting is inscribed on the back "Geo. Washington in prayer at Valley Forge/ by L. Sachs landscape by Paul Weber" (<u>Americana</u>, Sotheby Parke Bernet Sale Catalogue No. 3834, January 29-31, 1976, no. 355). The Pennsylvania Academy catalogue of 1854 lists only Sachs (who is also named as owner).

77. Numerous scholars have discussed this idea, for a summary, see B. Novak, "American Landscape: The Nationalist Garden and the Holy Book," <u>Art in America</u>, 60, February, 1972, 46-57.

78. McGuire, <u>Religious Opinions of Washington</u>, 159-160.

79. Sparks, <u>Life of Washington</u>, 371.

80. Headley, <u>Washington and His Generals</u>, 1, 77.

81. The drawing is reproduced as figure 91 in Slavin," Thompkins Harrison Matteson."

82. The Chicago Historical Society, the present owner of the work, dates it as 1865. The date is a puzzle, as Chappel was not in the habit of duplicating a composition at a later time.

83. "The Trumbull Gallery and its Founder," <u>The New-Yorker</u>, 10, October 17, 1840, 76.

84. S. L. Knapp, <u>Lectures on American History, with Remarks on Some Passages of American History</u>, New York, 1829, 206.

85. C. E. Lester, <u>The Artists of America: A Series of Biographical Sketches of American Artists with Portraits and Designs in Steel</u>, New York, 1846, 159.

86. <u>Catalogue of Paintings of Colonel Trumbull</u>, New Haven, 1864, 26-27. In 1864, the suit worn by Washington at his resignation was displayed at the Great Central Fair for the benefit of the United

States Sanitary Commission (see "The Last Day of the Fair," The Philadelphia Inquirer, June 25, 1864, 2).

87. A note appearing in an 1857 journal implies that White had just received the commission ("Domestic Art Gossip," The Crayon, 4, April, 1857, 123). However, the artist's study for the large painting at Annapolis is signed and dated 1856 (American Art Association catalogue, May 17, 1934, no. 212).

88. Jarves, The Art-Idea, 177.

89. "Sketchings--Domestic Art Gossip," The Crayon, 6, October, 1859, 319.

90. "Domestic Art Gossip," Cosmopolitan Art Journal, 3, September, 1859, 183, noted that the painting was to be exhibited in, presumably, New York, before it was sent to Annapolis.

91. "Fine Arts," The Albion, 37, October 1, 1859, 477.

92. Griswold, The Republican Court, 5.

93. The Crayon, October, 1859, 319.

94. Ibid.

95. Ibid.; quoted from the Evening Post, in "Sketchings--Domestic Art Gossip," The Crayon, 6, July, 1859, 221.

96. "The Fine Arts--The Washington Pictures," The Century, 1, February 26, 1859, 3, col. 3.

97. "The Washington Tableaux," The Daily Journal [Wilmington, N.C.], 10, October 1, 1860, 2 col. 1; 3, col. 2.

98. "A Hard Subject to Paint," Godey's Lady's Book, 30, February, 1845, 60.

CHAPTER IV

WASHINGTON DOMESTICATED

> . . . the public want, at present, being less to
> gaze upon the oft-repeated battle-fields and
> occasions of state and great event, than to have a
> nearer look at the domestic daily life of the
> great Chieftain . . .
> The Home Journal, November 26, 1859

When J. B. Stearns completed his Washington as a Farmer, at
Mount Vernon (1851; fig. 95), he presaged an intense interest in
Mount Vernon which culminated in its purchase by the Mount Vernon
Ladies' Association in 1858. Stearns's work reveals the nineteenth-
century concern for and veneration of Mount Vernon and of the attempt
at domesticating George Washington. In this chapter, consideration
will be given to Mount Vernon as fact and idea in art, as well as to
the artistic familiarization of Washington, continuing the earlier
theme of a humanized hero.

George Washington had inherited the property named in honor
of the English admiral Lord Vernon from his older brother Lawrence.
With the canonization of Washington, an extremely swift process
following his death in 1799,[1] his estate likewise assumed a religious
aura. References to Mount Vernon as a "sacred spot!" and a "Mecca
of Republicanism" were typical.[2] For artists and writers, Mount

Vernon became a favorite subject, maintaining its popularity throughout the Civil War period.[3] The Virginia site afforded the artist an
opportunity, unrivalled in American art, of rendering a landscape
imbued with the sentiment of a nationalistic religion: "What need
we say of Mount Vernon? And yet how can we--how can any American
forebear to speak of a spot, around which cluster so many dearly
cherished and hallowed associations."[4] An abundance of paintings
and prints depicting Mount Vernon appeared in nineteenth-century
America. These works can be described as historical landscapes, as
the site rendered cannot be disassociated from the history of its
owner. Such paintings function as visual impulses for the viewer's
musings on past glory: "Mount Vernon! While the eye delights in
the beauty of the engraving, memory is busy recalling the lofty and
manly form that once dwelt there in active life . . . "[5] An image
of Mount Vernon was, in essence, a representation of Washington and
all that he signified:

> By the natural impulse of the heart, the reverence with
> which we look upon great men--benefactors of their kind and
> shedding lustre by their actions upon humanity--extends itself
> to some degree to objects with which they have been closely
> associated.[6]

Thus, John Gadsby Chapman, who regarded himself primarily as a history
painter, could render a "life" of Washington by depictions of appropriate architecture and landscape.[7] Of the nine paintings related
to Washington that Chapman executed between 1833 and 1834 (thus,
shortly after the one hundredth anniversary of the hero's birth),
a third treated Mount Vernon.[8] The estate was observed first from

a distance as though from a boat on the Potomac (fig. 96). Next
the artist portrayed the room where Washington died (fig. 97). In
this romantic conception, "with all the furniture as it was"[9] and
an open window and a cloak draped over the chair, one feels the
presence of the deceased hero. Finally, Chapman represented for the
viewer's contemplation the tomb of Washington (fig. 98). Chapman's
views are didactic in nature and nostalgic in sentiment: didactic
because the viewer is intended to ponder, by association, the greatness of Washington, and nostalgic owing to the growing awareness in
the second quarter of the nineteenth century of a sense of an
American history.

Through the first half of the nineteenth century, writers
continually lamented Mount Vernon's increasing state of disrepair:
"once an Eden, now a wilderness."[10] Nearly all visual representations of the estate, however, depicted the buildings and grounds as
in pristine condition. Artists rendered Mount Vernon as it was,
rather than as it existed. Despite its actual deterioration, Washington's home was not allowed, in art, to assume the appearance of
a ruin. Certainly, Mount Vernon was linked to an Old World ruin
in purpose, yet American nostalgia was related to the beginnings
of a "new" history, not to the ebb and flow of some ancient past.
A sense of the truncated, but eminently usable, American history is
evident in an 1849 writer's description of Mount Vernon as: "A
ruin! an old ruin stood before us! It was not a feudal castle [with
its attendant romanticism, described at length] . . . It was grander,
better, and dearer than all this romantic legend."[11] Although the

decay of Mount Vernon formed part of early nineteenth-century American consciousness, not until 1853, with the founding of the Mount Vernon Ladies' Association by Ann Pamela Cunningham, did a concern for restoring the site become a national campaign. This women's organization won high praise, not only for drawing attention to the physical state of Mount Vernon, but also for re-awakening American patriotism. During the second quarter of the century, writers often noticed Americans's "insensibility to the truths and traditions of the past,"[12] a trait particularly worrisome in the difficult days of the 1850s. The effort of the Mount Vernon Ladies' Association was seen as a reversal of that trend; Beverly R. Wellford, Jr., asserted in an 1855 article that the women were:

> . . . engaged in the sacred work of reviving revolutionary associations and rekindling revolutionary feelings. Upon the success of such a policy, now eminently depends the destiny of twenty millions of living men. If the past be forgotten, who may predict the future before us. We live in troublous times. Our lot is cast in a crisis of our country's destiny. The Ship of State is plunged headlong upon an angry sea, amid tempest tost waves and threatening clouds.[13]

Aside from this larger issue of American patriotism, another concern, more specific in character, emerged: the future ownership of Mount Vernon.

Congress had been urged, from the early years of the century, to acquire Mount Vernon and turn it into a memorial. However, Virginia opposed yielding the property and Congress failed to press the issue. A mounting fear developed over the purchase of the land by a private-enterprise group:

> If such a group was to get it, the place which should be a
> Mecca to our children and children's children forever will
> inevitably become a show-ground, the scenes of bacchanalian
> orgies, and the gambler's den. Nothing but vice can pay the
> interest which private speculation must have at heart . . .[14]

Gleason's Pictorial Drawing-Room Companion had earlier voiced similar

sentiments, noting that "no matter how sacred the spot may be to

history, no matter how dear the ground may be from past associations,

the question is, how much will it bring per foot!"[15] Ultimately,

such fears were not realized, for in 1858, the Mount Vernon Ladies'

Association was able to purchase the estate.

J. B. Stearns's Washington as a Farmer, at Mount Vernon

entrance into American culture marks, then, the long interest in the

estate and anticipates the more vocal concern for its preservation.

The painting represents the hero as a gentleman-farmer, the role he

most preferred.[16] The composition depicts Washington tending to the

management of his land: "When breakfast was over, his horse was

ready at the door, and he rode to his farms, and gave directions for

the day to the managers and laborers."[17] Stearns's Washington, a

well-dressed planter with a tricorn, strikes a "domestic Lansdowne"

pose as he addresses the overseer. Nearby, slaves busily harvest

wheat, while others quench thirsts. The figural group engaged in

the latter activity are particularly heroic in attitude and handsome

in appearance. Playing in the left portion of the scene are a small

boy and girl, Washington's adopted children. Visible in the panoramic

background are the mansion and the Potomac River. The painting

interprets Washington as a domestic, rather than military, leader

presiding over a scene of bountiful harvest. Despite ever enlarging
sectional differences at the time Stearns painted this work, a sense
of well-being characterizes the painting. As a contemporary wrote,
pictures of Washington's childhood had become standard modes of
household instruction, "while his own household in his riper years
is made the example, almost, of an earthly paradise."[18]

In 1851, America was still an agriculturally-based economy,
and Stearns's painting can be comprehended as an apotheosis of this
American way of life, with Washington as "first farmer of his country."
Washington honors farming as farming honors him. Americans could
readily identify with this farmer:

> . . . Washington on his farm at Mount Vernon, performing his
> duties as a virtuous and useful citizen, is not less worthy of
> contemplation than Washington leading his country to indepen-
> dence, and showing her how to enjoy it afterwards. The former
> example is indeed more extensively useful, because it comes
> home to the business and bosoms of ordinary men, and is within
> the reach of their imitation.[19]

Domesticating the hero resulted in no loss of his inspiring
qualities and, in fact, enhanced those traits by making them more
accessible: only one could be Father of his Country, yet many could
be virtuous citizen-farmers.

Washington became a potent symbol of the positive and
patriotic values of agriculture after resigning his military commission in 1783 and returning to his farm. Contemporaries likened
him to Lucius Quinctius Cincinnatus, the fifth century B.C. Roman
statesman who successfully led the State through a major crisis only
to willingly yield power and resume his farming. In 1783, the Order

of the Cincinnati was formed in this country, with Washington as the

president of this organization composed of former Revolutionary

officers. While comparisons between their hero and those of the

past riled some Americans--". . . the pedants of republicanism were

calling him the American Cincinnatus . . . as if our Washington were

honored in playing the adjective to any Roman however illustrious!"[20]--

most Americans during the first half of the nineteenth century would

have concurred with, indeed, been shaped by, Parson Weems's remarks

on Washington as Cincinnatus:

> He abhors war; but, if war be necessary, to this end he bravely
> encounters it. His ruling passion must be obeyed. He beats
> his ploughshare into a sword, and exchanges the peace and
> pleasure of his fame for the din and dangers of the camp.
> Having won the great prize for which he contended, he returns
> to the plough. His military habits are laid by with the same
> ease as he would throw off an old coat . . . The useful citizen
> is the high character he wishes to act-- his sword turned into
> a ploughshare is his favourite instrument, and his beloved
> farm his stage.[21]

In art, one of the earliest images of Washington which

incorporated this useful citizen/Cincinnatus theme was Jean-Antoine

Houdon's life-size statue (1786-95; fig. 99).[22] The French sculptor

originally intended to depict the modern Cincinnatus in antique

garb. However, Washington preferred contemporary attire, noting to

Thomas Jefferson that "this taste for modern costume, which has been

introduced in painting by West I understand is received with applause,

and prevails extensively."[23] Houdon submitted to Washington's taste,

and represented the hero as a modern man, albeit imbued with a class-

icistic sensibility, standing before his plow.

Another late eighteenth-century linkage of Washington and his plow is made in an engraving designed by John J. Barralet and engraved by Alexander Lawson, General Washington's Resignation (fig. 100). This small (6 2/16-by-3 3/16 inches) work appeared in The Philadelphia Magazine and Review, or Monthly Repository of Information and Amusement, for January 1799.[24] In this allegorical scene, a uniformed Washington stands before a personification of America at an altar of public gratitude, near the Temple of Fame. In the foreground appears the eagle with shield and a cornucopia. At Washington's feet lie a chivalric helmet and sword, emblems of the power he is resigning. The hero gestures down towards them with one arm and, with the other, to Mount Vernon in the distance. Before his estate stands a team of oxen harnessed to a plow, but a plow which awaits its master. The Cincinnatus imagery is plain: Washington has left his plow idle during his military leadership, but now after resigning his commission, he must return to the farm to again take up the reins.

An early nineteenth-century engraving which also casts Washington in the Cincinnatus mould is Ralph Rawdon's (c.1816; fig. 101). A gentlemanly Washington, with plow, appears in a grain-framed medallion set in the midst of an allegorical countryside. This compositional device of an image, bearing iconic value, within another has a long tradition in western art: Peter Paul Rubens's altarpiece for the Chiesa Nuova, Rome, being but one example (fig. 102). In Rawdon's engraving, symbols of America's prosperity abound.

The print is, in fact, close in content and form to another by John
J. Barralet, <u>America Guided by Wisdom: an Allegorical Representation
of the United States Denoting Their Independence and Prosperity</u>
(c.1815; fig. 103). Both include an image of Washington and symbols
of commerce and industry, such as the spinning wheel, beehive, cornu-
copiae and ships. The major difference is the specific emphasis on
farming and Washington in the Rawdon work. A classicistic maiden
occupies a spinning wheel, while being crowned by a putto. On the
opposite side of the medallion, another winged child holds aloft a
banner proclaiming "VENERATE THE PLOUGH." This motto apparently
originated with the design of a medal awarded in 1786 by the Philadelphia Society for the Promotion of Agriculture, the earliest
organization involved with reforming agricultural practices in
America.[25] An engraving of this premium (fig. 104) depicts "INDUSTRY,
driving a yoke of oxen . . . PLENTY, following, crowned with the
<u>New Constellation</u>, and supporting over her right arm a Cornucopiae,
teeming with the choicest products of the earth."[26] The exergue
reads "VENERATE THE PLOUGH."[27] Retaining the personification of
Plenty being crowned, Rawdon substituted Washington leaning on his
plow for Industry. Rawdon's engraving was published in Albany,
probably shortly before the 1819 appearance in the same city of the
first issue of the farm journal <u>The Plough Boy</u>. The work of Rawdon
may have triggered an editorial remark which explicitly linked
Washington, Cincinnatus, and the motto: "Was not CINCINNATUS a

Plough Boy?--Was not WASHINGTON a Plough Boy? And was not the first lesson which the Roman and the American learned; and the last which they bequeathed to posterity; VENERATE THE PLOUGH!"[28] This direct connection between Washington and Cincinnatus was also expressed in an Alonzo Chappel illustration for John F. Schroeder's Life and Times of Washington (1859, fig. 105). Chappel's title-page design features a marmoreal, though floating, Washington holding his plow, with the abundant fruits of his labor scattered at his feet. Represented below, in "bas-relief," is the story of Cincinnatus. Chappel, then essentially, illustrates the idea voiced by The Plough Boy writer.

The actual depiction of the Cincinnatus legend in conjunction with an image of Washington is rare, and really unnecessary. However, another artist who, like Chappel, chose to render it was Constantino Brumidi, the so-called "Michelangelo of the Capitol."[29] Brumidi executed numerous paintings in the United States Capitol Building during the years 1855 to 1880. These works, roundly criticized by Americans for their "foreign-ness," included a wall fresco in the then Agriculture Committee Room, Calling of Cincinnatus from the Plow (1855; fig. 106). This scene served as a companion piece to another fresco in the room, which depicted not Washington, but the Calling of Putnam from the Plow to the Revolution (1855; fig. 107).[30] Although far from approaching the status of Washington, Israel Putnam was a Revolutionary hero whose abandonment of the plow to join the fight was a favorite tale. Paintings of Putnam dropping his plow have not been discovered; however, the popularity of this theme is witnessed by its treatment in prints and illustrations. Invariably, the incident is presented as urgent drama, displaying Putnam's immediate willingness to serve. Examples of this subject include Alonzo Chappel's "painting" for Spencer's History of the United States (1858; fig.108)and an engraving in Headley's Illustrated Life of Washington (1859; fig. 109). The application of the Cincinnatus idea to Putnam indicates that although the Roman figure was most closely identified with Washington, it was not exclusively confined to him, and, in fact, came to represent all farmers. The Western Farmer of 1839 praised farmers as Cincinnatus-like defenders of the land: "There is one class of men on whom we can yet rely . . . It is the same class that stood on the green at Lexington--that gathered on the heights of Bunker Hill, and poured down the hills of New England."[31] Again popular graphic art provides an index to the prevalence of the theme (fig. 110). Almost always the farmer responds to news from Lexington. Thus, the Cincinnatus concept is associated with the beginnings of the Revolution, and is culminated when Washington resigns his commission. The linkage of American farmer and Cincinnatus demonstrates yet another example of Revolutionary America's desire, continued during the years of the Early Republic as well, to identify itself with and justify its actions by involing the spirit of the Roman Republic.

Washington as Farmer, at Mount Vernon by J. B. Stearns makes no specific references to Cincinnatus, that is, no plow is used by the American hero. However, well before 1851, the joining of

Washington and Cincinnatus had become secured in American mythology, so that any representation of Washington as a farmer caused the viewer to reflect upon the hero's Cincinnatus-like virutes and his being, in Byron's phrase, "the Cincinnatus of the West."[32]

Despite illustrating the past, Stearns's composition does relate to a common artistic interest of his day--the depiction of rural life. Typically, pre-Civil War paintings of American farming showed a benign life style. For example, William Sidney Mount's paintings, generally relating leisure moments rather than physical work, were major statements in American artists's concern with farm life. Cider Making (1841) by Mount is similar to Stearns in rendering work and relaxation, and in the inclusion of children. Other contemporary works of art treating aspects of farming are Otis A. Bullard's Loading Hay (1846), and Asher B. Durand's Dance of the Haymakers (1851). Only rarely broached, slavery tended to appear as in Stearns's painting: exemplifying the plantation myth of a "pastoral tradition and feudal romance."[33]

Washington as Farmer, at Mount Vernon also relates, at least superficially, to European art. The Stearns painting seems akin in interest to the numerous agricultural scenes like Jean-Francois Millet's The Gleaners (1857; fig. 111). However, the American's work lacks the powerful monumentalism and sociopolitical nature of Millet's. Although Stearns does picture the central group of slaves as heroic, this representation is tied more to Washington as a benevolent master than to ideals of the dignity of labor postulated

by the Revolution of 1848 in France and expressed in the art of
Millet, Gustave Courbet and others.[34] Clearly, a case could be
argued for a political reading of the Stearns's painting. With the
recent debates over and the passage of the Compromise of 1850,
slavery was certainly a major issue of increasing gravity. Yet,
Stearns, in spite of the placement and attitudes of the central
black group, fails to communicate a potent image in the manner of
his European contemporaries. Aside from inherent artistic limitations, part of Stearns's problem stems from Washington's ambiguous
position as a slaveholder, a role which both North and South could
defend, though from opposite points-of-view, during the 1850s and
Civil War. Because Washington, like the Bible, could mean all things
to all people, Stearns's painting offers a multiplicity of readings:
a statement of the virtues of Washington as a farmer; the benefits
of farming in general; Washington as the patriarchal slaveholder; a
depiction of a threatened mode of life. Stearns's painting, although
touching contemporary issues, represented the past, a significant
difference between his work and that of the mid-nineteenth century
European Realists. Yet, as a sign of the non-static structure of
art at that time, Millet and Courbet's works were essentially genre
subjects raised to the level of serious history painting, while
Stearns's was a move in the opposite direction, history as genre.

　　　While J. B. Stearns's painting appears to be the first to
render Washington actively supervising his farm, it was not the
earliest work to put Washington into a farming context. The

frontispiece to an 1834 collection of fables, entitled <u>Aesop, Junior,</u>

<u>in America</u>, showed the "Chief of the Patriot Host" seated in front

of his mansion. This engraving (fig. 112) served as the counterpart

to the title page illustration depicting Aesop, Jr., conversing with

animals. While Washington does not chat with the creatures, various

animals are evident behind him, gazing serenely, thus, placing the

hero in an agricultural ambience. Near him, two foxes run away from

his seat. Traditional symbols of deceit and cunning, foxes flee

from the truth, here personified by Washington. The obvious allegori-

cal nature of this crudely drawn work is not part of Stearns's

aesthetic and it is his work which was to inspire other depictions

of Farmer Washington.

In 1852, Nathaniel Currier published a color lithograph

called <u>Washington at Mount Vernon 1787</u> (fig. 113). Perhaps con-

ceived in reaction to Stearns's work of the previous year, Currier's

print presents a more rustic scene than Stearns's, with a mounted

Washington inspecting his holdings. In the border of the work

appears a quotation from Washington: "Agriculture is the most

healthy, the most useful and the most noble employment of man."

Currier's illustration tends to conform generally to the description

of Washington relayed by George Washington Parke Custis:

> Fancy to yourself a fine, noble-looking old cavalier, well
> mounted, sitting firm and erect in his saddle, the personifica-
> tion of power, mellowed yet not impaired by time, the equip-
> ments of his steed all proper and in perfect orders, his
> clothes plain and those of a gentleman, a broad-brimmed white
> hat, with a small gold buckle in front, a riding switch cut
> from the forest, entirely unattended, and thus you have Washing-
> ton on his farm, in the last days at Mount Vernon.[35]

While Currier's print represents an essentially hard-working farmer, John McNevin's interpretation emphasizes the gentlemanliness of the gentleman-farmer (1859; fig. 114).[36] McNevin creates a bustling harvest scene through which stroll an elegantly appointed Washington arm in arm with his adopted daughter. This romantic interpretation reflects Henry T. Tuckerman's observations on Virginia in Washington's time, made two years earlier:

> The aristocratic sentiment had a more emphatic recognition there than in any other of the English Cis-atlantic colonies: the distinctions of the landed property and of gentle blood were deeply felt; the responsibility of a high caste, and of personal authority and influence over a subject race, kept alive chivalric pride and loyalty; and, with the duties of the agriculturist, the pleasures of the hunt and of the table, and of the rites of an established and unlimited hospitality, was mingled in the thoughts and the conversation of the people that interest in political affairs whence arise public spirit and patriotic enthusiasm.[37]

In its aristocratic sentiment, Washington at Mount Vernon can be seen as a descendent of such pictures as Chapman's Washington in His Youth and Stearns's Marriage of Washington. Related to the notion of aristocracy is that of Washington's paternalism, a feeling also evident in the McNevin print. The engraving illustrates Horatio Hastings Weld's words of a decade earlier: "His domestic government was patriarchal; the people of his establishment were his children, equally the subjects of his authority and the objects of his affection."[38] Mount Vernon becomes then the domestic microcosm of the United States for the "Father of his Country." In Cannibals All! or Slaves without Masters (1856), George Fitzhugh asserted the moralism of the slaveholder by relying on an argument of partiachism:

> His whole life is spent in providing for the minutest wants of
> others . . . Hence he is the least selfish of men . . . Is not
> the head of a large family almost always kind and benevolent?
> And is not the slaveholder the head of the largest family?[39]

Pro-slavery advocates often voiced such words in the 1850s and

during the Civil War period in justifying the "peculiar institution,"

and, by way of evidence, emphasized Washington's slave-owner status.

Intentional or not, McNevin's engraving supports this benign view

of slavery. While this print ultimately derives from the Stearns's

work, McNevin eliminates any sort of physical participation by Wash-

ington in the actual process of farming. Washington does not direct

the field operation, but merely stops to observe. The work does, by

the inclusion of children, refer, like the Stearns, to Washington's

family life at Mount Vernon. The depiction of Washington as pater-

familias forms another body of works of art domesticating the hero.

The first to render Washington and his family was Edward

Savage. The artist's large The Washington Family was completed

around 1795 (fig. 115) and published as an engraving in 1798.

Savage's work, which places the family in a fictive, baroque interior,

achieved popularity and celebrity, being copied often in the nine-

teenth century (Henry Inman and George C. Lambdin made copies;

Christian Schuessele executed a modified version (1865; fig. 116).

Savage's work recalls colonial group painting, such as John Smibert's

"Bermuda Group" (1730), and John Singleton Copley's Mr. and Mrs.

Ralph Izard (1775), Formally, Savage's resembles Copley's, yet the

Izards contemplate a classical object, while the Washingtons study

the Ellicott plan of the new national capitol; hence they look to the

future rather than to the past. Savage's work obviously influenced
Jeremiah Paul's conversation piece (1800; fig. 117), which depicts
the General bidding his family farewell. The grand, pillared space
and the costumes and features of Martha and George Washington derive
from the earlier work. Differing from Savage's group, Paul's scene
includes an additional figure, probably Martha Washington's daughter-
in-law, and elements of action. Paul's painting was engraved in
London by E. Bell and published by Atkins and Nightingale of London
and Philadelphia two weeks after the death of the hero.

While neither Savage or Paul rendered Mount Vernon, or any
known structure, in an identifiable sense, two late eighteenth-
century artists who did depict Washington at a recognizable Mount
Vernon were G. I. Parkyns and Francis Guy (figs. 118 and 119). In
both artists' works, small-scale figures occupy the foreground with
Mount Vernon behind. Even though the figure of Washington is dis-
cernible in each, emphasis is placed on the landscape, the space
which Washington inhabited, rather than the man himself. Reproduced
often in the first half of the nineteenth century, Parkyn's print
apparently fulfilled a desire for the picturesque.

One of the most romantic renderings of Washington and his
family is Thomas Sully's 1850 composition (fig. 120). Similar in
subject to the Jeremiah Paul work, Sully depicts Washington bidding
farewell to his kin. A sense of movement pervades the scene as
Washington turns to his family before setting off on a journey
(perhaps to New York to assume the Presidency). As a moment of

parting, the subject is one of potential sadness; however, Sully interprets it as one of excitement and grandeur. Washington appears more determined than melancholy and displays the countenance and bearing of a man with great and lofty deeds to perform. Though a domestic subject, with children and animals included, Sully imbues the event with a monumental sense of grandeur.

Quite different from the fluidity of the Sully is the more labored and detailed scene created by Alonzo Chappel and engraved by H. B. Hall (1867; fig. 121). This domestic portrait "catches" the Washingtons relaxing: holding her knitting, Mrs. Washington casually leans on the chair occupied by her husband, who, in turn, puts down his book, marking the page with his fingers. The interior is sumptuous, betokening a refined upper class. The mantle section visible in Chappel's composition attests to the artist's attempt at historical accuracy. Samuel Vaughan had given to Washington an Italian marble chimney piece which feature high relief scenes of agricultural life. Chappel could have studied this mantle whether or not he travelled to Mount Vernon, for the piece was illustrated and described in Benson J. Lossing's Mount Vernon and Its Associations of 1859 (fig. 127).[40] Any sense of familiarity engendered by this domestic environment is, however, abated by the gaze, almost supercilious in nature, of the "Chief Host." Ambivalence characterizes the picture: the home-space implies relaxation, yet Washington's attitude makes the viewer uncomfortable, at least, unwelcome, at worst. In fact, many visitors to Mount Vernon were uneasy in Washington's presence. In part, their feeling owed to Washington's formal, reserved and, consequently, aloof air. Even as paterfamilias, psychological distance existed between him and others. Visitors were also conditioned to respond respectfully by the elevated status of the "Father of his Country" (a term first used, apparently, in 1779). In domesticating George Washington, Chappel, like other artists, had to treat an individual whose personality (real and mythic) severely restrained familiarization.

Scenes of Mount Vernon family life other than of a portrait nature also exist. An engraving by H. B. Hall after a drawing by A. Henning renders Mount Vernon in the Olden Times (1856; fig. 123). In this game- and conservation piece, Washington appears as a Natty Bumppo-figure just returned from the hunt. His charming, young wife, elegantly dressed, enters bearing refreshments. The artist strongly contrasts the "wilderness," represented by Washington with his dogs, dead game, knife and boots hanging on the wall, and the "garden," personified by Martha Washington and reinforced by her two finely attired children and the tame landscape, with its classical architectural form, visible through the doorway behind the young wife. The works treat a constant American ambiguity--the land as both frontier and arcadia.

Henning's composition attempts to render history as genre. A supposedly ordinary occurrence in the earlier days of Washington is offered the viewer. Carrying little didactic value, the scene aims at making interesting other sides of Washington's life. In domesticating the hero, the artist is very much in step with his times: European art of the first half of the nineteenth century witnessed a familiarization of the head of state, as an appeal to the middle class.[41] Commenting on this phenomenon at the Salon of 1817, the critic E. F. Miel remarked: "They have shown us kings at home and made us see the man in the hero. Simpler, closer to us, these his- toric personalities please us more."[42] Such thoughts were common in mid-century America as well. A European example rather close to the Henning design is Edwin Landseer's well-known Queen Victoria and Family at Windsor (1843; fig. 124). In both, the man sits as the woman stands, each man has returned from hunting and has strewn dead creatures about the room, a child (or two) is present, dogs pay homage to their masters, and an orderly, classicistic environment appears outside. These formal resemblances make for a similarity in content: the domestication of the ruler. While no direct influence of the English work on the American can be documented, the affinities shared demonstrate parallel cultural values.

Henning's composition anticipated, perhaps influenced, a later work portraying Washington as a sportsman.[43] In an 1868 lithograph by Charles P. Tholey, Washington and a group of friends are pictured after a day's hunt (fig. 125).[44] Included in this imaginary scene are Wayne, Lafayette, Washington, Green, La Grange and Pulaski. As in the Henning, the rewards of a successful hunt are evident. Tholey attempts to render Washington as an entertaining story-teller among his cohorts. However, due to the artist's awkward composition and his

inability to achieve any sense of psychological interaction between
the gentleman-hunters, this interesting effort at rendering history
as genre fails.

A much greater success at such scenes was Thomas P. Rossiter,
an artist, who by his paintings and writings, expressed a deep
interest in the estate of Washington. Rossiter first displayed his
concern for Mount Vernon in a lengthy contribution to The Crayon
of September 1858, entitled "Mount Vernon, Past and Present." The
artist-writer commenced his discourse by chastizing his countrymen
for allowing the dilapidated condition of Washington's home:

> A blush of shame would burn on every patriot's cheek could
> he contemplate the forlorn picture it presents . . . he would
> feel degraded at the sight of his father's house thus permitted
> for sixty years to waste and corrode into a ruin without the
> nation's taking cognizance of it, or caring enough for its
> hallowed walls to rescue them from the spoilings of Time.[45]

Rossiter's harangue echoed sentiments expressed often during the
1840s and 1850s. As the Cincinnati-based The Ladies' Repository
charged in 1854: "Virginia has failed herself to protect and preserve
the home and the grave of her distinguished son, and the Pater Patriae.
His mansion is crumbling away."[46] Eastman Johnson chronicled the
decayed state of Mount Vernon, Eastman Johnson in his Kitchen at Mount
Vernon (c.1857; fig. 126). Beginning in 1853, concerted efforts to
purchase and restore the estate were begun and spearheaded by Ann
Pamela Cunningham (known as "The Southern Matron") and her organization, the Mount Vernon Ladies' Association. In 1858, through
numerous money-raising projects, most notably Edward Everett's
heroic stump-speaking across the land, the Association acquired the

"hallowed" site. In his article, Rossiter noted with pleasure the
success of the women and, with exuberance, urged them to erect "on
one of the promontories, or on a site overlooking the Potomac, a
WALHALIA, or hall of the nation's dead."[47]

Rossiter's interest in Washington at home was also reflected
by five paintings: Washington Reading to his Family Under the Trees
at Mount Vernon (1859); Palmy Days of Mount Vernon (exhibited at
Yale University, 1867); The Library at Mount Vernon (exhibited at
Yale University, 1867); Washington and Family in the Summer House
at Mount Vernon.[48] All of these works portrayed a domesticated
Washington and illustrate the artist's words voiced in The Crayon
article:

> The liberties of his country achieved, and he the agent, now
> a simple citizen among his own people. The little adopted
> ones climbing on his knees, and the good wife, consoler and
> sustainer in camp, cabinet, and field occupying the other
> chair beside the home-hearth. O Epic Muse! O Genius of
> History! O Goddess of Art! was ever more glorious theme to
> record before the admiring nations?[49]

In the past, such an outpouring of sentiment would have celebrated
history painting as the aesthetic record of man's noblest moments.
Rossiter, however, praises history as genre, and his remarks
superbly indicate the status achieved by such history painting by
the mid-nineteenth century. Further Rossiter's statement mirrors
popular conceptions of history; history as less grand and more
accessible.

Richard Rush's 1857 Washington in Domestic Life exemplifies
this interest, as does the reviewer who wrote of the book: "Despite

the proverb that no man is a hero to his valet, we hold that these little episodes of history are precisely those which endear the objects of them to our hearts."[50] Earlier, in an 1854 letter to Rufus W. Griswold, author of The Republican Court, or American Society in the Time of Washington, Charles G. Leland praised Griswold's work as a step toward writing American history as it should be written, not a recitation of the "bricks and mortar," but the more personal character.[51] Likewise, Elizabeth F. Ellet stated, with regard to her "Firesides and Facts of the Revolution," appearing in Godey's Lady's Book of 1858, that she aimed to illustrate the "domestic state of those troubled times . . . "[52] Rossiter's words and paintings express, then, the contemporary interest in a domestication of history.

An 1867 Yale catalogue described Rossiter's The Library at Mount Vernon as: "Washington talking to Nellie Custis. Mrs. Washington and Mrs. Custis listening. The architecture from a sketch made at Mt. Vernon and the various objects introduced, taken from reliable sources."[53] Palmy Days of Mount Vernon also appeared in this same catalogue, with a long, society column-like description:

> Washington entertaining Madison, Hamilton and Patrick Henry, seated by a table on the lawn near the summer house. Mrs. Washington, with Nellie Custis standing behind her chair. In the summer house are Richard Henry Lee, talking to Laurence Lewis, who afterwards married Miss Custis. Mrs. George A. Washington, widow of a favorite nephew, leans against a pillar of the summer house, watching her children; one son, Lafayette Washington, is teaching a dog tricks, while a girl looks on with her skirt full of flowers. George Washington Lafayette, a guest at Mount Vernon, is talking to Mrs. Madison in the summer house. The figures beyond are Mrs. Sophia Chew, Lord Fairfax and his sister.

> The group on the lawn is composed of Dr. Stuart and his wife, formerly Mrs. Custis, mother of Nellie and George Washington Parke Custis, who is at her feet looking at some game which the Doctor and his companion, Tobias Lear, have shot. The young lady is the daughter of Dr. Stuart.
> In the middle distance is the Mansion, the Potomac, and the Maryland Hills beyond.[54]

Depicting a veritable "who's who" of Early Republic luminaries, Palmy Days of Mount Vernon seems to be a rural counterpart to Daniel Huntington's The Republican Court (1861; fig. 146) and an expanded conception of Rossiter's best known painting, Washington and Lafayette at Mount Vernon (fig. 127).[55]

In creating this large (87-by-146 1/2-inches) work of Lafayette's 1784 visit to the estate, Rossiter collaborated with Louis Remy Mignot.[56] The former handled the figures, while the latter rendered the landscape. The painting received considerable publicity during its progress and following its completion. Contemporaries praised the work for its form and content. Over a decade later, when interest in history painting was waning, reactions to the work were less than kind: "Washington at home at Mount Vernon is positively execrable;" "The father of his country was as stately, and Lafayette as idiotic-looking, as usual."[57] Contemporary critics, however, found much to recommend the picture, noting that it was "sure to be popular, and which to the elements of popularity adds intrinsic merit as a work of art."[58] The Home Journal of November 26, 1859, greatly lauded the artist's choice of subject, saying that Rossiter and Mignot "have prepared a feast for which the public appetite was particularly ready."[59] In this respect, the painting favorably

compared to Benson J. Lossing's contemporary book, <u>Mount Vernon and</u>
<u>Its Associations</u>. Writers stressed that while Washington appears as
<u>paterfamilias</u>, he still maintains "all his native dignity:"

> The family are upon that favorite American lounging place
> (if Washington could ever lounge), the verrandah, or as it is
> here somewhat unaccountably called, the piazza . . . So charming
> is the attitude and manner of the young French Marquis, that
> in spite of the idolization of Washington, he will surely be
> the favourite of all beholders, except those who maybe won by
> the charms of Mrs. Custis.[59]

The most interesting and revealing line in the passage is the paren-
thetical remark "if Washington could ever lounge." This statement
succinctly states the difficulty encountered by artists attempting
to domesticate or humanize Washington; the character of Washington
simply did not easily lend itself to familiarization. Hence, in
scenes like Rossiter and Mignot's, Washington still appears, despite
the artistic intention, a figure above the general level of humanity.
Washington could be pictured in a relaxed situation, but nothing in
his character allowed an American artist the familiarity evident in
Jean-Auguste-Dominque Ingres's or Richard Parke Bonnington's scenes
of Henry IV playing with his children. Mrs. Kirkland summed up the
artist's problem of humanizing Washington, when she observed, in
1855, that compared to the heroic side of Washington, the domestic
was "less grand, but not less symmetrical, and wonderfully free from
those lowering discrepancies which bring near to our own level all
other great, conspicuous men."[61] Washington then could be humanized,
but could never be commonplace; he could be accessible, but he would
be still elevated. Washington's persona did not permit a depiction

of a carefree and jocular individual. As Marcus Cunliffe has written, with Washington, man and monument became one.[62] The artist, then, relied on the environment he selected to signify a domestication of the hero.

Complementing the painting of Washington and Lafayette was a descriptive tract written by Rossiter, in which he detailed the extensive research involved in creating the scene of Washington and Lafayette "in colloquy."[63] The newspaper, The Pennsylvania Gazette, which Lafayette holds, indicates the two veterans (lest the viewer forget, a powder horn, with "1776" inscribed, appears in the foreground him) discussing a topic of the day. On the porch are seen Mrs. Washington, her daughter-in-law and her granddaughter. Her grandson plays on the lawn with a servant. The realistically painted scene, "like a photograph from the Past,"[64] is one of domestic tranquility and harmony. In his pamphlet, Rossiter waxes poetic on Washington and Mount Vernon: "What thoughts of a Hero's repose are awakened at mention of the beloved Home of the venerated and idolized Father of the Nation! What a Mecca of the Western Hemisphere is its site!"[65] Rossiter deems Washington "the most perfect Man of History!"[66] and, referring to Byron's poem, which is included in the tract, he places his scene in 1784, when "the modern Cincinnatus exchanged the sword for the pruning hook."[67] The painting's claim to historical authenticity, which validates its status as a history painting, is asserted by Rossiter who mentions not only Mignot having travelled to Mount Vernon, but his own research through available

primary data and his basing his depiction of Washington's features on
Houdon's bust of the hero.[68] The artist presumably also relied on
Stuart's conception of Washington, for Rossiter notes that the Stuart
image has "passed from excellent portraiture into the type of the
Hero . . . "[69] The mid-century interest in phrenology becomes
apparent in Rossiter's remarks that in all Washington's portraits,
the leader conveys "unmistakably determination, force, and indomitable
will. In this respect, like Napoleon's mask, and that of all great
commanders, it is a striking example . . . ,"[70] further, "like the
head of Napoleon, Washington's will ever remain a standard from which
to compare other men's cranial and facial combinations."[71] As Rossiter's interest in "cranial and facial combinations" providing guides
to character reflects his society's interests, so does his linking of
Washington and Napoleon. This latter point will be discussed
further in Chapter VI.

Although remaining in Rossiter's possession until his death
in 1871,[72] the painting was, nevertheless, well-known. Before the
large work reached completion, a finished sketch was sent to London
to be engraved by Thomas Oldham Barlow, whose large folio version
appeared in 1859. The Crayon felt that "so far as effect is concerned, the engraving will be superior to the picture, some of the
beauties that appertain to composition being more forcibly expressed
in chiaroscuro."[73] The painting was exhibited at the National
Academy of Design from December 1859, to January 1860, when it
traveled to Washington, D.C., "where, we trust [wrote The Home

<u>Journal</u>], it will become the property of the nation."[74] Ilene Fort
has plausibly suggested that the exhibition of the painting in Washington was intended to prove to the government and the recently-
established Art Commission that an American artist could, in fact,
execute a large-scale painting of an American historical subject.[75]
The painting may have been, indeed, not just exhibited for this purpose, but actually undertaken specifically as a demonstration piece,
linked to his ideas concerning the Capitol extension decoration
elucidated in <u>The Crayon</u> of 1858.[76]

In October 1860, when Albert Edward, the Prince of Wales,
visited Washington, D.C., he was presented a unique large photograph
of Rossiter's painting.[77] This speaks well of its celebrity. The
presentation, perhaps, also indicated a desire to fulfill the historical content of the painting in the contemporary sense: like
Lafayette, the Prince was a reminder of the Revolution as well as
a signifier of unity between America and Europe. The painting also
achieved fame because in lobbying for the picture's purchase by the
federal government, the artist succeeded in having the work hung in
the United States Capitol Rotunda, again, for a few weeks in early
1867.

The impact of Rossiter's work appears in a large folio
lithograph drawn by Charles P. Tholey and published by G. Spohni in
1868, titled <u>Genl. Lafayette's Departure from Mount Vernon 1784</u> (fig.
128). The composition, although reversed, is fundamentally the same
as that of the Rossiter painting. Lafayette's departure had been

treated earlier, in 1847, by an illustration in Life of General Lafayette (fig. 129). Although this depiction only generally connects with Tholey, the drawing does derive from a representation of Washington at Mount Vernon, Jeremiah Paul's The Washington Family (fig. 117). The illustrator of the Lafayette scene took the 1800 engraving after Paul and substituted Washington for his wife and put Lafayette in Washington's former place, leaving the remainder of the composition virtually intact. Another work depicting Washington and Lafayette does show the general influence of the Rossiter: Otto Knirsch's 1867 lithograph Mount Vernon (fig. 130).[78] Although Knirsch moves the family down from the porch, and changes the grouping (except for young George Washington Parke Custis on the left), the spirit of the piece is essentially that of the Rossiter painting.

Like J. B. Stearns's Washington as a Farmer, at Mount Vernon, the painting by Thomas Rossiter renders a domesticated Washington. Rossiter's composition is, however, much larger in size and scale, and with this work history as genre reached monumental proportions, affirming the mid-nineteenth century breakdown of distinctions between history and genre, as well as asserting the status achieved by the contemporary interest in domesticating the hero.

Notes--Chapter IV

1. 340 extant sermons and funeral orations on Washington published shortly after his death were fundamental in this process.

2. R. Criswell, Jr., "Mount Vernon," Godey's Lady's Book, 39, October, 1849, 247; B. R. Wellford, Jr., "Address Delivered Before the Ladies' Mount Vernon Association July 4, 1855," The Southern Literary Messenger, 21, September, 1855, 566.

3. The elevated status of Mount Vernon was clearly demonstrated during the War when it was deemed neutral territory and a peaceful meeting place for soldiers of both sides (R. Harley, "George Washington, Lived Here, Some Early Prints of Mount Vernon, Part I," Antiques, 47, February, 1945, 103).

4. "Mount Vernon," The Columbian Magazine, 4, September, 1845, 139.

5. Ibid.

6. "The Birth-Place of Washington," The Columbian Magazine, 3, February, 1845, 92.

7. The series was painted for James K. Paulding, who in fact, wrote a biography of Washington in 1835.
   Stearns may have contemplated executing paintings similar to Chapman's. In 1851, Stearns made a "professional visit" to Mount Vernon "where he designs making drawings of the interior of the residence of the Father of his Country for future studies" (Art and Artists, The Home Journal, no. 288, August 16, 1851, 3, col. 3). The visit was, of course, also related to his painting of Washington as farmer.

8. Seven of these paintings, including the three views of Mount Vernon, were exhibited at the National Academy of Design in 1835.

9. "The Artist's Studio--John G. Chapman," The New-York Mirror, 12, March 21, 1835, 302.

10. Address of Hon. John W. Houston, on the Purchase of Mount Vernon, by the Ladies of the United States, Delivered Before the Ladies of Milford, Del., on the Evening of February 22d, 1856, Wilmington, Del., 1856, 11.

11. "Mount Vernon," The Columbian Magazine, 10, February, 1849, 87.

12. Wellford, Southern Literary Messenger, 565.

13. Ibid.

14. "The Home of Washington," The Ladies' Repository, 14 March, 1858, 138.

15. "Mount Vernon," Gleason's Pictorial Drawing-Room Companion, 5, October 29, 1853, 273.

16. The painting was exhibited at both the National Academy of Design and the Pennsylvania Academy of the Fine Arts in 1854. This same year the artist was elected an honorary member of the Pennsylvania Academy.

17. J. Sparks, The Life of George Washington, Boston, 1843, 389.

18. "George Washington," The Amaranth, Boston, 1851, 275.

19. [H. H. Weld], The Life of George Washington, Philadelphia, 1845, 146.

20. Washington and the Principles of the Revolution--an Oration delivered before the Municipal Authorities of the City of Boston at the Celebration of the Seventy-Fourth Anniversary of the Declaration of American Independence, July 4, 1850, by Edwin F. Whipple, Boston, 1850, 20. Similar sentiments were expressed by Charles Burroughs in 1832: "He has been called a Fabius, an Aristides, a Marcus Aurelius, an Epaminodas; but all do him injustice, who call him, anything, but WASHINGTON" (C. Burroughs, An Oration on the Moral Grandeur of George Washington on the Centennial Anniversary of his Birth Day, February 22, 1832 at the request of the Citizens of Portsmouth N.H. Portsmouth, 1832, 41).

21. M. L. Weems, The Life of Washington (M. Cunliffe, ed), Cambridge, Mass., 1962, 128. In an earlier passage treating the French and Indian War (p. 37), Weems wrote: "Here, Cincinnatus-like, he betook him to his favourite plough . . . "

22. For a recent, detailed discussion of the sculpture, see H. H. Arnason, The Sculptures of Houdon, New York, 1975, 72-77.

23. Ibid., 76: the letter is dated August 1, 1786.

24. The engraving itself gives a publication date of February 1, 1799. In "The Explanation of the Frontispiece," a writer describes the engraving as being based on a large transparency that was part of the evening's entertainment celebrating Washington's retiring from the Presidency in March, 1797. The writer refers to the work as an "emblem of the American Cincinnatus retiring from public life," and notes that although it was created to commemorate Washington's giving up the Presidency, the composition alludes more particularly to his resigning his military

commission ("The Explanation of the Frontispiece," The Philadelphia Magazine and Review, or Monthly Repository of Information and Amusement, 1, January, 1799, v-vi).

25. L. F. Ellsworth, "The Philadelphia Society for the Promotion of
    Agriculture and Agricultural Reform, 1785-1793," Agricultural
    History, 42, July, 1968, 189.

26. Minutes of the Philadelphia Society for the Promotion of
    Agriculture from Its Institution in February, 1785 to March,
    1810, Philadelphia, 1854, 11: meeting of September 5, 1785.

27. Ibid.: on January 5, 1786, this motto was approved over the
    original selection, INTEREST OMNIUM.

28. H. H. Jr., "Original," The Plough Boy, 1, June 5, 1819, 2.

29. See M. C. Murdock, Constantino Brumidi, Michelangelo of the United
    States Capitol, Washington, D.C., 1950.

30. Typical criticism of Brumidi's work appeared in the Cosmopolitan
    Art Journal of 1858, where his Putnam was regarded as "Italian
    in tone" and "the landscape, the grouping, the attitudes, and
    the expression, are of the Roman campagna, and not of Connecticut,
    as they should be" (Art-Desecration of the Capitol," Cosmopolitan
    Art Journal, 2, March-June, 1858, 136.

31. Quoted in R. H. Abbott, "The Agricultural Press Views the Yeoman:
    1819-1859," Agricultural History, 42, January, 1968, 41.

32. T. Moore, The Works of Byron: With His Letters And Journals,
    and His Life, 10, London, 1832, 15. The line appears in a poem
    originally published in 1814.

33. H. N. Smith, Virgin Land, New York, 1950, 172. This point of
    view was propagated in American fiction especially from the
    1830s on.

34. For a discussion of labor depicted in mid-nineteenth-century
    art, see L. Nochlin, Realism, Harmondsworth, England, 1971, 111-
    137.

35. G. W. P. Custis, Recollections and Private Memoirs of Washington,
    Washington, D.C., 1859, 75. Articles by Custis, which were to
    form this book, were published during the early nineteenth cen-
    tury, especially in the United States Gazette and the National
    Intelligencer. They were also known through their being quoted
    by other authors.

36. The work may relate to the series of paintings the artist exhibited in 1859 called "Washington and the Revolutionary Campaigns," (popularly known as "The Washington Pictures"). A contemporary illustration of Washington as a farmer which completely contrasts the McNevin by showing the hero involved in manual labor is found in J. T. Headley, The Illustrated Life of Washington, New York, 1859.

37. H. T. Tuckerman, Essays, Biographical and Critical, Boston, 1857, 7.

38. [Weld], Life of Washington, 145

39. Quoted in I. H. Bartlett, The American Mind in the Mid-Nineteenth Century, New York, 1967, 91.

40. In Lossing the illustration of the entire mantlepiece, the section rendered in the Chappel (a boy harnessing horses to a plow) correctly appears on the other side. However, an illustration of this section and the text description place it on the left as Chappel has done.

41. This issue has been considered in Nochlin, Realism, M. Levey, Painting at Court, London, 1971, and R. Kaufmann, "Henry IV and President Carter: The Loving Father as a Political Image," Arts Magazine, 51, March, 1977, 114-119.

42. Kaufmann, 114.

43. Tholey may have been inspired by a chapter on Washington as Sportsman in G. W. P. Custis's Recollections and Memoirs of Washington, 1861 edition.

44. The lithograph was printed by G. Spohni and published by John Smith of Philadelphia.

45. T. P. Rossiter, "Mount Vernon, Past and Present," The Crayon, 5, September, 1858, 243.

46. "The Home of Washington," The Ladies' Repository, 14 March, 1854, 138.

47. Rossiter, The Crayon, 252. In calling for Mount Vernon-as-Walhalla, Rossiter again reflected popular notions: in 1855, "Augusta" urged that Mount Vernon be "the Westminster Abbey of America," with each state memorializing in sculpture a native son (An Appeal for the Preservation of the Home and Grave of Washington, Philadelphia, 1855, 17). Similarly, G. W. Doane urged: "Let our Westminster be Mount Vernon!" (G. W. Doane, One World: One Washington: The Oration, in the

City Hall, Burlington, on Washington's Birthday, 1859, Burlington, N.J., 1859, 30). Horatio Stone advocated placing tombs of all the Presidents at Mount Vernon (H. Stone, Inaugural Address, Delivered February 24, 1857, and An Address on National Art, before the Washington Art Association, February 10, 1858, Washington, D.C., 1858, 8).

48. The artist also executed a study of Washington as Farmer, which was sold in a 1859 sale of his works. All are unlocated, except Washington and Lafayette at Mount Vernon (The Metropolitan Museum of Art, New York) and Washington and Family in the Summer House (Malcolm Matheson, Jr., Ferry Point, Va.).

49. Rossiter, The Crayon, 247.

50. "Review of Washington in Domestic Life. From Original Letters and Manuscripts. By Richard Rush. Philadelphia, 1857," The Historical Magazine, 1, June, 1857, 191.

51. Charles G. Leland to Rufus W. Griswold, December 28, 1854, Joseph Jackson Collection, The Historical Society of Pennsylvania, Philadelphia.

52. E. F. Ellet, "Firesides and Facts of the Revolution," Godey's Lady's Book, 56, February, 1858, 121.

53. First Annual Exhibition of the Yale School of the Fine Arts, New Haven, 1867, no. 40. The work was listed as being for sale by the artist.

54. Ibid., no. 78. Also for sale by the artist.

55. The work was originally called The Home of Washington After the War.

56. Mignot had accompanied Eastman Johnson to Mount Vernon in 1857, spending several weeks there. Johnson intended to paint a scene of Washington and Lafayette at Mount Vernon, but never did. It is not known if Mignot was to collaborate with Johnson on this effort, nor what influence Mignot had, if any, on Rossiter's choice subject and on their collaborating on the work. See Highly Important Eighteenth and Nineteenth Century American Paintings (Sotheby Parke Bernet Sale Catalogue, No. 3561), October 25, 1973, no. 33.

57. "Art at the National Capitol," The International Review, 1, April, 1874, 333; "Brooklyn Art Association," The Aldine, 7, 1874, 48.

58. "Fine Arts--Rossiter and Mignot's 'Home of Washington After the War'," The Albion, 37, November 26, 1859, 573.

59. "Mere Mention--George Washington at Home," The Home Journal, no. 720, November 26, 1859, 2, col. 4.

60. The Albion, November 26, 1859, 573.

61. Homes of American Statesmen, Hartford, 1855, 7.

62. M. Cunliffe, George Washington, Man and Monument, New York, 1958.

63. T. P. Rossiter, A Description of the Picture of the Home of Washington After the War. Painted by T. P. Rossiter and L. R. Mignot. With Historical Sketches of the Personages Introduced, New York, 1859, 4.

64. The Home Journal, November 26, 1859, 2.

65. Rossiter, Description of the Picture, 9.

66. Ibid.

67. Ibid., 13.

68. In a letter to James Mulcahy, dated September 9, 1855, Rossiter's granddaughter, Edith Rossiter Bevan, stated that her father (the artist's son) and his twin sister posed for the little Custis children (Rossiter file, Independence National Historical Park, Philadelphia).

69. Rossiter, Description of the Picture, 30.

70. Ibid., 30-31.

71. Ibid., 31. For a detailed phrenological consideration of Washington, see G. Combe, Notes on the United States of America during a Phrenological Visit in 1838-9-40, 1, Philadelphia, 1841, 208-210.

72. No. 223 in the 1873 catalogue of the artist's estate sale, the painting was purchased by William Nelson who bequeathed it to the Metropolitan Museum of Art in 1905.

73. "Domestic Art Gossip," The Crayon, 6, October, 1859, 319.

74. "Mere Mention--The Home of Washington," The Home Journal, no. 728, January 21, 1860, 2, col. 7.

75. I. S. Fort, "High Art and the American Experience: The Career of Thomas Pritchard Rossiter" (M.A. Thesis, Queens College, New York, 1975), 111-115.

76. T. P. Rossiter, "Plan for a National School of Art," The Crayon, 5, October, 1858, 299.

77. "The Prince and the President," The New York Herald, no. 8793, October 5, 1860, 6, col. 5, states that the photograph was 30-by-40-inches and the only one taken.

78. Knirsch was affliated with Currier and Ives, although this particular print was published by Thomas Lawler of San Francisco.

CHAPTER V

WASHINGTON THE CIVIL HERO

> Trumbull's Congressional pictures were derisively
> called "shin-pieces" because the mind disdained to
> see nothing but a row of solemn gentlemen in tight
> black small clothes, when it looked to see the men
> who laid the foundation of the republic. Those con-
> script fathers did, indeed, wear knee-breeches and
> buckles, but when we think of them, they have an
> air of lofty and devoted manhood. If an artist
> cannot deepen this feeling, he ought not to paint
> the picture,--unless he can content himself with
> that success which renders satin, velvet and
> feathers with deceptive imitation.

New York Daily Tribune, 1852

As indicated in his 1849 letter to the Executive Committee
of the American Art-Union, J. B. Stearns intended to paint four scenes
from the life of Washington. Yet in 1856, two years after the four
had appeared as lithographs published by Goupil-Knoedler, the artist
completed a painting, which by its size, rounded upper corners, and
subject matter, was clearly to be read as part of the cycle. The
event and the hero's role illustrated by Stearns in this final painting is Washington as Statesman, at the Constitutional Convention (1856;
fig. 131).[1] Commencing with an examination of this painting, I shall
discuss in this chapter the nature of paintings treating Washington's
political career.

Although narrative, Stearns's painting is essentially a historical group portrait, recalling earlier American examples like Edward Savage's (in collaboration with Robert Edge Pine) Congress Voting Independence (c.1817; fig. 132) and John Trumbull's Declaration of Independence, 4 July, 1776 (1818; fig. 133), as well as a more contemporary and much-publicized painting by G. P. A. Healy, Webster's Reply to Hayne (1851; fig. 134). Further, although Benjamin West's Death of Wolfe of 1770 and his Penn's Treaty with the Indians (c.1771) are early examples of this form, the type, in terms of large crowd size, was established and popularized by John Singleton Copley's Death of the Earl of Chatham (1781). Owing to John Randolph's oft-repeated, denigration of Trumbull's Declaration of Independence, the historical group portrait was often called a "shin piece." Stearns displays in Washington as Statesman the problems which led Randolph to coin such a term. These include a sense of figural randomness, woodenness, and even awkwardness (as in the two seated, right foreground figures). Yet, despite these difficulties, Stearns clearly directs the attention of the participants, as well as the viewer, toward George Washington. And in rendering this hero, the artist has accepted and perpetuated the godlike image of Washington as mythologized in writings such as this from 1844:

> Alike calm, dignified and self-possessed amid the excitement of enterprize and danger . . . ever keeping his eye fixed steadfastly upon the highest aim of a being created for immortality, and ever advancing toward it with a constancy that no inducement could turn aside, as with a vigor of progress that no obstacle could for a moment check, in him we see exemplified the dignity of man, as he was designed to be when the Almighty said "Let us make man in our image, after our likeness."[2]

The very presence of Washington at the convention, serving
as its president, assured its success. Stearns portrays the climactic
moment, when Washington, having just broken months-long, self-imposed,
official silence and addressed the delegates, offered the document
for approval. Positioned on a dias, the elevated hero personifies
stability and leadership in a time of chaos. In his book The
Republican Court, or American Society in the Time of Washington, published the year preceding Stearns's painting, Rufus W. Griswold
described Washington at the convention: "He is the central attractive
figure, and wields a mighty moral influence over these statesmen, not
unlike in its effects that which he exercised over the officers of
the army. He binds them into union."[3] Griswold's words, which
Stearns undoubtedly knew, effectively elucidate the content of Washington as Statesman.

For all the risk-taking and radical political significance
of this 1787 convention, Stearns's representation is only minimally
dramatic. The artist interprets the scene as cool and rational
democracy at work. Being true to the nature (mythical, if not
factual) of the episode, the artist faced a problem inherent in the
depiction of such deliberative assemblages--lack of visual excitement.[4] In reviewing Healy's huge (15-by-27-feet) Webster's Reply
to Hayne, an 1851 writer succinctly stated the problem of such
paintings: "'Actions speak louder than words,' is an old maxim,
and the picture of an action is more impressive than the picture of
a speech."[5] The writer felt, then, that the subject matter conditioned

the form. Only rarely did a legislative subject allow a dramatic
visual interpretation. Peter F. Rothermel took advantage of such an
instance in his Patrick Henry Delivering his Address Before the House
of Burgesses (1851; fig. 135).[6] The artist successfully and dynam-
ically perpetuates the mythic power of the moment by means of a composition recalling Peter Paul Rubens's Mystical Marriage of St.
Catherine (fig. 136)[7] and Godfried Guffens's Rouget de Lisle Singing
the "Marseillaise" (1849), a very popular painting owned by the Pennsylvania Academy of the Fine Arts at mid-century (fig. 137).

The weight that the critic of Healy's painting placed on
subject matter typified mid-nineteenth century art criticism. With
form and content usually understood as dichotomous, writers generally
emphasized the latter, particularly with regard to history painting.
A discussion of history painting in The Literary World of April 1847,
noted that:

> In casting about for subjects, the historical painter is
> frequently struck with graphic historical situations of char-
> acters; and if he can content himself with that, he may make
> a very tolerable picture for the eye, but he must have stronger
> appeals than this to reach the mind and heart. Picture seers
> may be abundantly content with that element of painting which
> appeals only to the eye; but one who appreciates the true end
> of art will never be caught by such flimsy traps.[8]

With the true end of historical art being fundamentally a
moral didacticism, it was natural that Washington should figure
prominently in such art. As a moral exemplar, George Washington
was unimpeachable. Frequently, in discussing paintings treating
Washington and those depicting European heroes writers constructed a

polarity in which the moral, but unpicturesque uniqueness of the
American stood against the amoral, "flimsy traps" of European visual
splendor and panoply. The claim could then be made that:

> The tableaux of Washington's life . . . differ from the prom-
> inent and dramatic events in other lives of warriors and states-
> men in a latent significance and a prophetic interest that appeal
> to the heart more than to the eye . . . It is the absolute mean-
> ing, the wide scope, the glorious issue, and not the mere pictorial
> effect, that absorbs the mind intent on these historical pictures
> . . . In comparison with them, more dazzling and gorgeous illus-
> trations of the life of nations are as evanescent in effect as
> the mirage that paints its dissolving views on the horizon, or
> as pyrotechnic glare beside the stars of the firmament.[9]

The prosaic form of Stearns's Washington as Statesman was then over-
shadowed by the subject; the subject being not merely the specific
historical event, but, in a real sense, the moral leadership of
George Washington and its effect on the United States.

What motivated Stearns to render this scene at this particular
moment remains unknown. Certainly a subject of national union, symbolized by the Constitution, was appropriate for a time when growing
sectionalism threatened the fabric of the Republic. The artist may
have felt that the climate of opinion called for an invocation of the
past in order to speak to the present. But perhaps a more immediate
catalyst (though certainly related to the general influence of impending national disunity) was the establishment of the Assembly Room, the
room of the Constitutional Convention, as a national shrine on Washington's birthday, February 22, 1855. The inspiration for Stearns's
work may have been this event.

The room as it existed at the time of Stearns's 1856 painting
only vaguely resembled the rather sparse interior of 1787, when the

Convention occupied the space. The serenity of that earlier environment was jarred by a busy mid-century interior of tiled floor, Liberty
Bell, walls crammed with portraits from Charles Willson Peale's old
museum, and, at the east end (flanking William Rush's life-size,
carved figure of Washington) two large portraits of Penn and Lafayette
by Henry Inman and Thomas Sully, respectively. No dias existed; portraits and John Haviland-panelling covered doorways and fireplaces
on the east wall. One is tempted, then, when comparing Stearns's
painting with a contemporary lithograph of the space, to believe the
painter has accurately re-created the room (fig. 138). Stearns typically devoted much time to research in order to secure the validity
of his historical compositions. In Washington as Statesman an attempt
at historical fidelity is indicated by the artist's representation of
the delegates.[10] Most are, indeed, identifiable portraits. Apparently, the artist relied on the best known likeness of an individual,
which generally meant the most accessible. For instance, the renderings of James Madison, seated fifth from the left, and of Rufus King,
seated third from the right, came directly from portraits by Gilbert
Stuart, these appearing as engravings in James Herring and James B.
Longacre's popular volumes, The National Portrait Gallery of Distinguished Americans (1852 ed.). Stearns's reconstruction of the
room is, however, another matter. While capturing the spirit of the
space, the artist misrepresented certain details. The chair at the
left is nineteenth, not eighteenth, century, the table coverings
appear to be fabrications of the artist (or influenced, perhaps, by

those in Trumbull's Declaration of Independence) and the east wall
behind Washington is without real architectural fact.[11] Stearns does,
however, correctly render a wooden floor and the two-step dias. He
may have derived these features from either Savage's Congress Voting
Independence or Trumbull's Declaration of Independence, both of which
show the Assembly Room, although from opposite ends. However, had he
studied the Savage work, which is architecturally accurate, Stearns
surely would have rendered the walls and chairs in his painting
differently. More likely, the artist looked at Trumbull's painting
or its engraving by Asher B. Durand (1823). In both Washington as
Statesman and The Declaration of Independence, the dias, the table
coverings and draperies are similar. Also, the general compositional
affinity between the two works indicates a knowledge of the earlier
work by Stearns. In each painting, a small group of standing men in
the center of the "stage" (both take a tableau vivant form) confronts
a single figure. Each composition uses paper as a space-filling device
between the two groups. Such formal similarities, as well as the
celebrity and availability of Trumbull, make the Declaration of Independence a plausible general influence on Stearns. There is, however,
a major difference between the two paintings: the reversal of roles
taken by the two groups. Trumbull gave to the standing group greater
significance, while Stearns assigns more importance to the single
figure. What little drama exists in Stearns's work results from the
standing figure of Washington. Further, by having Washington erect,
thus revealing his chair, the artist imbues additional meaning to the

historical event, for the chair (although unfaithfully drawn) has a sunburst emblem, a device which figures not only in the history of the Constitutional Convention, but also in Washington iconography. The meaning of the chair will be discussed fully in regard to a painting by Thomas P. Rossiter.

A decade after Stearns's painting, Thomas P. Rossiter rendered his interpretation of the same assemblage of statesmen. His Signing of the Constitution is known today by an oil sketch in the collection of the Independence National Historical Park (fig. 139). A larger, finished version is unlocated today.[12] The date of the sketch is fairly certain: Rossiter informed a friend in a letter dated December 28, 1866, that his "study picture of the Constitutional Convention" was far advanced, would be exhibited at the Century Club in New York City on January 5, and that he was thinking of taking it to Washington, D.C.[13] Hoping to receive a commission for a large-scale version, Rossiter took the study to the Capitol, where it was exhibited in the Room of the Senate Committee on Patents in January, 1867.[14] At this same time, the artist's Washington and Lafayette at Mount Vernon was on display in the Capitol Rotunda. Rossiter had earlier attempted to obtain a government commission. In 1855, he had applied, noting that: "Historical compositions have been my constant study, and years spent in Italy, Germany, and this country have been devoted to historic art and its kindred department."[15] In 1858, he published a plan for federal patronage and the decoration of the nearly completed Capitol extension.[16] Rossiter's efforts at securing government patronage proved fruitless.

Superficially, the Rossiter convention scene resembles the Stearns, noticeably in a semi-circular figural arrangement opening to the viewer. Rossiter's figures are, however, smaller in scale and his Washington sits benignly on a very high dias, farther back from the picture plane than Stearns's. Displaying less rigidity and more movement of figures than Stearns, Rossiter treats a different episode of the convention. Washington has already spoken and presented the document; the members are now putting their signatures to paper. The work, like the Stearns takes liberty with history.

Despite evidence found in Rossiter's letters indicating his engaging in rather thorough research before executing the work,[17] the room, its furnishings, and the sunburst backdrop behind Washington are completely imaginary.[18] Rendering true likenesses of the participants concerned Rossiter more than correct details of architecture, and the sunburst form, although based on fact, is historically inaccurate.

The prominent inclusion of the radiant sun motif (fig. 140) suggests levels of meaning transcending its formal value as a device for focussing attention on Washington (which is accomplished by the great dias). Indeed, the sunburst is an age-old attribute of heroes and leaders and, as such, figures strongly in Washington imagery. Typical of the blazing sun motif haloing Washington is a tailpiece from John Frost's Remarkable Events in the History of America, from the Earliest Times to the Year 1848 (fig. 141). This particular illustration may directly bear on Rossiter's Signing of the

Constitution: the engraving appeared at the end of the chapter treating the formation of the Constitution, and the artist owned Frost's book (listed in Rossiter's estate sale catalogue of 1873). The sun image was, by no means, limited to John Frost's volume; time and again, writers and speakers referred to George Washington in solar or luminar terms--Washington was not only the "Father of his Country," he was also its "Sun." Parson Weems mentioned the hero as "the sun beam in council,"[19] while Richard Rush spoke of his "full-orbed glory."[20] Washington was "the one man whose sun-like integrity and capacity shot rays of heat through everything they shone upon," opined The Literary World in 1850.[21] Though speaking of the Revolution, Reverend George Washington Doane's words suit the hero as a civil leader as well: "He was the Sun of the whole system; about which all revolved; and, by which, all were kept together."[22] Likewise, Noah Schenck asserted, in 1861, that like the sun, Washington "was at once the radiating and gravitating center of the system of which he was a member."[23] The well-known Christian symbolism of the sun became easily linked to Washington, the national saint, the Saviour of his country.[24] L. Carroll Judson remarked in his 1851 book, The Sages and Heroes of the American Revolution, that the name of Washington "is encircled by a sacred halo."[25] Judson continued:

> It would require an angel's pen dipped in ethereal fire and an angel's hand to guide it to fully delineate the noble frame work and perfect finish of this great and good man. Like the sun at high meridian, the lustre of his virtues can be seen and felt but not clearly described.[26]

The writer then added: "Like a blazing luminary--his refulgence dims the surrounding stars and illuminates the horizon of biography with a light ineffable."[27] The sunburst in Rossiter's painting then serves formally to distinguish Washington from the others and, more significantly, exemplifies the iconographic tradition of Washington as the solar center of his universe. Further, the sunburst emblem does relate, however greatly modified by the artist, to the historical realities of the 1787 event.

The 1873 auction catalogue of the Rossiter estate describes Signing the Constitution by noting that Benjamin Franklin, in the left foreground, calls Gouverneur Morris's attention to the effigy of the sun, indicating that those members painted in shadow or remote from the spectator did not sign.[28] This remark is rendered moot, at least, by the inconsistent shadows in the sketch, and wrong, at worst, by history itself. The cataloguer confused and combined two passages which appeared in a descriptive broadside accompanying the oil sketch when it was exhibited in Washington in 1867. The flyer stated:

> Near the left foreground Franklin is calling Gouverneur Morris' attention to the effigy of the sun painted behind Washington, saying as narrated by Mr. Madison, 'I have often and often in the course of the session, and the vicissitudes of my hopes and fears as to its issue, looked at the sun behind the President without being able to tell whether it was rising or setting; at length I have the happiness to know that it is the rising and not the setting sun.'
> Those painted in shadow or remote from the spectator did not sign.[29]

Taken from James Madison's final entry in his Constitution journal, the often-repeated Franklin observation became quite famous in the nineteenth century, practically symbolizing the whole convention. Washington Irving, for example, in his popular Life of George

Washington of 1860, hardly mentioned the convention, but does give full play to this anecdote.[30] The passage as published in the 1867 description of Rossiter's painting unfaithfully renders Madison's words. The future president does not mention Gouveneur Morris, while he does specify the sun as being on Washington's chair. Madison wrote:

> Whilst the last members were signing it, Dr. Franklin looking toward the President's chair, at the back of which a rising sun happened to be painted, observed to a few members near him that painters had found it difficult to distinguish in their art a rising from a setting sun. I have, said he, often and often . . . [31]

By having the sunburst appear as a tapestry or wall painting behind Washington rather than on his chair, Rossiter inaccurately re-creates the scene. Compared with Rossiter's work, J. B. Stearns's composition, with its sun chair, appears to display a higher degree of historical fidelity. Such is not the case, however.

The chair occupied by Washington at the Constitutional Convention is known as the "Rising Sun Chair" and is found today in the Assembly Room of Independence Hall (fig. 142). Crafted by John Folwell in 1779 for the State House, this American Chippendale piece resembles neither Rossiter's nor Stearns's chair. A carved and gilded sun, with eyes, partial nose, and rays of equal length, occupies the crest rail, below a liberty cap. From 1854 on, attempts were made to bring the chair, which had passed to the Pennsylvania House of Representatives in Harrisburg, back to Independence Hall. These efforts culminated in the return of the chair on February 22, 1867. Traveling back to New York from Washington, Rossiter may have seen the chair in Philadelphia, and perhaps a correct rendering of the chair appears in his larger painting of the Convention. Stearns would not have seen the piece had he visited Independence Hall preparatory to his work. Max Rosenthal's lithograph (c.1856; fig. 138) shows a chair similar to the "Rising Sun Chair" on the south wall, while at the east end are two chairs which are somewhat close to Stearns's. Although rendering the chair inaccurately, Stearns did maintain the correct general relationship between the sun motif and its support. Rossiter, on the other hand, expands the scale of the device, completely over-shadowing the chair.

By locating the large sun emblem behind George Washington, Rossiter assigned the device three interrelated functions. Firstly, the sun serves to quickly draw the viewer's eye to the leader. Secondly, the motif, a traditional heroic and spiritual symbol, per-petuates the mythic nature of Washington. Thirdly, the sunburst illustrates the well-known prophetic comment of Franklin. In delin-eating and giving prominence to the Franklin observation, Rossiter speaks to his contemporaries. In 1867, with the extreme difficulties and trials of Reconstruction just underway, one could only hope for the reconstitution of the nation's "rising sun."

Few paintings treat Washington's tenure as President of the United States, paralleling the lack of discussion accorded Washington as administrator in American schoolbooks.[32] Like J. B. Stearns's and Thomas P. Rossiter's representations of the Constitutional

Convention, scenes depicting the hero as President necessarily aimed
at displaying his executive steadiness, and consequently resulted in
canvases appealing more to the mind than to the eye. The paucity of
visual images illustrating Washington's Presidency can be explained
by the subject's undramatic and unpicturesque aspect. Artists found
difficulty rendering a visually exciting form when their content was:
"In the management of the civil government, he [Washington] manifested
the practical good sense, and that sound, judgment, which are justly
esteemed the most valuable qualities of the human mind."[33] Thomas
P. Rossiter's Washington and his First Cabinet (n.d.; fig. 143)
exemplifies such an "Administration" painting: the content, with its
nationalistic associational values, is significant, yet the form lacks
vitality.[34] Portraying the men who set the nation's course, this conversation group shows, left to right, Attorney General Edmund Randolph,
President George Washington, Vice-President John Adams, Postmaster
General Samuel Osgood, Secretary of State Thomas Jefferson, Secretary
of War Henry Knox and Secretary of the Treasury Alexander Hamilton.
An 1837 journal boasted that:

> The Cabinet of Washington was one of extraordinary splendor,
> talent and patriotism; and which in the force of its character,
> and indefatigable industry, the unspotted purity of its motives,
> and the prophetic wisdom of its councils, has never been surpassed
> or equalled, by the cabinet of this or perhaps of any European
> nation.[35]

Without this passage's spirit, Rossiter employed the august body
in council as a vehicle for a historical conversation piece, rather
than depicting a specific historical incident. The picture could,
conceivably, depict the first meeting of the Cabinet. However, there

is no indication that this is the intention of the artist. A European
work of a somewhat similar form, but representing a definite historical
moment, in David Wilkie's The First Council of Queen Victoria (1838;
fig. 144). In reality, the Cabinet meetings had their stormy moments
and Washington his piques of temper; Jefferson wrote of Washington
at the meeting of April 2, 1793: "The President was much inflamed,
got into one of those passions when he cannot command himself . . . "[36]
However, the public image of Washington emphasized stability. The
new nation needed to conceive the Executive in such terms, and for
Rossiter,painting during sectional upheavals a half-century later, such
a conception was likewise desirable. The non-dynamic form taken by
"Administration" paintings, exemplified here by the Rossiter, reflected
the myth of a stable, logical and calm leadership.

Tompkins H. Matteson treated the newly-elected President his
Washington Delivering his Inaugural Address (1848/1849; fig. 145).
Engraved by H. S. Sadd and published by John Neale, for whom the work
was painted, this print became well-known in its day.[37] In its general compositional form, the Sadd engraving may have influenced J.
B. Stearns in his Washington as Statesman. Both display an elevated
Washington surrounded by seating and standing figures with another
group standing in the hero's line of vision. Both were also in the
historic event-cum-group portrait tradition of John Trumbull's Declaration of Independence. Contemporaries noted that Matteson's com-
pacted composition, with its "Lansdowne"-like Washington, descended
from Trumbull. The Literary World of May 19, 1849, described the

engraving, acknowledged its antecedent, and commented on the problems of the genre:

> A large and well executed Engraving of a well known historical scene, after the model of Col. Trumbull's Signing of the Declaration of Independence. In works of this kind, where portraits are to be introduced, it is hard to avoid stiffness in composition and great sameness of expression. The present work is not exempt from these faults.[38]

The criticism offered by this writer typified the period. Critics felt this type of historical subject had certain inherent limitations. Another such obstacle cited in regard to the Matteson, was that of historical costume: "Mr. Matteson deserves great credit for his very difficult task of giving pictorial effect to an assemblage of men in the ungainly garments that our forefathers wore."[39] While the problems of "stiffness in composition" and "sameness of expression" might be considered intrinsic to the nature of painting, the issue of costume is extrinsic--the historical epoch dictated the garb, at least, this had been true since Benjamin West's Death of Wolfe of 1770. One solution to "ungainly garments" problem was to remove the subject from the "deliberative assemblage" sphere and place it in a more picturesque social context. Daniel Huntington's The Republican Court moved in this direction.

One of Daniel Huntington's best known paintings, The Republican Court in the Time of Washington, or Lady Washington's Reception (1861; fig. 146) was exhibited at The Derby Gallery, New York, 1865-66, and the Paris Universal Exposition of 1867. The work gained further celebrity through a large steel engraving (titled Lady Washington's Reception) executed by Alexander H. Ritchie in 1866. The painting had been, in fact, commissioned by this highly regarded

New York engraver around 1858.[40] Ritchie must have intended the print
as a counterpart to his earlier Washington and His Generals (c.1855;
fig. 147).[41] Once referred to as Huntington's "areal masterpiece,"[42]
The Republican Court crowds sixty-four figures into its bounds.

Like J. B. Stearns's Washington as Statesman, The Republican
Court represents a gathering of notables. Now, however, the civil
deliberations have given way to social niceties and a domestic, albeit
courtly, ambience. Drab garments are sloughed off in favor of more
elegant costumes. Huntington's opulent conversation piece falls into
a European tradition, exemplified by Marcellus Laroon's The Duke of
Buckingham's Levee of the early eighteenth century (fig. 148). In
representing a group of notables in an essentially honorific scene,
the painting can also be generally related to Delaroche's Hemicycle
of 1841, a work with which Huntington was familiar.[43] With regard to
American art, Ritchie's Washington and His Generals offers a model as
does, even more specifically, Washington's Reception for Mr. and Mrs.
Alexander Hamilton (1856; fig. 149) by Dennis Malone Carter, a well-
known history painter of the mid-century. Carter presages all the
pomp and circumstance of the Huntington. Carter also painted a work
which, by its title, indicates even closer affinity with Huntington:
in the 1862 Pennsylvania Academy of the Fine Arts annual exhibition
Carter showed Mrs. Washington's Friday Afternoon.[44] The catalogue
entry for this now unlocated work included a passage from George
Washington Parke Custis's Recollections and Private Memoirs of Washington:

Washington, in his diary in the autumn of 1789 and the winter of 1790, often makes a simple record, thus: The visitors this afternoon were not numerous but respectable. In the evening great numbers of ladies and many gentlemen visited Mrs. Washington.[45]

The temporal relationship between the "Receptions" of these two artists is unknown; however, due to Huntington's prominence in the American art world, one suspects that the Carter followed the Huntington.[46]

When exhibited at the Derby Gallery in New York, 1865-66, Huntington's The Republican Court was accompanied by a descriptive pamphlet and key.[47] This pamphlet clearly indicates that Huntington represents an ideal assemblage in Philadelphia.[48] Like Rossiter's Washington and His First Cabinet, Huntington's painting renders a recurrent event. Habitually, Martha Washington, or Lady Washington, as her contemporaries addressed her, held Friday evening "levees," from eight until nine or ten o'clock. In re-creating such an event, the artist certainly must have relied upon the well-known and popular 1855 book by Rufus W. Griswold, The Republican Court, or American Society in the Time of Washington. Huntington's title alone manifests a familiarity with Griswold. The artist depicted Washington as described by Griswold at such soirees--appearing in a private rather than an official capacity, without hat or sword, and conversing "without restraint" with women.[49] Further, while the authenticity of the elegant interior Huntington paints is questionable, and was, in fact, doubted by his peers,[50] the painting does visualize Sally McKean's description, quoted in Griswold, of the first levee held in the room:

You never could have had such a drawing-room [in New York]; it was brilliant beyond any thing you can imagine; and though there was a great deal of extravagence, there was so much of Phila-delphia taste in every thing that it must have been confessed the most delightful occasion of the kind ever known in this country.[51]

Little doubt exists that Rufus Griswold's The Republican Court had a strong impact and bearing on The Republican Court of Daniel Hunt-ington.

All of the sixty-four figures in the painting are portraits.[52] The artist copied works by Copley, Stuart, Malbone and others, and "when the resemblance had been transmitted through two generations, a granddaughter would sit for her grandmother's picture."[53] The versimilitude aimed for in individual likenesses was not necessarily true of the painting as a whole. The pamphlet accompanying the paint-ing acknowledged that all those depicted could not really have been present in the same place at the same time. The Duke of Kent (father of Queen Victoria) and the Duc d'Orleans (later Louis Philippe, King of France), who appear behind Washington and Harriet Chew, could not (as the pamphlet points out) have met in Philadelphia. General Greene who stands near this group, had died shortly before the time the work depicts. These inaccuracies did not, however, detract from the painting, according to the pamphlet:

The artist and the poet alike claim a certain degree of license, and the world of art and of letters has always willingly granted it. The liberties taken by Mr. Huntington in this pic-ture with the facts of history are few and immaterial; the slight anachronisms that occur are hardly worthy of notice. The artist's purpose was to represent in one frame the principal statesmen and belles who formed the Republican Court in Washington's second term.[54]

Discussing the painting in his Book of the Artists (1867), Henry T.
Tuckerman accepted this traditional argument for artistic license.
Further, noting that the work was completed just prior to the Civil
War, Tuckerman deemed the painting:

> . . . eminently a national picture, appealing so forcibly to the
> florious past in our history--in its social manifestation--as
> caused tears of sorrow and indignation to start in the eyes of
> every lover of his country as he looked with pride and delight
> upon the beautiful work of Huntington, and contrasted its high
> and endeared associations with the melancholy facts of that
> hour.[55]

Yet, despite Tuckerman's praise and the pamphlet's invocation of
artistic license, not all of the artist's contemporaries approved
the work.

Basing his criticism on the "volunteered admissions" of the
pamphlet, a writer in The Nation of October 12, 1865, questioned the
validity of the painting as historical art. The writer, believing
more anachronisms could probably be found and doubting the representation of the room, felt that Huntington's interest in historical
accuracy was slight. The writer continued:

> Now, let the reader think how pleasant and instructive it would
> be to have as perfect a reproduction as is possible of Washing-
> ton's drawing-room as it really was, or as perfect a conception
> as possible of what it might have been. That would be histor-
> ical art. This picture, let it be confessed, does not pretend
> to be historical art, it pretends to be portraiture only . . .
> The reader will see in print-shop windows a photographic pic-
> ture which represents a crowd of heads of generals, another of
> statesmen, etc.; these are made by cutting out the heads of
> small portrait photographs of the whole. Mr. Huntington's is,
> as historical art, precisely on a par with those "popular"
> works; as portraiture, it is necessarily of but little value
> as compared with them. And we must wait for our historical
> picture of Washington's "Court," thinking how pleasant it would
> be to have one.[56]

The author of The Nation article found, then, Huntington's subject
entirely suitable, but, with a mid-nineteenth-century sense of the
real, he could not accept the factual lapses in the painting.

    The critic of the New-York Daily Tribune of October 21, 1865,
likewise faulted the form of the painting, stating that the artist
"avowedly discards" historical accuracy, while finding the subject
appropriate for his day: "We do not think of any subject for a picture, outside of landscape, which would be so likely to interest all
native Americans as this, which Mr. Huntington has chosen."[57]
Sarcastically praising the work for its snob-appeal, the writer argued
that the depiction of a "Court" in the olden days comforts that growing
class desirous of more pomp and circumstance in government.[58] The
writer bitingly accuses Huntington of pandering to this sentiment.
The journalist also charges that the figural groups are arranged to
flatter certain wealthy families of the day. However, the general
compositional form of the work most concerned the reviewer.

    The chief complaint voiced involved the placement of Martha
Washington, "whom no effort of the imagination can make look like a
queen."[59] Looking embarassed on her dias, she does not, the writer
argued, command the attention that she should: no one addresses her,
no one looks at her, no one does anything in reference to her. This
is, of course, an exaggeration. Washington, striking a Lansdownian
pose, or as the Tribune critic remarked, "delivering his Farewell
Address to an imaginary audience,"[60] does gesture toward his wife,
and various ladies opposite her appear to, at least, recognize her.
Yet, fundamentally, one does accept the writer's criticism of the

painting. The work does lack a basic trait of history painting, a
sense of the narrative. As Frank Leslie, the American Commissioner
of Art for the 1867 Paris Universal Exposition, stated in his official
report: "[the painting] illustrates no event, and tells no story . . .
it is more a costume picture than a historical composition."[61] The
problems of the picture perhaps stem from Huntington's decision to
expand his conception from twenty figures to sixty-four. The artist's
compositional drawings (fig. 150) indicate a shallow room with a small
crowd.[62] In the more finished of these two pencil sketches, the eye
is quickly drawn to Lady Washington and a sense of psychological interaction exists between her and the woman facing her across a rather
wide space. In the sketches the point of view assumed by the beholder
is that of the participants themselves; one looks slightly up to
Mrs. Washington. The viewpoint of the painting differs by being more
elevated and panoramic, in order to accomodate the additional figures.
This shift lessens whatever immediacy the drawings evince. The
inclusion of more figures in the painting created problems of arrangement and, as the Tribune critic rightly emphasized, groups function
as independent units and not as well-integrated forms.

Like the Nation's critic, the author of the Tribune article
considered Huntington's work of little historical worth and of little
value as a collection of portraits. As a costume study the writer
deemed it "inexcusably uninteresting and wanting in character," and
he felt that the artist's reputation as a costume painter would consequently suffer: "A French painter of Mr. Huntington's rank would

have left no stone unturned to get accuracy in his details."[63] The

Tribune writer concluded his criticisms by asserting:

> We should have had first-rate portraits, logical arrangements,
> and beautiful and characteristic costumes painted with con-
> scientious fidelity and care. Nothing more is needed to show
> the raw and provincial character of our Art than the fact that
> the President of our only National Academy, after four years'
> labor, has produced so imcomplete and so uninteresting a record
> of the men and women who made the splendor of our Nation's
> early day.[64]

Despite the _Tribune_ critic's devastating remarks, Hunting-

ton's painting and the engraving received much acclaim. Perhaps, as

the critic charged, the scene did appeal to certain aristocratic

pretentions or yearnings rooted in American society. Certainly a

work like Rufus W. Griswold's _The Republican Court_ of 1855, fostered

an interest in the fashionable social aspect of the past. Rendering

not the usual military or political gathering and assigning prom-

inence to women rather than men, Huntington struck a chord pleasing

to his peers. Women had been increasingly before the public's eye

as significant motivators and organizers of the Mount Vernon Ladies's

Association (1853+) and the United States Sanitary Commission (1861+).

Interest in women of the past appeared not only in Griswold's volume,

but also in Elizabeth F. Ellet's _The Women of the Revolution_ (1848-50),

a popular multi-volumed work, and serialized in periodical literature.

Martha Washington herself was essayed in her grandson's _Recollections_

and Private Memoirs of Washington (1860) and in Benson J. Lossing's

1861 biography. The popularity of Huntington's work relates to

its timely entrance into the matrix of American culture as well as

being the creation of one of America's major and celebrated artists.

A mark of the fame attained by Huntington's The Republican Court is evinced by an 1875 tableau vivant production of the painting, performed under the direction of the artist, by the ladies of the St. John's Guild of New York.[65]

Aside from a work like The Republican Court by Daniel Huntington, visualizations of Washington's civil career, in keeping with their subject, generally appear unpicturesque in form. Yet, for the mid-century American, harassed by sectionalism, such images provided didactic and inspiring reminders of the nation's fundamentally virtuous basis. As literature painted a picture of the prudent and stable leader, so works of art reinforced and perpetuated the myth of George Washington's benign and moral civil guidance.

Notes--Chapter V

1. Another signed version, of the same size (37 1/2-by-54inches) and year is owned by Clarence Dillon, Far Hills, New Jersey. Stearns's duplicating this composition recalls his so doing with his Marriage of Washington. The Dillon painting was perhaps executed first, as it is dated, while the other is not. The Dillon work was exhibited at the centennial celebration of the inauguration of Washington as first President, held at the Metropolitan Opera House, 1889. It was also seen at the Corcoran Gallery's "Commemoration of the 150th Anniversary of the Formation of the Constitution of the United States," in 1938.

2. [J. Inman], "Washington," The Columbian Magazine, 2, July, 1844, 23.

3. R. W. Griswold, The Republican Court, or American Society in the Time of Washington, New York, 1855, 67.

4. One way of mitigating this problem was by depicting a moment related to, but after, the more deliberative one. Examples include Peter F. Rothermel's Reading the Declaration of Independence (c.1864), and E. L. Henry's Independence Hall, July 8, 1776 (1871). Rothermel depicts a rather chaotic scene. Henry's painting shows the signers coming out of the hall and proceeding to announce their decision. Both artists include recognizable figures in their works.

5. "Art and Artists in America," Bulletin of the American Art-Union, November, 1851, 182.

6. The work was engraved, by Alfred Jones, and distributed by the Art Union of Philadelphia in 1852.

7. John W. McCoubrey of the University of Pennsylvania pointed this out to me in October, 1973.

8. "Exhibition at the National Academy," The Literary World, 1, April 24,1847, 279.

9. "The Character of Washington," North American Review, 83, July, 1856, 7.

10. The catalogue of the centennial celebration of Washington's inauguration claims, incredibly, that the artist spent fifteen years collecting portraits of the delegates ("Centennial Celebration of the Inauguration of George Washington as First President of the United States at the Metropolitan Opera House," New York, April 17-May 8, 1889, 61).

11. John C. Milley, Museum Curator of Independence National Historical Park, Philadelphia, kindly provided me with information relative to the room's interior.

12. Both sketch and finished painting were sold at the Rossiter estate sale of 1873, even though the finished work was not listed in the catalogue (George A. Leavitt to Frank M. Etting, May 1, 1874, Etting Collection, The Historical Society of Pennsylvania, Philadelphia). Mrs. William F. (Edith Rossiter) Bevan, the artist's granddaughter, noted that the final painting had been in a hotel in Ely, Minn., and was offered for sale by a Mrs. Nixon of that town in 1952 (Mrs. W. F. Bevan, "Biography of T. P. Rossiter and A Checklist of His Paintings," March, 1957, Archives of American Art, Washington, D.C.).

13. Rossiter file, Independence National Historical Park, Philadelphia. The friend to whom Rossiter writes is unknown, but may be Benson J. Lossing, who Rossiter had corresponded with concerning the painting.

14. Rossiter to James A. McAllister, January 25, 1867, Society Collection, The Historical Society of Pennsylvania, Philadelphia.

15. A. H. Savoie, "A Biographical Sketch of Thomas P. Rossiter" (Paper for the Department of Art, Geroge Washington University, January, 1968), National Collection of Fine Arts, Washington, D.C.

16. T. P. Rossiter, "Plan for a National School of Art," The Crayon, 5, October, 1858, 299.

17. Rossiter to an unknown friend, December 28, 1866, Independence National Historical Park, Philadelphia; Rossiter to Ferdinand J. Dreer, October 5, 1866, The Historical Society of Pennsylvania; Rossiter to James A. McAllister, December 12, 1866, The Historical Society of Pennsylvania, Philadelphia. In this last letter, the artist mentions that woodcuts serve him well enough for the "study picture but should I paint a large one I will look up all the originals . . . "

18. John Milley to H. Dordan Dyke, March 3, 1967, Rossiter File, Independence National Historical Park, Philadelphia.

19. M. L. Weems, The Life of Washington (M. Cunliffe, ed.), Cambridge, Mass., 1962, 3.

20. Quoted in Griswold, The Republican Court, 242.

21. "Washington [from Whipple's Oration at Boston]," The Literary World, 7, July 20, 1850, 55.

22. G. W. Doane, One World: One Washington: The Oration, in the City Hall, Burlington, on Washington's Birth-Day, 1859, Burlington N.J., 1859, 15.

23. The Memory of Washington: An Oration, by the Rev. Noah Hunt Schenck, A.M., Rector of Emmanuel Church, Delivered in Baltimore on the Evening of February 22, 1861, Baltimore, 1861, 9.

24. Without pressing the point, Rossiter's composition may vaguely recall Raphael's Disputa (c.1508), in its general semi-circular arrangement, figure in glory (i.e., Washington elevated with an "aureole"), and figure pointing out the scene (Franklin).

25. L. C. Judson, The Sages and Heroes of the American Revolution, Philadelphia, 1851; Port Washington, N.Y., 1970 reprint, 369.

26. Ibid., 378.

27. Ibid., 379.

28. The Valuable Collection of Engravings, Etchings, Paintings, Antique Furniture, Armor, Bronzes, Rich Brocades, Draperies, Costumes, Etc., A Valuable Library, the Studio Furniture Stock of Artists' Materials, Etc., Etc., Belonging to the late Thomas Prichard Rossiter, Esq. (George A. Leavitt and Co., Auctioneers, Clinton Hall, N.Y.), February 5-8, 1873, no. 222.

29. The Signing of the Constitution. Sept. 17, 1787. A Study Sketch, Painted by Thomas P. Rossiter, N.A., Etting Collection, The Historical Society of Pennsylvania

30. W. Irving, Life of George Washington, 4, New York, 1860, 458.

31. I. Brant, James Madison: Father of the Constitution, 1787-1800, Indianapolis and New York, 1950, 153.

32. R. M. Elson , Guardians of Tradition, American Schoolbooks of the Nineteenth Century, Lincoln, Neb., 1964, 199.

33. S. Worcester, A Fourth Book of Lessons for Reading, Boston, 1842, 95.

34. Another painting by Rossiter rendering the first Presidency, and probably more dramatic, is Washington's Farewell Dinner. This work, undated and unlocated today, is described in the 1868 Rossiter catalogue as showing the President "drinking the health

and taking leave of Members of Cabinet and Diplomatic Body."
The scene is then a civil parallel to the farewell to the officers.
The catalogue lists the following as being delineated in this
48-by-54-inch painting: John Adams, Jefferson, Hamilton, Ells-
worth, Pickering, Cushing, Liston, British Ambassador and wife,
Marquis D'Yrujo, Spanish Minister, Marchioness D'Yrujo, Mr. and
Mrs. McHenry, Mr. and Mrs. Bingham, Mrs. Ellsworth, Mrs. Picker-
ing, Mrs. Cushing, and Bishop White (Catalogue of the Entire
Collection of Paintings, Studies and Sketches of Mr. T. P.
Rossiter, Cold Spring on Hudson (Leavitt, Strebeigh and Co.,
New York), April 24, 1868, no. 75).

35. "Gen. Washington," The Monument, 1, July 29, 1837, 344.

36. W. A. Bryan, George Washington in Literature, 1775-1860, New York,
    1952, 47.

37. Neale (or Neal) was a New York publisher. An advertisement in
    The Literary World, 4, May 5, 1849, 400, informs that the plate
    was 22-by-28-inches and a descriptive key came with each impres-
    sion. This work relates to, perhaps as a pendant, Matteson's
    The First Prayer in Congress (1848?), engraved by Sadd and printed
    by Neals and William Pate in 1848. Like Washington Delivering
    his Inaugural Address, the painting of the First Prayer was
    executed expressly for the engraving. Purchased by the American
    Art-Union, The First Prayer in Congress went to Samuel Pilsbury
    of Biddeford, Me., in the 1850 distribution. A version of the
    work, dating from the early 1930s, takes the form of a stained
    glass window in Christ Church, Philadelphia.

38. "Washington Delivering his Inaugural Address," The Literary
    World, 4, May 19, 1849, 435.

39. "Fine Arts--Washington's Inaugural Address," The Albion, 8,
    May 5, 1849, 213.

40. By 1866, Ritchie had sold the work to A. T. Stewart of New York
    City, for $25,000.

41. The earlier plate measures 24-by-36-inches, while Lady Washing-
    ton's Reception is 21-by-35-inches. The earliest reference to
    Washington and His Generals appears in "Fine Arts--A National
    Engraving," The Albion, 14, August 11, 1855, 381. The subject
    is taken from J. T. Headley's comment: "Washington, standing
    amid his band of patriot generals, is to me the sublimest
    spectacle the history of the world furnishes."

42. E. D. Branch, The Sentimental Years, 1836-1860, New York and
    London, 1934, 166. The painting is 66-by-109-inches.

43. D. Huntington, "Sketches of the Great Masters--Rembrandt,"
    The Crayon, 1, January 17, 1855, 41, indicates the artist's
    awareness of the Hemicycle. A connection between Delaroche and
    Huntington is also made in L. Stober, "Daniel Huntington's
    History Paintings: A Survey" (The Graduate Center, The City
    University of New York, 1975), 31.

44. Also known as Mrs. Washington's Reception, the undated work
    was owned by the artist and offered for sale. The painting was
    also shown at the Brooklyn Art Association exhibition of 1866,
    and again at the Pennsylvania Academy in 1867.

45. Catalogue of the Thirty-Ninth Annual Exhibition of the Penn-
    sylvania Academy of the Fine Arts, Philadelphia, 1862, 11.
    Although its content is the same, the passage as it appears in
    the catalogue is not correctly quoted. Further, Custis itali-
    cized the word "great," the Academy did not.

46. Huntington was not only financially successful as an artist,
    but was also president of the National Academy of Design. The
    artist's stature was indicated in remarks made by the critic of
    the New-York Daily Tribune on The Republican Court: "The
    pecuniary success of the affair was already secured when the
    subject had been chosen, and Mr. Huntington selected to paint
    it . . . " ("The Fine Arts," New-York Daily Tribune, 25, October
    21, 1865, 9.)
        Huntington's work did influence Peter F. Rothermel's The
    Republican Court in the Time of Lincoln (c.1867, unlocated).
    A broadside called the Rothermel "a comparison work" to Hunt-
    ington's (Peter Frederick Rothermel's "The Republican Court in
    the Days of Lincoln," New York, n.d., Broadside Collection,
    Library of Congress). In a lengthy review in the New-York Daily
    Tribune of March 12, 1867, a writer protested Rothermel's title
    (he also suggested that the title may have been given by Derby,
    where, presumably, the work was on exhibition; Huntington's
    work had been seen at Derby's Gallery in 1865-1866), saying
    something like a court did exist in Washington's day, but cer-
    tainly not in Lincoln's. The reviewer feels the Rothermel super-
    ior "in every artistic quality" to the "unfortunate picture" of
    Huntington. After claiming the work as the "best of the long
    history of similar pictures painted in our country," the writer
    says it is not wholly successful. However, Rothermel is not
    to feel discouraged, for even Delaroche's Hemicycle, "the only
    interesting picture of the class," has problems, and "if Dela-
    roche has not in all respects satisfied the conditions of such
    a work, how can we expect smaller men to do it, even with a
    smaller subject? We do not expect it . . . " (Fine Arts--Mr.
    Rothermel's 'Republican Court in the Time of Lincoln'," New-
    York Daily Tribune, 26, March 12, 1867, 2).

47. A reading of "Fine Arts--Works of Art Now on Exhibition," The
    Nation, 1, October 12, 1865, 473-474, suggests the pamphlet to
    be that published by Emil Seitz (who also published the engrav-
    ing), Description of Mr. Huntington's Picture of Lady Washing-
    ton's Reception Day, Engraved by A. H. Ritchie, New York, n.d.

48. Sources sometimes state that the interior is that of the McComb
    House in New York, the dwelling occupied by the President for
    six months in 1790. Mrs. Washington did give receptions there,
    but the pamphlet reveals the gathering to be in Philadelphia.

49. Griswold, The Republican Court, 270.

50. The Nation, October 12, 1865: "The rooms are not vouched for;
    indeed, President Washington's parlors at Philadelphia could
    hardly have been like these; the portraits on the walls, and
    the strange bust on a stranger substructure (is it a stove?),
    have no one to answer for them" The numerous paintings in the
    rooms have not been identified. The Nation article claims
    that Charles I hangs behind Mrs. Washington and portraits of
    George II and his Queen possibly flank the archway. The
    "Queen" derives, formally, from the mezzotint by Smith of
    1703, after a Kneller painting of the Duchess of Bolton.

51. Griswold, The Republican Court, 270-271.

52. Among the multitude are two artists: John Trumbull leans over
    his father, the old gentleman seated to the right of Lady Wash-
    ington; Gilbert Stuart, to the right of the archway, has his
    face half-obscured.

53. Description of Mr. Huntington's Picture of Lady Washington's
    Reception Day, 2.

54. Ibid. This explanation strengthens the notion that Ritchie
    intended The Republican Court to relate to Washington and His
    Generals. That earlier work also showed a historical group
    composed of figures who could not have been in the company of
    one another at any one time. However, a writer rationalized
    the grouping as: "artistic license having high authority,
    that of Raffaele in his 'School of Athens'" ("Fine Arts,"
    The Albion, 36, December 18, 1858, 609).

55. H. T. Tuckerman, Book of the Artists, New York, 1966 reprint,
    323. "Domestic Art Gossip," The Crayon, 8, July, 1861, 151,
    had presaged Tuckerman (The Crayon writer may, in fact, have
    been Tuckerman) by noting:
        "Among the recent works of art kept from public view by
        the present political crisis is Mr. Huntington's great

historical picture of Mrs. Washington's Reception. We believe this work to be exhibited as soon as order is restored, and regular forces of civilization again in healthy operation. The picture is a striking, effective composition, and one which we are confident will attract the public admiration to a greater degree than any other national painting produced here of late years."

56. "Fine Arts--Works of Art Now on Exhibition," The Nation, 1, October 12, 1865, 473.

57. "The Fine Arts," New-York Daily Tribune, 25, October 21, 1865, 9.

58. Ibid.

59. Ibid. B. J. Lossing, Martha Washington, New York, 1861, 21, states that at her levees, Mrs. Washington was "adverse to all ostentatious show and parade, yet she fully appreciated the gravity of her position, and was careful to exact those court-esies to which she was entitled."

60. New-York Daily Tribune, 9.

61. F. Leslie, "Report on the Fine Arts," Reports of the United States Commissioners to the Paris Universal Exposition, 1867 (W. Blake, ed.), 1, Washington, D.C., 1870, 13.

62. These drawings are in the collection of the Cooper-Hewitt Museum of Design, New York. The Museum also owns a rough sketch of the event; a rather finished compositional drawing; a drawing of a boy holding a salver; a drawing of the women behind Mrs. Washington; and a sketch of Mrs. George Clinton (the dour, seated figure at the right, in the painting).

63. New-York Daily Tribune, 9.

64. Ibid. The writer confuses the period of the engraving's execution with that of the painting.

65. "Lady Washington's Reception-Day," Harper's Weekly, 19 Feb-ruary 17, 1875, 178. This issue also included a double-page reproduction of the painting and an accompanying key.

CHAPTER VI

WASHINGTON MEMORIALIZED

> It was meet, that the close of one century should be marked by
> the death of the noblest patriot and statesman which it had
> produced, and that another should commence filled with his
> glorious memory, and with the elevating example which he set,
> not for his countrymen only, but for all time and for all
> people.

> J. A. Spencer, History of the United States, 1858

Images pertaining to the death of George Washington on December

14, 1799, may be broadly categorized: mourning pictures, apotheoses, and

deathbed scenes. Mourning pictures characteristically depict people grief-

stricken or reflective before a symbol of Washington's remains. Apotheoses,

showing Washington in glory, provided a sense of high emotional release.

Generally less allegorical than either of these two modes, deathbed scenes

appeared more reportage-like in character. Yet, in realistic works of

art like J. B. Stearns's Washington on His Deathbed, the moral didacticism

of the hero's death is fully stated.

The last historical event depicted in Junius Brutus Stearns's

cycle of the "Father of his Country," is Washington on His Deathbed (1851;

fig. 151).[1] Here the spotlighted hero expires among family and friends.

Martha Washington, rendered profil perdu, hovers near her husband's head;

Tobias Lear, superintendent of Washington's private affairs, holds the

dying man's hand, and Dr. James Craik, lifelong friend and attending

183

physician, ponders the moment as he stands at the bedside. The remaining figures in the composition display various attitudes of anxiety and melancholy.

Lear's and Craik's eyewitness accounts of the death of Washington were well-known by the time of Stearns's painting, having been published in eulogies and newspapers immediately following the hero's death, as well as being a standard part of subsequent histories of Washington. G. W. P. Custis published a narrative, based on these accounts, of his stepfather's expiration in the National Intelligencer of February, 1827. Jared Sparks related Lear's and Craik's reports in his edition of Washington's writings (1837) and his popular biography of the hero (1839). A first-hand description of Washington's demise was readily available to the artist, and little doubt exists that Stearns familiarized himself with the literature before commencing his picture.

However, with regard to the figures in the room, Washington on His Deathbed inaccurately portrays the event. Behind Dr. Craik stand two young people who appear to be Mrs. Washington's grandchildren. However, neither G. W. P. Custis nor his sister Nellie, who Stearns casts in a Magdalene-like pose, were present in the death room. According to Craik, who added to and certified Lear's account, those present at the time of Washington's passing were Lear, Craik, Mrs. Washington, the servants Christopher, Caroline, Molly and Charlotte, and the housekeeper Mrs. Forbes. Stearns probably included Washington's stepchildren to underscore familyness. An 1846 Currier print of the scene may also have influenced the children's inclusion (see below). In addition to changing the

participants, the artist also moved Mrs. Washington from the foot of the
bed to the head. By so doing, Stearns effectively closed off the composition and framed Washington with loved ones. Despite these historical
inconsistencies, Washington on His Deathbed conveys the essential nature
of the scene as described by Tobias Lear:

> About ten minutes before he expired (which was between ten and
> and eleven o'clock), his breathing became easier. He lay quietly;
> he withdrew his hand from mine, and felt his own pulse. I saw his
> countenance change. I spoke to Dr. Craik, who sat by the fire.
> He came to the bedside. The General's hand fell from his wrist. I
> took it in mine and pressed it to my bosom. Dr. Craik put his hands
> over his eyes, and he expired without a struggle.[2]

Although not an exact visual translation of this passage, Stearns's painting does evince the mood of the moment. As in Lear's writing, Washington
appears quiet, almost benign and the painting is as unemotional as Lear's
dry account. This last quality differentiates Washington on His Deathbed
from two other versions from the 1840s.[3]

Two popular prints of the death of the hero appeared in 1846:
Nathaniel Currier's lithograph, Death of Washington, Dec. 14. A.D. 1799
(fig. 152)[4] and Tompkins H. Matteson's design for a H. S. Sadd engraving,
appearing in the May 1846 issue of The Columbian Magazine (fig. 153).[5]
Both display figures weeping openly, something eschewed by Stearns, and
both share similar compositional features. In fact, an examination of
the two works reveals that one has influenced the other. Each includes
an identical group of crying servants standing in the doorway, the figure
of Dr. Craik on the left (called the "Quaker--an intimate friend of
Washington" in the Currier) is the same in each, as is Mrs. Washington's
chair. To determine which print came first is not possible here; Currier

(and later, Currier and Ives) regularly based work on well-known images. This printmaker had, however, earlier (in 1841) executed a variation on this same theme. The Matteson and the Currier do differ in their historical authencity, the former being the more accurate of the pair. Matteson depicts the very moment of death, as Lear takes Washington's hand to his bosom and Mrs. Washington inquires (as Lear also reported): "Is he gone?" Currier, on the other hand, includes the Quaker (the border inscription identifies him as such, but does not explain his inclusion), places Craik in Lear's position, and shows a weeping Martha Washington and grandchildren (the incorporation of the children may have influenced Stearns's representation). The grieving family of Washington adds a sentimental flavor to the work, an aura missing from the Stearns composition.

The emotional understating and the realism of Washington on His Deathbed evokes, perhaps, a Realist depiction of death. As in a Realist painting, Stearns's composition chronicles the process of dying, as well as specifying the time and location of the occurrence. Despite this objectivity and concreteness, Washington on His Deathbed fundamentally differs from a Realist work by representing the past, not the present. Further, Stearns's intention is unlike that of the Realist artist, who, in Nochlin's words, "severs its [the deathbed scene's] transcendental connections and posits the non-value of the dead person and the meaninglessness of his experience."[6] Typical of the mid-nineteenth century, an artist utilizes modern forms, i.e., Realism, yet still aims to convey a traditional ideal content through his subject matter.

By realistically portraying the dying Washington (who admitted he died hard, but was not afraid) as stoically benign, Stearns perpetuates the ideas and ideals of the hero's steadfastness, his Christianity, as well as rendering the mid-century American conception of the deathbed moment.

Despite his fantastic allegorical representation of the hero's death, Parson Weems accurately remarked: "It has been said that a man's death, is generally a copy of his life. It was Washington's case exactly. In his last illness he behaved with the firmness of a soldier, and the resignation of a Christian."[7] Weems probably based his observation on a published letter of Tobias Lear to John Adams, in which Lear claimed Washington died in perfect resignation and in complete control of his faculties. Lewis O. Saum has evaluated the potency of the Parson's transmission on this account: " . . . Parson Weems's Washington, one might contend, endeared himself quite as much to the two succeeding generations for his deathbed patience and submission as for his inability to tell a lie."[8] Throughout the middle decades, Washington's grip on death was repeatedly held up as a model of stability and Christianity. In death as in life, the hero remained America's greatest exemplum virtutis. This notion imbues Stearns's depiction.

In order to reinforce the notion of a calm Washington resigned to his fate, the artist renders the other figures in the composition with muted emotions. They, as surrogates for mid-century viewers, follow Washington's example. For Stearns's audience, Washington on His Deathbed reassured the positive value of a "triumphant" death, that is, a death distinguished by Christian resignation.[9] Indeed, when the painting appeared as a lithograph in 1853, its subtitle was The Christian. Further, in visually perpetuating Washington's Christianity, the painting argues against mid-century debunkers and revisionists who spoke of the hero's lack of religious inclinations. Additionally, by illustrating the "levelling effect of death,"[10] the painting humanized Washington, although his success in meeting death represents an ideal humanity. A morally didactic work, Washington on His Deathbed spoke to contemporaries of the hero's firmness and Christianity, and the glory of a resigned death.

Mourning pictures related to Washington's passing, usually show weeping figures before the remains or a symbol of the hero.[11] Such scenes, composed of an imaginary landscape setting and often including allegorical architectural forms, were generally very sentimentalized, patriotic homages to the deceased (figs. 154 and 155). Mourning pictures experienced a great vogue in the first two decades of the nineteenth century, reflecting the classistic spirit of the Federal period.

From the 1820s on, corresponding with the growth of landscape and, later, with the development of the cemetary as a social institution, the earlier, overtly symbolic mourning pictures became supplanted by views of Mount Vernon and Washington's tomb. Such works of art had existed previously, but they appeared in much greater numbers in the middle decades. Small-scale figures are depicted standing respectfully before the earlier, more picturesque tomb or the later (after 1832) more formal structure (figs. 156 and 157). The scene offered the artist a real landscape imbued with the sentiment of a nationalistic religion.

A type of picture which occupies a middle ground between the mourning form and the apotheosis is seen in an illustration from John Frost's 1857 Pictorial Life of George Washington (fig. 22). Here a child engages in the worship of the national ancestor, the "Father of his Country." Gabriel Harrison's photograph (fig. 24), which must be based on the illustration from Frost, more closely resembles mourning pictures with the inclusion of the girl and flowers. The sense of filial devotion evidenced in the Frost and Harrison works recalls earlier European paintings such as Francois Kinson's The Duchess of Berry and her Daughter Marie-Louise Stretching out her Arms towards the Bust of the Duke of Berry (fig. 158) and an anonymous nineteenth-century painting showing the future Carlo III of Parma offering flowers to a bust of Maria Luisa di Borbone (fig. 159). An apotheosizing image is seen in Robert W. Weir's design for the title vignette of The New-York Mirror (fig. 160). This "allegorical representation of the present 1832 period in the history of our country," shows the Genius of Liberty crowning the hero "with a halo of glory, whose brilliant beams spread far and wide, lighting up the whole picture with radiant beauty."[12] Although an apotheosis is not a mourning picture, the composition does reflect that allegorical and classicistic sensibility associated with genre. Here the eagle represents American literature. History, with Truth by her side, has written Washington's name first on her tablet. Painting reclines with her board, near Poetry and Music. Niagara Falls thunders in the distance, while "the poor Indians . . . are wending their melancholic way to the setting sun."[13] Appropriately, on the hundredth anniversary of his birth, the marmoreal image of Washington illuminates this scene of nationalism and the arts.

The third major type of images treating Washington's death are true apotheoses featuring an ascendant hero. Apotheoses, not particularly popular in the Protestant nation, did afford an opportunity of representing, in grandiose religious and emotional terms, Washington in glory. Parson Weems's account of Washington's death expresses the mood of celestial apotheoses:

> Swift on angels' wings the brightening saint ascended; while voices more than human were heard . . . warbling through the happy regions, and hymning the great procession towards the gates of heaven. His glorious coming was seen far off, and myriads of mighty angels hastened forth, with golden harps, to welcome the honoured stranger.[14]

Two early nineteenth-century works depicting the apotheosis of Washington are David Edwin's 1800 engraving after a Rembrandt Peale painting (fig. 88) and John J. Barralet's engraving of 1802 (fig. 161). While Barralet, showing Washington on a cushion of clouds above his tomb, is a dynamic, bombastic, and symbol-laden affair, the Edwin print features a Guido Reni-like maudlin saint wafted heavenward. Except for the Peale design influencing Lambert Sachs's Washington at Valley Forge, these prints exhibited little impact on Washington visual imagery. At mid-century, three more apotheoses of the hero appeared, which like the earlier one, seemed too foreign to American taste to have any lasting influence on American art.

These mid-century works are: James Burns's Washington Crowned of 1849 (fig. 162); Rembrandt Lockwood's 1854 The Last Judgment (fig. 163); and Constantino Brumidi's Apotheosis of Washington, 1865 (fig.

164).[15] Burns's allegorical painting, based on a poem by George Rogers,[16] depicts Washington surrounded by a heavenly host of heroes and leaders of the past, being crowned by the angelic forms of Equality, Fraternity and Liberty.[17] In this celestial scene, those supporting Washington as "the brightest stars of the firmament of freedom" are Columbus, Vespucci, Lafayette, Tell, Bolivar, DeWitt, Hofer, Emmett, Hermann, Dussault, Butzaris, Sidney and Pellico.[18] The painting, apparently colossal in size, received favorable press notices. While Burns's painting is an apotheosis of Washington, Rembrandt Lockwood's work places the apotheosis in a Biblical context. This huge painting (twenty-seven-by-seventeen-feet) depicts the Last Judgment, with a semi-nude Washington in the lower center of the composition.[19] The hero, being delivered up by an angelic form, acts as a symbol of Liberty.[20] Although a pamphlet published to describe the painting includes laudatory (as one might expect) newspaper reviews of the work, reception to the painting was mixed. The Albion critic of November 1854, remarked that the painting exemplified "patriotic folly."[21] The writer further claimed that the inclusion of the "champion of human liberty" among the "coming Kingdom of Heaven, seriously mars the unity of the design."[22] Underlying the negative criticism was the work's unreal basis, that is, the painting did not relate to the American experience of the mid-century. This same attitude prevailed in regard to Constantino Brumidi's Apotheosis of Washington.

Completed in 1865, the Italian-born Brumidi's work found little favor with comtemporaries. Americans related the allegorical painting in the dome of the United States Capitol Rotunda to the art of Italy, not of the United States. In fact, Brumidi's figure of the hero is based on Horatio Greenough's ill-fated statue of Washington executed two decades earlier. Brumidi learned, at least, from Greenough's experience and, although he wraps Washington in a toga, he also dresses the hero in his military uniform; he may be George "Jupiter" Washington, but he's more than fully clothed.

Undoubtedly, one of the most interesting paintings treating the memorialization of Washington is a mid-century representation of a contemporary event. On September 20, 1860, His Royal Highness, Albert Edward, Prince of Wales, arrived in Detroit, commencing a month-long tour of the United States. President James Buchanan, learning of the Prince's official visit to Canada, had invited him to the United States. The invitation was conditionally accepted; Queen Victoria insisted that the Prince travel and study the United States in the guise of a student and use the incognito, Lord Renfrew. Americans, however, would not be denied the rare opportunity of paying homage to royalty and conveniently ignored the alias, constantly referring to the nineteen-year old as the Prince of Wales. Touring numerous cities throughout the land during his brief stay, the Prince was warmly and enthusiastically received. Despite 1860 being an important election year, the Prince's visit was not at all slighted by public and press. Of all the many incidents associated with the Prince's tour, the one which most impressed people was his visit on October 5 to the tomb of George Washington at Mount Vernon. As James Buchanan Henry, the President's nephew and one-time private secretary, recalled:

I well remember the whole part--the tall, venerable form of the President, the youthful Prince, and the other guests representing the highest social order in Great Britain, standing bare-headed in front of the tomb of Washington. It was a most impressive and singular spectacle, and I have often thought it would make a very striking subject for a large historical painting.[23]

In fact, at least one artist did render this particular scene. In 1861, Thomas P. Rossiter completed his painting Visit of the Prince of Wales, President Buchanan and Dignitaries to the Tomb of Washington at Mount Vernon, October, 1860 (fig. 165).

The Prince of Wales at Washington's Tomb was, apparently, Rossiter's only painting of contemporary history. According to the artist's grand-daughter, Rossiter actually witnessed the ceremony and sketched the participants.[24] Seemingly an example of straightforward realism, The Prince of Wales at Washington's Tomb, in fact, goes beyond mere documentation.

The circumstances surrounding the execution of Rossiter's painting are unclear. The New York Times of October 19, 1860, states that the "Government has ordered from ROSSITER a historical picture of the Prince and Mr. BUCHANAN standing at the Tomb of WASHINGTON. The Prince has already granted Mr. ROSSITER several appointments for the progress of the work."[25] The Daily National Intelligencer mentions the same information,[26] while The Home Journal of November 3, 1860, states that the idea of the painting had been discussed during the Prince's visit to Washington, that Rossiter had supervised the Prince's posing at the New York photographic studio of Mathew Brady, and that the royal party was interested in the subject and wished to be kept informed of the painting's progress.[27] The newspapers are, nevertheless, vague on the

commission. The subject matter would have certainly appealed to both
the American and British governments. In 1855 Queen Victoria had earlier
commissioned the English artist Edward Matthew Ward to render her visit
to the tomb of Napoleon. Like Rossiter's, Ward's painting was completed
in 1861, and displayed a similar content: a descendent of a British
monarch paying homage to that earlier ruler's enemy (fig. 166). Despite
the newspapers' accounts, no documentation can be found showing a commission from either government. Indeed, the painting remained in
Rossiter's possession until his death and was part of his estate sale
of 1873.[28] James Buchanan Henry, the President's nephew, indicated by
his remarks quoted above no knowledge of such a painting.[29] Yet, the
painting came to the Smithsonian Institution in 1906, as a bequest of
Buchanan's niece, Harriet Lane Johnston. Harriet Lane acted as hostess
for the President during his term and is seen as the fifth woman from
the left, with parasol. Thus, while it remains a mystery who, if any-
one, commissioned the painting, it is not surprising that Thomas P.
Rossiter who undertook the subject. As set forth in Chapter IV, this
artist displayed a deep interest in Washington and Mount Vernon, by his
paintings and writings of the late 1850s.

Of his several paintings treating Mount Vernon, Rossiter's
Washington and Lafayette at Mount Vernon (fig. 127) makes the most interesting comparison with The Prince of Wales at Washington's Tomb. In
both works treat foreigners and their relationship to Washington
Americans admired Lafayette and deemed him the "adopted son" of Washington (Lafayette, in turn, named his son George Washington). As a living

reminder of the American Revolution, Lafayette made a triumphful tour
of this country in 1824-25.[30] Like Lafayette, the Prince of Wales represented a link to the past. With the generation of Revolutionary soldiers
all but vanished by 1860, nostalgic recollections of the Revolution were
rekindled by the sight of the great-grandson of George III standing, head
bowed, before the tomb of Washington. Further, as Lafayette represented
France as an American ally, so the Prince's visit to the tomb exhibited
a new kinship between America and Great Britain--soon to be tested by
the Civil War. In fact, were it not for the great difference in size
between the two paintings, one would be tempted to regard them as pendants. Appropriately, a large photograph of both Rossiter's and Mignot's
work was presented to the Prince while in Washington.[31]

Contemporaries hailed the moral progress of the age that enabled
the "heir-apparent to the British throne [to visit] the grave of a
victorious British rebel!"[32] "His Royal Highness's presence at the tomb
of George Washington will be chronicled as one of the marvellous spec-
tacles of the age, and as a sign of advancing humanity. And so it truly
is, or will be--paralleled only by the visit of the Prince's royal
mother to the tomb of the First Napoleon."[33] A newspaper correspondent
succinctly summed up the hyperbole of the day by asking: "When Kings
visit Presidents, when royal princes visit the graves of rebel democrats,
may not the Millennum be dawning?"[34] British journalists also noted
the psychological nature of the event:

> It is easy moralizing on this visit, for there is something
> grandly suggestive of historical retribution in the reverential
> awe of the Prince of Wales, the great grandson of George III, stand-
> ing bareheaded at the foot of the coffin of Washington . . . For a

> few moments the party stood mute and motionless, and the Prince then
> proceeded to plant a chestnut tree by the side of the tomb. It
> seemed when the Royal youth closed in the earth around the little
> germ that he was burying the last trace of discord between us and
> our great brethren in the West.[35]

The impact of the event on the British is also evident in the competition

of English verse held at Cambridge. His Royal Highness, Albert, the

Prince Consort, as the Chancellor of the University, approved as the

subject for 1861, "The Prince of Wales at the Tomb of Washington."[36]

The Prince's visit to the tomb then suggested the past as well

as holding forth hope for the future. The attainment of international

harmony at the tomb certainly heartened those Americans then striving to

maintain national unity. With the United States, in 1860, near the

devastating schism of Civil War, the Prince's visit naturally entered

into the political arena of the day. Precisely what political effect

the visit had on Anglo-American relationships during the War between the

States is uncertain, although it appears Victoria and Albert did develop

a liking, absent before, for the North due to their son's journey.[37]

And certainly the youthful and impressionable Prince retained an extremely

favorable sense of the United States that continued during his reign as

Edward VII.

During the first half of the nineteenth century, a journey to

Washington's tomb was de rigueur for visitors to the Capitol area. As

witnessed in their written accounts, visitors to the tomb usually came

from a deep respect to pay homage. One traveler noted in 1856:

> I stood at the Tomb of Washington. It was holy ground. I experi-
> enced a momentary shock as a woman uttered some pleasantry & laughed
> close by the grating which encloses the sacrophagus, but soon she
> turned away and my own feelings of sacred pleasure made me forget

others.[38]

Over and over, pilgrims to the tomb remarked on the profound and awful
sensation the site evoked. For these reasons the tomb was a popular subject for painters and engravers.[39]

The painting The Prince of Wales at Washington's Tomb seems to
be an accurate portrayal of the event.[40] The President, the Prince and
other dignitaries, after reaching Mount Vernon on the steamer "Harriet
Lane," toured the house and grounds before proceeding to the tomb. As
the congregation wound its way to the "holy ground," the Marine band,
hidden in a thicket, played a dirge. Hats were removed and voices
quieted as the tomb "of the great world's noblest sleeper"[41] was contemplated by all. The Prince planted a chestnut tree before the tomb
and took seeds to plant another at Windsor Park.[42] Before leaving, the
group received the customary sticks from the tomb as relics. The scene,
by all accounts, was truly impressive and the only specific incident of
the Prince's tour mentioned in correspondence between Buchanan and
Victoria.[43] Rossiter's painting captures the solemnity of the occasion
in a tight, photographic style. In fact, Rossiter worked from photographs provided by Mathew Brady and, very likely, George Barnard.

A Washington, D.C. newspaper, The Evening Star, of March 30, 1861,
states that Rossiter received assistance from Barnard, a photographer
associated with Brady's Washington gallery and considered one of the
finest stereoscopic operators in the country.[44] The sharp focus of the
foreground and the receding planes evident in Rossiter's composition may
indicate an influence of stereoscopy. When in New York, Brady photographed

the Prince and his suite and the full length image of the Prince taken
then is nearly identical to his form in Rossiter's painting (fig. 167).
Indeed, The Home Journal of November 3, 1860, informs that the Prince
had arranged for Rossiter to be at Brady's "where he stood for a full
length figure in the attitude desired by the painter."[45] Brady had
earlier made photographs of Buchanan and his Cabinet. Also the firm of
Gurney and Son of New York had photographed the Royal group.[46] An
availability of photographic images existed then for the artist concerned
with the veracity of this historical assemblage at the tomb of
Washington.

Another source possibly tapped by Rossiter was the fashion
plate, found in such popular periodicals as Godey's Lady's Book,
Peterson's Magazine and Harper's Monthly. Certainly the poses of the
women, particularly the woman in the left foreground with her back to
the viewer, thus defeating a sense of portraiture, support this sup-
position. The painting's purpose as a group portrait should not be
forgotten, and undoubtedly accounted for Rossiter exercising artistic
license in the placement of the memorial shafts. Rather than properly
siting these obelisk forms as symmetrically flanking the tomb, the
painter moves them back, splaying the composition to allow an uninter-
rupted view of the important dignitaries.

Despite an appearance of objective realism, the painting is more
than mere reportage. And Rossiter creatively accentuates the importance
of the event by the inclusion of a single, subtle motif which shifts the
work from reality to ideality. In the central area of the composition,

in the sky, above the space between the two major figural groups, the
artist has delineated in the form of a cloud, a recumbent profile of
George Washington (fig. 168). The real occurence becomes imbued,
figuratively, with the spirit of Washington. The presence of the hero,
felt by all standing before his tomb, is made literal by the artist's
ethereal cloud.

Jasper F. Cropsey, the American landscapist, wrote, in 1855, of
clouds as:

> . . . grand masses of dreamy forms floating by each other, some-
> times looking like magic palaces . . . with light and shadow
> playing amid them, as though it were a spirit world of its own
> . . . In boyhood, we have often watched this dream-world, and
> peopled it with angels.[47]

For American landscape artists, clouds represented not only a physical
phenomenon, but also a spiritual one, the idea of God in nature. By
1861, Washington's status had assumed divine proportions; Americans
often spoke of him in celestial terms, such as the polar star, and
likened him to the sun. In terms of nineteenth-century Washington
memorial iconography, the hero had appeared in the clouds before, however, not with the same understated quality of Rossiter's image.

Apotheoses, like Barralet's, Peale's and Burns's, offered the
artist an opportunity of rendering a celestial Washington. An 1860
lithograph entitled Spirit of the Union (fig. 169) shows the General
hovering over Mount Vernon and his tomb, and below the Capitol, as the
symbol of national unity.[48] Again, unity, although primarily international in scope, is a significant component of Rossiter's painting.
Unlike the Rossiter picture, none of these works attempt to render

Washington as an anthropomorphic cloud. However, an example of such an effort does exist; a work which may, in fact, have served as a source for Rossiter's motif. The Cosmopolitan Art Journal of June 1859, had as its frontispiece the engraving The American Eagle. Guarding the Spirit of Washington (fig. 170).[49] Dedicated to the Mount Vernon Ladies' Association, the print shows a recumbent profile of Washington sil- houetted against a radiant sun, as the American Eagle, up among the clouds, stands watch. Well-known and published in New York, the Cosmopolitan Art Journal was a periodical Rossiter undoubtedly read, a suspicion further suggested by the strong visual correlation of print and painting.

In rendering the spirit of Washington at his own tomb, Rossiter employed a popular print tradition of the time: portrayals of the "shade," or ghost, of Washington, formed by two trees, looking at his tomb. Two such "puzzle" prints were published by C. N. Robinson (be- fore 1857) and W. Schaus (1861; figs. 171 and 172). Currier and Ives later, in 1876, issued such an engraving. These anthropomorphic works were probably influenced by similar images of Napoleon contemplating his grave.[50] Kennedy and Lucas's lithograph, A Natural Curiosity in St. Helena (c. 1829-35; fig. 173), provides an example of this popular genre. Even closer in conception to the Rossiter is an undated German print, with its border title, Napoleon Buried Upon St. Helena, given in both German and English (fig. 174). Here the cloud-formed head of the hero gazes over his tomb. That this Washington memorial type should be related to Napoleon is not unexpected. During the first half of the nineteenth century, writers continually compared the two leaders. Although Washington inevitably emerged as the superior of the pair, American writers did enthusiastically admire certain traits of Napoleon, especially his charismatic quality; Washington was: "Above Napoleon, though he dazzled less."[51] Thus, by utilizing this Napoleonic form, Washington's stature remained undiminished.

One final image of the spirit of Washington at his tomb should be noted. An illustration in R. J. de Cordova's 1861 humorous poem, The Prince's Visit, shows His Royal Highness before the tomb, out of which rises the spirit of Washington (fig. 175). De Cordova penned:

> Now I'm not superstituous; have no faith in ghosts;
> Don't believe in the rappings of angelic hosts;
> But that WASHINGTON'S spirit was there to receive
> This offering of peace the tree, I am free to believe;
> And I know, if it witnessed the scene by the grave,
> That the soul of the great man forgot and forgave.
> "Of evil repented, the angels are glad!"
> Says WASHINGTON'S spirit, and blesses the lad.[52]

In The Prince of Wales at Washington's Tomb, Rossiter combines the three memorial types: his painting aligns with the tradition of the mourning picture, yet the anthropomorphic cloud also relates the work to the deathbed and apotheosis modes. Conjuring up both patriotic and religious associations, the painting typifies Washington memorial iconography with its sense of nationalism as religion. By literally incorporating the spirit of George Washington into his otherwise realistic work, Rossiter also elevates the painting from pure documentation. That the artist should combine the real and the spiritual, the present and the living past, indicates a desire to render the contemporary event in some semblance of traditional history painting. However, a mid-nineteenth-century artist, American or European,[53] could not lean too far from a realist stance, hence, the subtlety of the Washington image. Nonetheless, once known, this anthropomorphic cloud changes the character and expands the meaning of the entire composition.

Reflecting on the national dilemma which existed as Rossiter completed his painting in 1861, one is struck by the poignancy of a journalist's description of the tomb visit: "A sad cloud softened the sunlight; the sweet solemn strains of the beautiful dirge floated around, bringing unconscious tears to eyes unused to weep."[54] That anthropomorphic image did indeed become a "sad cloud" when the sense of peace and harmony manifested at the tomb in October 1860, was shattered six months later with the shelling of Fort Sumter.

Rossiter's painting remarkably visualizes the contemporary notion of Washington's spirit animating America. Rossiter, as well as Stearns and the other works discussed here, attests to the viability of George Washington as an exemplum virtutis transcending even death.

Notes - Chapter VI

1. The painting was exhibited as <u>The Deathbed of Washington</u> at the
   National Academy of Design exhibition of 1854, as <u>The Last Moments</u>
   <u>of Washington</u> at the Pennsylvania Academy of the Fine Arts annual
   of the same year, and as <u>The Last Hours of Washington</u> at the 1859
   Washington Art Association Annual Exhibition.

2. J. Sparks, <u>The Writings of Washington</u>, 1, 1837, 559.

3. One of the earliest visual representations of the scene, even if
   known to Stearns, had little apparent influence on his work:
   Pember and Luzarder's colored etching and stipple engraving titled
   <u>G. Washington in his last Illness attended by Doc.^{rs} Craik and</u>
   <u>Brown</u> (1800).

4. The work is reproduced here as a painting by John Meister.

5. An article accompanied the engraving (J. I[nman]., "Washington's
   Death Bed," <u>The Columbian Magazine</u>, 5, May, 1846, 236-237). A
   crudely executed reversal of Matteson's design appeared in R.
   Sears, <u>A New and Popular Pictorial Description of the United States</u>,
   New York, 1848, 343.

6. L. Nochlin, <u>Realism</u>, Harmondsworth, England, 1971, 65.

7. M. L. Weems, <u>The Life of Washington</u> (M. Cunliffe, ed.), Cambridge,
   Mass., 1962, 165.

8. L. O. Saum, "Death in the Popular Mind of Pre-Civil War America,"
   <u>Death in America</u> (D. E. Stannard, ed.), Philadelphia, 1975, 43.

9. Ibid.

10. J. I., <u>The Columbian Magazine</u>, 236.

11. See B. I. Strauss, "The Memorial Iconography of George Washington"
    (M.A. Thesis, University of Delaware, 1966), A. Schorsch, "Mourn-
    ing Becomes America" (exhibition catalogue, Pennsylvania Historical
    and Museum Commission, 1976), and D. T. Deutsch, "Washington
    Memorial Prints," <u>Antiques</u>, 111, February, 1977, 324-331.

12. "The Vignette," <u>The New-York Mirror</u>, 10, July 7, 1832, 1.

13. Ibid.

14. Weems, <u>Life of Washington</u>, 168.

15. An additional apotheosis is Henry Brueckner's Washington received in Elysian Fields, which was offered to, but apparently rejected by, the American Art-Union in 1849 (Register of Works of Art, 1848-1851, American Art-Union Collection, The New-York Historical Society).

16. G. Rogers, George Washington Crowned by "Equality, Fraternity and Liberty." A Democratic Poem, New York, 1849.

17. Explanation of the Painting, by James Burns of Washington Crowned by Three Angels, Emblematic of Equality, Fraternity and Liberty, with a halo formed of the hues of the Rainbow surrounded by eminent Patriots of other Countries, New York, 1850.

18. Ibid.

19. The work is unlocated today. For a detailed discussion of this artist, see W. H. Gerdts, Jr., "Rembrandt Lockwood, An Artist of Newark," Proceedings of the New Jersey Historical Society, 76, October, 1958, 265-279.

20. Key to and Description of (by English, German, French and Spanish) "The Last Judgment;" A Scriptural Painting, by Rembrandt Lockwood, Newark, 1854, 1.

21. "Fine Arts," The Albion, 13, November 18, 1854, 549, col. 1.

22. Ibid.

23. G. T. Curtis, Life of James Buchanan, 2, New York, 1883, 238-239.

24. Edith Rossiter Bevan to James Mulcahy, October 22, 1955, Rossiter file, Independence National Historical Park, Philadelphia.

25. "The Prince in Boston," The New York Times, 10, October 19, 1860, 4, col. 6.

26. "Progress of the Prince," Daily National Intelligencer, 48, October 20, 1860, 3, col. 4.

27. "Fine Arts--An International Picture," The Home Journal, no. 769, November 3, 1860, 2, col. 5.

28. The Valuable Collection of Engravings, Etchings, Paintings, Antique Furniture, Armor, Bronzes, Rich Brocades, Draperies, Costumes, Etc., A Valuable Library, the Studio Furniture Stock of Artists' Materials, Etc., Etc., Belonging to the late Thomas Prichard Rossiter, Esq. (George A. Leavitt and Co., Auctioneers, Clinton Hall, N.Y.), February 5-8, 1873, no. 225. "Rossiter Art Sale," New-York Tribune, 32, February 7, 1873, 5, col. 2, states that Dr. Weiner purchased the work for 100 dollars. This was Joseph Weiner of New York City.

29. Henry stated, "large historical painting." The Rossiter is not too large, 27 1/4-by 54 3/8-inches; however, were he making a qualification, one would expect him to, at least, mention the Rossiter.

30. See R. F. Hay, "The American Revolution Twice Recalled: Lafayette's Visit and the Election of 1824," The Indiana Magazine of History, 69, April, 1973, 43-62, for an excellent interpretation of the psychological aspect of the visit.

31. "The Spirit of the Morning Press," The Evening Star, 16, October 23, 1860, 2, col. 1. "The Prince and the President," The New York Herald, no. 8793, October 5, 1860, 6, col. 5, states that the photograph was 30-by-40-inches and was the only one taken. "The Prince of Wales," The New York Herald, no. 8794, October 6, 1860, 10, col. 1, notes that the Prince was particular about his gifts. His aide, General Bruce, had inquired after the presentation if any duplicates could be obtained, explaining that the Prince accepted no presents which could be purchased by him.

32. "Washington," The Evening Post, 59, October 6, 1860, 2, col. 4. D. W. B., "From Our Washington Correspondent," The Independent, 12, October 11, 1860, 1, col. 6: "Behold how good and pleasant it is for brethren to dwell together in unity! . . . The new order of things is more consonant with Christianity."

33. "Baron Renfrew in the United States," The Albion, 38, October 6, 1860, 475, col. 1. Ward's depiction of Victoria visiting Napoleon's tomb in 1855, should be recalled here.

34. D. W. B., The Independent, October 11, 1860.

35. "The Prince's Visit to the United States," The Times, no. 23, 758, October 23, 1860, 7, cols. 5-6.

36. See W. Everett, The Prince of Wales at the Tomb of Washington, Cambridge, Mass., 1861.

37. The Prince's trip went only as far south as Richmond, a fact not lost on contemporaries. In Richmond, the Prince experienced belligerencies unfelt in other cities. Commenting on the "desecration" of the statue of Washington in Richmond which took place on the passage of the Secession Ordinance, Harper's Weekly of May 18, 1861, reminded its readers: "Richmond, it will be remembered, is the only place in the United States where the Prince of Wales was treated with discourtesy" ("Desecration of the Statue of Washington at Richmond, Virginia," Harper's Weekly, 5, May 18, 1861, 311.

38. "Arlington and Mount Vernon, 1856, As Described in a Letter of Augusta Blanche Herard" (C. Torrence, intro. and notes), The Virginia Magazine of History and Biography, 57, April, 1949, 155.

39. In its associative powers, Washington's tomb became the New World counterpart to such Old World tombs as those of Rousseau and Virgil. R. Rosenblum, in his Transformations in Late Eighteenth Century Art, Princeton, 1967, 117, cites late eighteenth-century notables who visited Rousseau's tomb to pay homage. European paintings which, like Rossiter's, have a sizeable group of figures before a tomb are rare; usually one or two figures are featured. Examples include: Joseph Wright of Derby's Virgil's Tomb (1779), Richard Wilson's Tomb of the Horatii and Curiatii (1754/1764), and Hubert Robert's pendants of the Rousseau Monument in the Tuillieries (1794).

40. Another depiction of the event is found in the October 13, 1860 issue of Harper's Weekly. Compared to Rossiter, the illustrator shows a much smaller crowd, omits women, and renders the tomb frontally.

41. K. Cornwallis, Royalty in the New World, London, 1860, 282.

42. Sources disagree as to whether the Prince was requested to plant the tree or whether he initiated the action himself.

43. The Works of James Buchanan (J. B. Moore, ed.), 2, Philadelphia and London, 1910, 4: Buchanan to Victoria, October 6, 1860; Victoria to Buchanan, November 19, 1860.

44. "Art Matters in Washington," The Evening Star, 17, March 30, 1861, 3, col. 1.

45. The Home Journal, November 3, 1860.

46. "City Items," New-York Daily Tribune, 21, October 12, 1861, 7, col. 6, notes that this firm was presented a gold medal by the Prince for their portraits of the Prince and his retinue and a volume of photographs.

47. J. F. Cropsey, "Up Among the Clouds," The Crayon, 2, August 8, 1855, 79.

48. The print is by E. Dechaux, New York, and has the poem at the bottom:
Lo! on high the glorious form,
  of WASHINGTON light all the gloom:
And words of warning seem to come,
  from out the portals of his tomb

Americans your fathers shed;
    Their blood to rear the UNIONS fame,
Then let your blood as free be given,
    The bond of UNION to remain

49. The engraving was designed by Thom (probably James C. Thom, 1835-
     1898) and engraved by John Rogers. "Catalogue of Premiums,"
     Supplement to the Cosmopolitan Art Journal, 3, December, 1859, 254,
     describes the work as: "An allegorical composition, representing
     the bird of our nationality guarding the spirit of Washington."

50. David Kiehl of the Metropolitan Museum of Art, New York, kindly
     pointed this out to me. Washington also appears as a profile in
     the trees in a Henry Inman lithograph of 1832 (published by Childs
     and Inman, Philadelphia). This work is unusual in that no tomb is
     evident, rather, Washington's spirit simply imbues the landscape
     of his estate.

51. "Lines on the Statue of Washington in the Capitol," The Southern
     Literary Messenger, 2, March, 1836, 253.

52. R. J. deCordova, The Prince's Visit: A Humorous Description of the
     Tour of His Royal Highness, The Prince of Wales, Through the United
     States of America, in 1860, New York, 1861, 29.

53. For a detailed discussion of this issue, see L. Nochlin, Realism,
     Harmondsworth, England, 1971.

54. "The Prince of Wales at the Tomb of Washington," Harper's Weekly,
     4, October 13, 1860, 642, col. 1.

CHAPTER VII

CONCLUSION

In the years after the Civil War, visualizations of George
Washington and American history ceased to exist in the numbers witnessed
at mid-century. An exception to this drop in productivity was the
Centennial year; however, even then, only about fourteen historical
scenes could be found among the hundreds of works exhibited in the
United States art gallery. Numerous historians have designated and discussed the War Between the States as marking the end of one era and the
commencement of another.[1] Despite traumatic means, the result of the
conflict insured a sense of Union, completing America's nationalizing
process.[2] With national identity achieved, the need for "national" works
of art dwindled. During the middle years of the century, when history
painting was so prevalent, an almost frentic effort to establish a
nationalistic sensibility characterized the country. The Civil War
functioned as a horrendous rite of passage, climaxed by a spending of
patriotic energies. With the Union secured, a modern America arose.
The postwar era, the Gilded Age, did not need, as the prewar age had,
visual images of American history to reinforce its identity. The tremendous material basis and growth of postbellum America provided this
security. Whereas, the mid-century citizen invoked the image or name
of George Washington as the nation's "talisman of power,"[3] his postwar

208

counterpart reveled in the physical prowess of the Corliss engine.

Not only was the "psyche" of postbellum America inimical to works depicting American history, but the aesthetic taste of the epoch also proved adverse. Although largely dependent on European art throughout its art history, America after the Civil War demonstrated an intensification of interest in contemporary foreign art. The mid-century encouragement of "American-ness" in art, which greatly contributed to the popularity of historical works, all but vanished in the last quarter of the century. As evident in the private and public collections of the postbellum period, American taste decidedly favored European art. In The Art Treasures of America (1879), edited by Edward Strahan (pseudonym of Earl Shinn), the choice of photogravures testifies overwhelmingly to the dominance of European work, for 141 foreign examples appear compared to just seven American. This preference for European art can be explained, in part, by the emphasis on figural compositions, a class of art considered of supreme importance and one in which Americans were deemed "most deficient."[4] Americans simply did not have access to the type of figure study required for art of the highest caliber, while Europeans, of course, did. J. J. Jarves blamed American artists' "inaptitude in treating the human figure" for the lack of American history paintings.[5] During the middle years, patriotic subject matter usually compensated for formal inadequacies; postwar Americans, however, seemed less tolerant of artistic deficiences. Americans now embraced the sophisticated, genteel style of Europe.

Ultimately, the rapid postwar decline of history painting can be interpreted as exposing the insecure position such art actually occupied in American culture. Even during its most fecund years at mid-century, historical art could not rival, in terms of quantity, portraiture, landscape or genre works. Its relative success at this time owed to the age's assertive nationalism, a trait which this art reflected and perpetuated. With the realization of Union, historical art lost its potency. Yet it was this very potency which, in part, had made the attainment of Union possible.

Junius Brutus Stearns's paintings of the life of Washington have been employed throughout this study as touchstones because they are paradigmatic of mid-century history painting. By treating George Washington, the series evinces the contemporary interest in the hero, American history and the establishment of a national identity. Painted in a realistic style which aims for historical flavor, if not authenticity, Stearns's works offer readily perceptible scenes of both a genre and a heroic nature. Typical of the period, these works are of a cabinet, rather than a monumental, size. While this trait sets it apart from traditional history painting, the series does carry the patriotic and moralistic didacticism associated with the form.

Individually, Stearns's paintings also mirror and eternalize cultural values. Romanticism is implicit in all the works dealing as they do with the past; but, this spirit is particularly bound up with The Marriage of Washington. The mid-century's admiration for military ability is reflected in Washington as a Soldier. As in the scene of marriage, Washington as a Farmer attempts to humanize and domesticate the hero, paralleling writers' efforts at making history accessible to all. This painting also appeals to the society's basis in and bias toward agriculture. Political unity and constitutionality, two pressing concerns of the day, imbue the depiction of Washington as Statesman. Finally, Washington on His Deathbed offers the hero as a Christian exemplar.

Whatever their aesthetic shortcomings may have been, Stearns's paintings and those like his were integral to the shaping and fixing of an American identity.

Notes--Chapter VII

1. See, for example, A. Nevins, "The Emergence of Modern America, 1865-1875," in The Historians' History of the United States (A. S. Berky and   J. P. Shenton, eds.), 2, New York, 1966, 806-815.

2. R. B. Nye, This Almost Chosen People, Essays in The History of American Ideas, East Lansing, Michigan, 1966, 78.

3. The Union of States: An Oration before the Order of United Americans, at the Academy of Music, New York, Feb. 22, 1855, on the Occasion of the Celebration of the One Hundred & Twenty-Third Anniversary of the Birthday of Washington, by the Hon. Thomas R. Whitney, New York, 1855, 5.

4. F. Leslie, "Report on the Fine Arts," Reports of the United States Commissioners to the Paris Universal Exposition, 1867 (W. P. Blake, ed.), 1, Washington, D.C., 1870, 15.

5. J. J. Jarves, The Art-Idea: Sculpture, Painting, and Architecture in America (2d ed.), New York, 1865, 241-242.

ILLUSTRATIONS

1. John Lewis Krimmel, Quilting Frolic, 1813, Henry Francis du Pont
    Winterthur Museum, Winterthur, Delaware, Courtesy, The Henry
    du Pont Winterthur Museum

2. Francis William Edmonds, Taking the Census, 1854, Private collection

3. <u>Home Again</u>, lithograph published by Endicott and Company, 1866,
   The Library of Congress, Washington, D.C.

4. <u>Dance in a Country Tavern</u>, lithograph published by Childs and Lehman after John Lewis Krimmel, c.1833-1836

5. John Quidor, <u>The Return of Rip Van Winkle</u>, 1829, National Gallery of Art, Washington, Andrew Mellon Collection

6. Gilbert Stuart, <u>George Washington</u> ("Athenaeum" Portrait), 1796, on loan to Museum of Fine Arts, Boston, Courtesy, Museum of Fine Arts, Boston

7. Carl H. Schmolze, <u>Washington Sitting for His Portrait to Gilbert Stuart</u>, 1858, The Pennsylvania Academy of the Fine Arts, Philadelphia, Courtesy, The Pennsylvania Academy of the Fine Arts, Philadelphia

8. Benjamin West, <u>The Death of Wolfe</u>, 1770, The National
Gallery of Canada, Ottawa

9. Jacob Eichholtz, <u>An Incident of the Revolution</u>, 1831, Museum of
Fine Arts, Boston, Courtesy, Museum of Fine Arts, Boston

10. John Gadsby Chapman, <u>Baptism of Pocahontas</u>, 1840, Rotunda, United States Capitol, Washington, D.C.

11. Robert W. Weir, <u>Embarkation of the Pilgrims at Delft Haven</u>, <u>Holland, July 22nd, 1620</u>, 1843, Rotunda, United States Capitol, Washington, D.C.

12. Asher B. Durand, <u>The Capture of Major André</u>, 1834,
Worcester Art Museum, Worcester, Massachusetts

13. William H. Powell, <u>Discovery of the Mississippi by
DeSoto</u>, 1853, Rotunda, United States Capitol,
Washington, D.C.

14. John Gadsby Chapman, <u>The Desertion of Sergeant
    Champe</u>, c. 1838, unlocated

15. Paul Delaroche,
    <u>Napoleon Crossing the</u>
    <u>Alps</u>, 1851, Walker Art
    Gallery, Liverpool

16. Jacques-Louis David,
    <u>Napoleon Crossing the</u>
    <u>Alps</u>, 1800, Musée
    National, Malmaison

223

17. <u>Napoleon Storming the Bridge at Arcole</u>,
lithograph after Horace Vernet, n.d.

18. <u>The Struggle at Concord Bridge</u>, W. J. Edwards
engraving after Alonzo Chappel, from Robert
Tomes, <u>Battles of America</u>, 1, New York, 1861,
opp. 145

19. Paul Delaroche,
    Napoleon Crossing the
    Alps, 1851, Walker Art
    Gallery, Liverpool

20. Washington on His Mission
    to the Ohio, engraving
    after Alonzo Chappel, from
    John Frederick Schroeder,
    Life and Times of
    Washington, 1, 1857,
    opp. 53

21. Francis William Edmonds, <u>The Image Peddler</u>, 1844, The
Collections of The New-York Historical Society,
New York

22. <u>Bust of Washington</u>, H. Bricher engraving
after William Croome, from John Frost,
<u>The Pictorial Life of Washington</u>, Phila-
delphia, 1857, 13

23. Southworth and Hawes, "A Girl with Portrait of Washington," daguerreotype, c.1852, The Metropolitan Museum of Art, New York

24. Gabriel Harrison, "Girl adoring a bust of Washington," daguerreotype, c.1853, The Collection of the International Museum of Photography, Rochester, New York

25. Richard Caton Woodville, <u>Old '76 and Young '48</u>,
     1849, The Walters Art Gallery, Baltimore

NOTE: Hirschl and Adler Galleries
could not permit the Magee work to
be reproduced here. The painting
can be seen in Hermann Warner
Williams, Jr., <u>Mirror to the Past</u>,
Greenwich, Connecticut, 1973, 81.

26. John L. Magee, <u>Reading of an Official Dispatch</u>
<u>(Mexican War News)</u>, c. 1849, Hirschl and Adler
Galleries, New York

27. The Spirit of '76, H. S. Sadd engraving after
Tompkins H. Matteson, from The Columbian Magazine,
5, April, 1846, opp. 185

28. David Claypool Johnston, <u>The Artist and the Tyro</u>,
 c. 1863, Private collection

29. Junius Brutus Stearns, <u>Washington in the Indian Council</u>,
     1847, Private collection

30. Junius Brutus Stearns, <u>Scene at the Battle of Brandywine</u>,
     1848, Joseph Sprain, Philadelphia

31. Junius Brutus Stearns, <u>The Marriage of Washington</u>, 1848, The Virginia Museum of Fine Arts, Richmond

32. <u>The Wedding</u>, J. B. Forrest engraving, from <u>The Columbian Magazine</u>, 3, May, 1845, frontispiece

33. George Washington Parke Custis, <u>Washington at the
    Battle of Trenton</u>, 1836(?), Dietrich Brothers,
    Americana Corporation, Philadelphia

34. George Washington Parke Custis, <u>Washington at the
    Battle of Princeton</u>, 1848(?), Dietrich Brothers,
    Americana Corporation, Philadelphia

35. <u>Washington's First Interview with Mrs. Custis</u>, W. H. Ellis engraving after F. O. C. Darley, from <u>Godey's Lady's Book</u>, 32, April, 1846, frontispiece

36. <u>Washington's First Interview with His Wife</u>, G. R. Hall engraving after John W. Ehninger, 1863, The Old Print Gallery, Washington, D.C.

37. The Frank Confession, Augustus Köllner engraving,
    from Anna C. Reed, The Life of George Washington,
    Philadelphia, 1842

38. "Washington and His Father," from Entertaining
    Anecdotes of Washington (new ed.), Boston, 1846,
    18

39. Early Days of Washington, W. Humphreys engraving after
Henry Inman, from The Gift, Philadelphia, 1844, opp. 139

40. Benjamin West's First Attempt at Drawing, engraving
     from Godey's Lady's Book, 40, March, 1850, 212

41. Watt's First Concep-
     tion of the Steam
     Engine, J. W. Steel
     engraving, from
     Godey's Lady's Book,
     44, April, 1852,
     frontispiece

42. Washington a Peacemaker, G. T. Devereux engraving after
William Croome, from John Frost, The Pictorial Life of
George Washington, New York, 1857, 23

43. Thomas W. Hope(?), Washington, The Boy Hero, n.d.,
Independence National Historical Park Collection,
Philadelphia

44. <u>Washington Subduing a Camp Brawl</u>, G. R. Hall engraving
after F. O. C. Darley, 1857, The Historical Society of
Pennsylvania, Philadelphia

45. John Gadsby Chapman,
<u>Washington in His
Youth</u>, 1841, The
Collections of The
New-York Historical
Society, New York

46. Robert Feke, <u>Isaac Winslow</u>, 1748, Museum of Fine Arts, Boston, Courtesy, Museum of Fine Arts, Boston

47. Thomas Doughty, <u>In Nature's Wonderland</u>, 1835, The Detroit Institute of Arts

48. William Ranney,
    Squire Boone Crossing
    the Mountains with
    Stores for His
    Brother Daniel,
    Encamped in the Wilds
    of Kentucky, 1852,
    Miss Amelia Peabody,
    Boston

49. Horatio Greenough,
    The Rescue, 1851,
    The United States
    Capitol, Washington,
    D.C.

50. Emanuel Leutze, <u>Washington as the Young Surveyor</u>, c. 1851, Cooper Union for the Advancement of Science and Art, New York

51. Harvey Birch's Warning to Young Wharton, Charles Burt
    engraving after Tompkins H. Matteson, from The Columbian
    Magazine, 5, February, 1846, opp. 90

52. The Benevolence of Washington, John Sartain engraving after
    Peter F. Rothermel, from The Eclectic Magazine, 34, January,
    1855, frontispiece

53. J. Beaufain Irving, <u>Washington Calling Upon
Colonel Rahl</u>, n.d., Cochran Collection,
Philipse Manor Hall State Historic Site,
Taconic State Parks and Recreation Commission,
New York State Office of Parks and Recreation

54. <u>Washington Taking Farewell of His Mother</u>,
Henry Linton engraving,
from <u>The Illustrated
Magazine of Art</u>, 4,
1854, opp. 73

55. William H. Powell, <u>Washington Receiving His Mother's Last Blessings</u>, 1864, Senate House State Historic Site, Palisades Interstate Park Commission, New York State Office of Parks and Recreation

56. Gilbert Stuart, <u>George Washington</u> ("Vaughan" Portrait), 1795, National Gallery of Art, Washington, D.C., Andrew Mellon Collection

57. Junius Brutus Stearns, <u>Washington as a Soldier</u>, c. 1851,
    The Virginia Museum of Fine Arts, Richmond

58. Emanuel Leutze, <u>Washington at the Battle of the Monongahela</u>,
    1858, General Braddock School District, Braddock, Pennsylvania

59. "The Battle of the Monongahela," from Entertaining Anecdotes
of Washington (new ed.), Boston, 1846, 47

60. Washington Crossing the Allegheny, Richard W. Dodson engraving
after Daniel Huntington, from The Gift, Philadelphia, 1845,
opp. 277

61. William Sidney Mount, <u>Washington and Gist Crossing the Allegheny</u>, 1863, Private collection, New York

62. William Sidney Mount after Daniel Huntington, "Sketch of Huntington's Washington," 1863, The Museums at Stony Brook, New York, Gift of the Estate of Ward Melville

63. William Ranney, <u>Gist Rescuing Washington from the Allegheny River</u>, 1854(?), Claude J. Ranney, Malvern, Pennsylvania

64. "Washington and Gist," from <u>Entertaining Anecdotes of Washington</u> (new ed.), Boston, 1846, 43

65. <u>Settlers Imploring Washington's Protection</u>, John Rogers engraving after John McNevin, from Benson J. Lossing, <u>Washington and the American Republic</u>, 1, New York, 1870, 211

66. Antoine Jean Gros, <u>Napoleon at Eylau</u>, 1808, Louvre, Paris

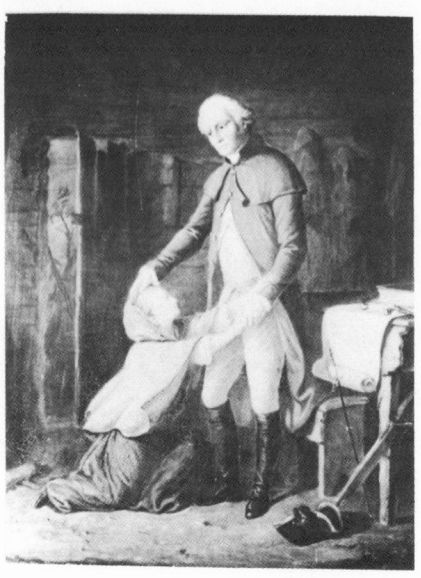

67. Tompkins H. Matteson, The Benevolence of Washington,
     1855(?), Sherburne Public Library, Sherburne, New York

68. "The Benevolence of Washington," J. W. Orr engraving after
     F. O. C. Darley, from J. Fenimore Cooper, The Spy, New York,
     1861 ed., 413

253

69. George Washington as a Surveyor, engraving after F. O. C. Darley,
     c.1854, Prints Division, The New York Public Library, Astor,
     Lenox and Tilden Foundations

70. William Ranney, <u>Washington with Soldiers</u>, n.d., Hirschl and Adler Galleries, New York

71. Emanuel Leutze, Washington at the Battle of Monmouth, 1854, University Art Museum, University of California, Berkeley

256

72. Emanuel Leutze, <u>Washington Crossing the Delaware</u>, 1851,
The Metropolitan Museum of Art, New York, Gift of
John S. Kennedy, 1897

73. Thomas Sully, <u>Washington's Passage of the Delaware</u>, 1819,
Museum of Fine Arts, Boston, Courtesy, Museum of Fine
Arts, Boston

74. <u>Washington Crossing the Delaware</u>, John Baker etching, 1832,
Baker Collection, The Historical Society of Pennsylvania,
Philadelphia

75. Théodore Géricault, <u>Raft of the Medusa</u>, 1818-1819, Louvre,
Paris

76. William Ranney, <u>Daniel Boone's First View of Kentucky</u>, 1849, Collection of National Cowboy Hall of Fame, Oklahoma City, Oklahoma

77. Emanuel Leutze, <u>Westward the Course of Empire Takes Its Way</u>, 1862, United States Capitol, Washington, D.C.

78. Thomas Eakins, <u>The Continental Army Crossing the Delaware</u>, 1893, bronze, The Trenton Battle Monument, Trenton, New Jersey

79. George Caleb Bingham, <u>Washington Crossing the Delaware</u>,
1855/1871, Private collection

80. George Caleb Bingham, <u>Daniel Boone Leading the Settlers</u>,
1851, Washington University, St. Louis

81. Tompkins H. Matteson, <u>Washington at Valley Forge</u>, 1855,
    Sherburne Public Library, Sherburne, New York

82. Tompkins H. Matteson, sketch for <u>Washington at Valley Forge</u>,
    1855, Sherburne Public Library, Sherburne, New York

83. Encampment at Valley Forge, Washington and His Wife Visiting
     the Troops, A. B. Walter engraving after Christian Schuessele,
     from Graham's Magazine, 45, August, 1854, opp. 113

84. Washington and the Committee of Congress at Valley Forge,
     engraving after William Powell, 1866, Prints Division, The
     New York Public Library, Astor, Lenox and Tilden Foundations

85. Lambert Sachs, <u>General Washington at Prayer at Valley Forge</u>, 1854, The Valley Forge Historical Society, Valley Forge, Pennsylvania

86. <u>Gen. Geo. Washington in Prayer at Valley Forge</u>, Peter Kramer
    lithograph after Lambert Sachs, 1854, The Library of Congress,
    Washington, D.C.

87. <u>Washington at Valley Forge</u>,
    Gilbert and Gihon engraving,
    from [Horatio Hasting Weld],
    <u>The Life of George Washington</u>,
    New York, 1847, opp. 88

88. <u>Apotheosis of Washington</u>, David Edwin engraving after
Rembrandt Peale, 1800, McAlpin Collection, Prints Division,
The New York Public Library, Astor, Lenox and Tilden
Foundations

89. <u>The Prayer at Valley Forge</u>, John C. McRae engraving after
     Henry Brueckner, 1866, The Old Print Gallery, Washington, D.C.

90. Tompkins H. Matteson, <u>Washington's Farewell to His Officers</u>,
     1855, Sheldon Swope Art Gallery, Terre Haute, Indiana

91. <u>Washington Taking Leave of the Officers of His Army</u>, at
     <u>Francis's Tavern, Broad Street, New York, Dec. 4th, 1783</u>,
     Nathaniel Currier lithograph, 1848

92. Alonzo Chappel, <u>Washington Taking Leave of His Officers</u>,
    1865(?), The Chicago Historical Society, Chicago

93. John Trumbull, <u>General Washington Resigning His Commission</u>, 1824, Rotunda, United States Capitol, Washington, D.C.

94. Edwin White, <u>Washington Resigning His Commission</u>, 1859, State House, Annapolis, Maryland

95. Junius Brutus Stearns, <u>Washington as a Farmer, at Mount
Vernon</u>, 1851, The Virginia Museum of Fine Arts, Richmond

96.   John Gadsby Chapman, <u>Distant View, Mount Vernon</u>, 1834, Private collection

97.   John Gadsby Chapman, <u>The Bed Chamber of Washington</u>, 1834, Private collection

98. John Gadsby Chapman, <u>Tomb of Washington</u>, 1834, Private collection

99. Jean-Antoine Houdon, <u>George Washington</u>, 1795, State Capitol, Richmond, Virginia

100. <u>General Washington's Resign-</u>
     <u>tion</u>, Alexander Lawson
     engraving after John J.
     Barralet, from <u>The Phila-</u>
     <u>delphia Magazine and Review,</u>
     <u>or Monthly Repository of</u>
     <u>Information and Amusement</u>, 1,
     January, 1799, frontispiece

101. "Venerate the Plough," Ralph Rawson engraving, c. 1816, Baker
     Collection, The Historical Society of Pennsylvania,
     Philadelphia

102. Peter Paul Rubens,
Madonna Adored by Angels,
oil sketch for Chiesa
Nuova altarpiece, 1608,
Academie der Bildenden
Kunste, Vienna

103. America Guided by Wisdom: An Allegorical Representation of the
United States Denoting Their Independence and Prosperity,
Benjamin Tanner engraving after John J. Barralet, c. 1815,
Atwater Kent Museum, Philadelphia

275

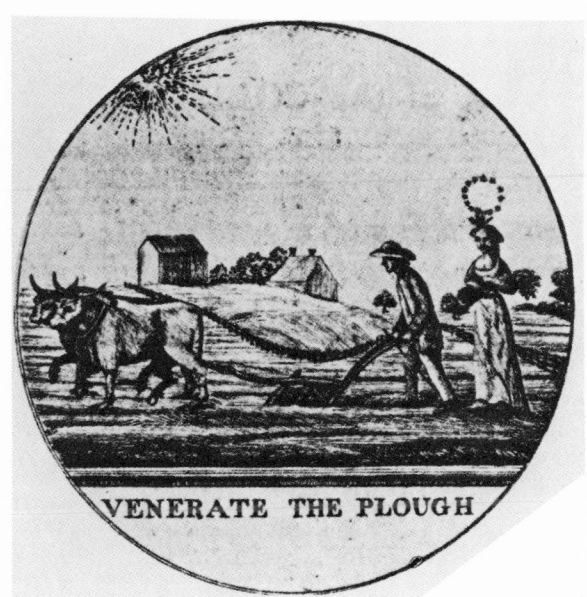

104. "Venerate the Plough," James Trenchard etching, from <u>The Columbian Magazine, or Monthly Miscellany</u>, 1, October, 1786, opp. 77

105. "Washington as Cincinnatus," James Smillie engraving after Alonzo Chappel, from John Frederick Schroeder, <u>Life and Times of Washington</u>, 2, 1857-1861, title page

106. Constantino Brumidi, <u>Calling Cincinnatus from the Plow</u>,
1855, United States Capitol, Washington, D.C.

107. Constantino Brumidi, <u>Calling of Putnam from the Plow to the
Revolution</u>, 1855, United States Capitol, Washington, D.C.

108. <u>News from Lexington--Putnam</u>
<u>Leaving the Plough</u>,
engraving after Alonzo
Chappel, from J. A. Spencer,
<u>History of the United</u>
<u>States</u>, 2, New York, 1858,
title page

109. <u>Putnam Receiving News of Lexington</u>, A. B. Walter engraving
after C. White, from J. T. Headley, <u>The Illustrated Life of</u>
<u>Washington</u>, New York, 1859, 175

110. <u>The Minute Man</u>, engraving from John Frost, <u>Remarkable Events in the History of America From the Earliest Times to the Year 1848</u>, 1, Philadelphia, 1848, 752

111. Jean-Francois Millet, <u>The Gleaners</u>, 1857, Louvre, Paris

112. Chief of the Patriot Host, engraving from Aesop, Junior in
     America: Being a Series of Fables written especially for
     the People of the United States of North America, New York,
     1834, frontispiece

113. <u>Washington at Mount Vernon 1787</u>, Nathaniel Currier lithograph, 1852, The Historical Society of Pennsylvania, Philadelphia

114. <u>Washington at Mount Vernon</u>, John Rogers engraving after John McNevin, 1859, The Historical Society of Pennsylvania, Philadelphia

115. Edward Savage, The Washington Family, c.1795, National Gallery of Art, Washington, Gift of Henry Prather Fletcher

116. The Washington Family, William Sartain engraving after Christian Schuessele, 1865, The Historical Society of Pennsylvania, Philadelphia

117. <u>The Washington Family</u>, E. Bell engraving after Jeremiah Paul, 1800

118. <u>Mount Vernon in 1796</u>, J. Duthie engraving after G. I. Parkyns, from Benson J. Lossing, <u>Mount Vernon and Its Associations, Historical, Biographical, and Pictorial</u>, New York, 1859, frontispiece

119. Francis Guy, <u>Mount Vernon</u>, c. 1798, unlocated

120. Thomas Sully, <u>Washington Bidding His Family Farewell</u>, 1850, Morristown National Historic Park, Morristown, New Jersey

121. <u>Washington at Home</u>, H. B. Hall engraving after Alonzo Chappel,
1867, Private collection

122. <u>Italian Chimney-piece</u>, engraving from Benson J. Lossing,
<u>Mount Vernon and Its Associations, Historical, Biographical,</u>
<u>and Pictorial</u>, New York, 1859, 172

123. <u>Mount Vernon in the Olden Time</u>, H. B. Hall engraving after
A. Henning, 1856, The Old Print Gallery, Washington, D.C.

124. Edwin Landseer, <u>Queen Victoria and Family at Windsor</u>, 1843,
Royal Collection, Windsor, Copyright Reserved

125. <u>Washington and Friends After a Day's Hunt in Virginia</u>,
Charles P. Tholey lithograph, 1868, The Old Print Gallery,
Washington, D.C.

126. Eastman Johnson, <u>Kitchen at Mount Vernon</u>, c.1857,
Sotheby Parke Bernet, Inc., New York

127. Thomas P. Rossiter and Louis R. Mignot, <u>Washington and Lafayette at Mount Vernon</u>, 1859, The Metropolitan Museum of Art, Bequest of William Nelson, 1905

128. <u>Genl. Lafayette's Departure from Mount Vernon 1784</u>, Charles P. Tholey lithograph, 1868, The Historical Society of Pennsylvania, Philadelphia

289

129. <u>Lafayette's Final Interview with Washington</u>, engraving from
<u>Life of General Lafayette</u>, Philadelphia, c. 1847, opp. 120

130. <u>Mount Vernon</u>, Otto Knirsch lithograph, 1867, The Library of
Congress, Washington, D.C.

131. Junius Brutus Stearns, <u>Washington as Statesman, at the
Constitutional Convention</u>, 1856, The Virginia Museum of
Fine Arts, Richmond

132. <u>Congress Voting Independence</u>, engraving after Edward Savage and Robert Edge Pine, unfinished, The Old Print Gallery, Washington, D.C.

133. John Trumbull, <u>Declaration of Independence</u>, <u>4 July, 1776</u>, 1818, Rotunda, United States Capitol, Washington, D.C.

134. George Peter Alexander Healy, <u>Webster's Reply to Hayne</u>, 1851, Faneuil Hall, Boston

135. Peter F. Rothermel, <u>Patrick Henry Delivering His Address Before the House of Burgesses</u>, 1851, Patrick Henry Memorial Shrine, Red Hill, Virginia

136. Peter Paul Rubens, The
Mystical Marriage of
St. Catherine, 1627-1628,
St. Augustine, Antwerp

137. Godfried Guffens, Rouget de Lisle Singing the "Marsellaise,"
1849, The Pennsylvania Academy of the Fine Arts,
Philadelphia, Courtesy of the Pennsylvania Academy of the
Fine Arts, Philadelphia

138. Interior View of Independence Hall, Philadelphia, Max
      Rosenthal chromolithograph, c. 1856, Independence National
      Historical Park Collection, Philadelphia

139. Thomas P. Rossiter, <u>Signing of the Constitution</u>, 1867,
     Independence National Historical Park Collection,
     Philadelphia

140. Detail of Rossiter, Signing of the Constitution

141. "Washington," engraving from John Frost, Remarkable Events
      in the History of America from the Earliest Times to the
      Year 1848, 2, Philadelphia, 1848, 374

142. John Folwell, "Rising Sun Chair," 1779, Independence
      National Historical Park Collection, Philadelphia

143. Thomas P. Rossiter, Washington and His First Cabinet, n.d.,
     Independence National Historical Park Collection, Philadelphia

144. David Wilkie, The First Council of Queen Victoria, 1838,
     Royal Collection, Windsor, Copyright Reserved

145. Washington Delivering His Inaugural Address, H. S. Sadd
engraving after Tompkins H. Matteson, 1848/1849, Private
collection

146.   Daniel Huntington, <u>The Republican Court in the Time of</u>
<u>Washington, or Lady Washington's Reception</u>, 1861, The
Brooklyn Museum, Gift of the Crescent-Hamilton Athletic Club

147.   <u>Washington and His Generals</u>, A. H. Ritchie engraving, 1855

146. Daniel Huntington, <u>The Republican Court in the Time of Washington, or Lady Washington's Reception</u>, 1861, The Brooklyn Museum, Gift of the Crescent-Hamilton Athletic Club

147. <u>Washington and His Generals</u>, A. H. Ritchie engraving, 1855

145. <u>Washington Delivering His Inaugural Address</u>, H. S. Sadd
engraving after Tompkins H. Matteson, 1848/1849, Private
collection

148. Marcellus Laroon, <u>The Duke of Buckingham's Levee</u>, early
     eighteenth century, Samuel Howard Whitbread, South Hill
     Park, Bedfordshire, England

302

149. Dennis Malone Carter, <u>Washington's Reception for Mr. and Mrs.</u>
<u>Alexander Hamilton</u>, 1856, unlocated

150. Daniel Huntington, Compositional sketches for The Republican
Court..., c.1860, Courtesy of Cooper-Hewitt Museum, The
Smithsonian Institution's National Museum of Design

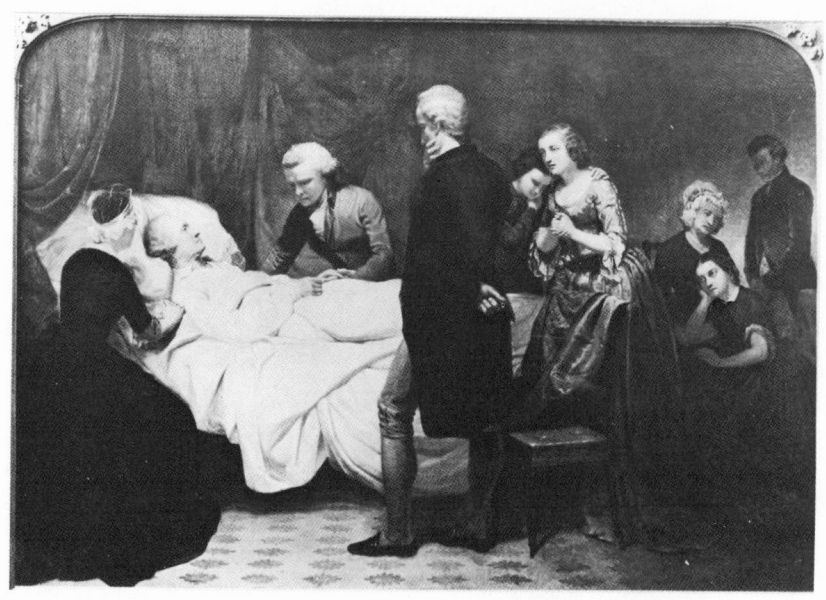

151.	Junius Brutus Stearns, <u>Washington on His Deathbed</u>, 1851,
Collection of The Dayton Art Institute, Gift of
Mr. Robert Badenhop, 1954

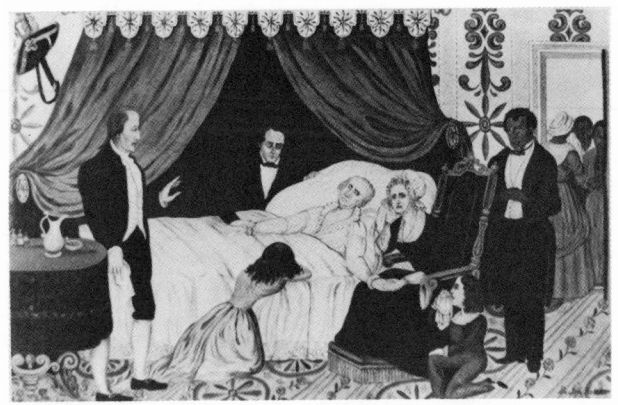

152. <u>George Washington on His Deathbed</u>, John Meister painting after an 1846 Nathaniel Currier lithograph, n.d., Mount Holyoke College, South Hadley, Massachusetts

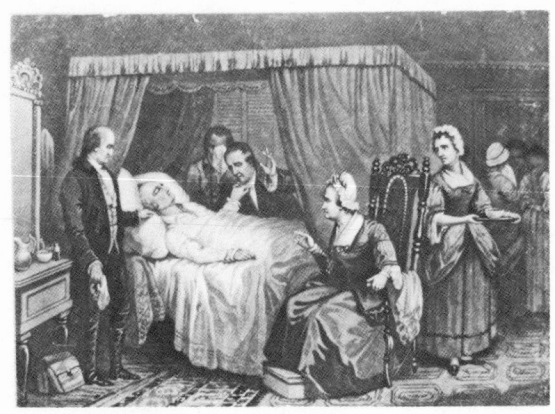

153. <u>Washington's Deathbed</u>, H. S. Sadd engraving after Tompkins H. Matteson, from <u>The Columbian Magazine</u>, 5, May, 1846, opp. 236

154. <u>Lived Respected and
Fear'd--Died Lamented
and rever'd</u>, etching and
engraving published by
Pember and Luzarder,
1800, Prints Division,
The New York Public
Library, Astor, Lenox
and Tilden Foundations

155. <u>Mourning Picture for
George Washington</u>,
E. G. Grindley engraving,
c.1800, Private
collection

156. <u>Washington's Tomb</u>, engraving, 1832, Private collection

157. Henry Inman,
    <u>Washington's Tomb at
    Mount Vernon</u>, 1841,
    Fisher Gallery, The
    University of
    Southern California,
    Los Angeles

158. <u>The Duchess of Berry and her Daughter Marie-Louise Stretching out her Arms towards the Bust of the Duke of Berry</u>, engraving after Francois Kinson, before 1839, Private collection

159. Anonymous, <u>Carlo Lodovico di Borbone Parma with his Wife,
     his Sister and the Future Carlo III of Parma Offering
     Flowers to the Bust of Maria Louisa di Borbone</u>, second
     quarter of the nineteenth century, Archducal Estate,
     Viareggio

160. "Title Vignette," Asher B. Durand engraving after Robert W.
     Weir, from <u>The New-York Mirror</u>, 10, 1832

161. <u>Apotheosis of Washington</u>, John J. Barralet engraving, 1802,
The Metropolitan Museum of Art, New York

162. Key to James Burns's <u>Washington Crowned</u>, 1850, McAlpin
Collection, Prints Division, The New York Public Library,
Astor, Lenox and Tilden Foundations

163. Rembrandt Lockwood, Compositional drawing for The Last
Judgment, 1854 or earlier, Collection of the Newark
Museum, Newark, New Jersey

164. Constantino Brumidi, detail of <u>Apotheosis of Washington</u>
      1865, Rotunda dome, United States Capitol, Washington, D.C.

165. Thomas P. Rossiter, <u>Visit of the Prince of Wales, President
Buchanan and Dignitaries to the Tomb of Washington at
Mount Vernon, October, 1860</u>, 1861, National Collection of
Fine Arts, Smithsonian Institution; Bequest of Harriet
Lane Johnston

166. Edward Matthew Ward, <u>Queen Victoria at the Tomb of Napoleon, 1855</u>, 1861, Royal Collection, Copyright Reserved

167. Mathew Brady, <u>The Prince of Wales</u>, photograph, 1860,
      The Library of Congress, Washington, D.C.

316

168. Rossiter, detail of <u>Visit of the Prince of Wales</u> . . . .

169.   Spirit of the Union, E.
       Dechaux lithograph, 1860,
       The Historical Society of
       Pennsylvania, Philadelphia

170.   The American Eagle,
       Guarding the Spirit
       of Washington, John
       Rogers engraving
       after Thom, from
       Cosmopolitan Art
       Journal, 3, June,
       1859, frontispiece

SHADE OF WASHINGTON.
Mount Vernon.

171. <u>Shade of Washington</u>, C. N. Robinson lithograph, before 1857,
The Library of Congress, Washington, D.C.

172. <u>The Shade at the Tomb, Mount Vernon</u>, lithograph published
by W. Schaus, 1861, The Library of Congress, Washington,
D.C.

173. <u>A Natural Curiosity in St.
    Helena</u>, Kennedy and Lucas
    engraving, c.1829-1835,
    Prints Division, The New
    York Public Library,
    Astor, Lenox and Tilden
    Foundations

174. <u>Napoleon Buried Upon St. Helena</u>, lithograph published by
    B. Krauss (Nurnberg), n.d., The Free Library of Philadelphia

175.   "The Prince at the Tomb," from R. J. de Cordova, <u>The
        Prince's Visit: A Humorous Description of the Tour of His
        Royal Highness, The Prince of Wales, Through the United
        States of America, in 1860</u>, New York, 1861, opp. 29

INDEX

A

Achenbach, Andreas, 91
Aesop, Junior, in America, 129
Albert Edward, Prince of Wales, 143, 192, 193, 195-198
Alberti, Leon Battista, 23
Alexandrian Gazette, 41
Allston, Washington, 18
American Art-Union, 9, 30-31, 88
The American Eagle. Guarding the Spirit of Washington, 200
Apotheoses, 183, 190-192, 199, 201
Arlington House, 41, 42
Art Union of Philadelphia, 60

B

Bacon, Reverend Henry, 18-19
Baker, John
  Washington Crossing the Delaware, 89
Bancroft, George, 22
Bank notes, 10
Barlow, Thomas Oldham, 142
Barnard, George, 197
Barralet, John J.
  America Guided by Wisdom . . ., 124
  Apotheosis of Washington, 190, 199
  General Washington's Resignation, 123
Benjamin West's First Attempt at Drawing, 51
Berkeley, Bishop, 91
Bingham, George Caleb
  Daniel Boone Leading the Settlers, 93
  Washington Crossing the Delaware, 93-94
Bonaparte, Napoleon, 142, 194, 195, 200-201
Bonnington, Richard Parke, 140
Braddock, General Sir Edward, 73-74
Brady, Mathew, 197, 198
Brueckner, Henry
  The Prayer at Valley Forge, 99, 101
  Washington received in Elysian Fields, 204
Brumidi, Constantino, 7, 34
  Apotheosis of Washington, 190-192
  Calling of Cincinnatus from the Plow, 125
  Calling of Putnam from the Plow to the Revolution, 125

321

Peale, Rembrandt
  Apotheosis of Washington, 100, 190, 199
Philadelphia Society for the Promotion of Agriculture, 124
The Plough Boy, 124-125
Powell, William
  Discovery of the Mississippi by DeSoto, 15, 16, 63
  Washington and the Committee of Congress at Valley Forge, 97-98
  Washington Receiving his Mother's Last Blessings, 63-65
Priest, Joshiah
  History of the Early Adventures of Washington among the Indians
    of the West, 45
Prescott, William, 16
Putnam, Israel, 125-126

Q

Queen Victoria, 192, 194, 196, 197

R

Randolph, John, 153
Ranney, William
  Daniel Boone's First View of Kentucky, 57
  Gist Rescuing Washington from the Allegheny River, 79
  Squire Boone Crossing the Mountains, 57
  Washington and Soldiers, 83
  Washington's Mission to the Indians, 72, 108
Ratti, Augusti
  Guido Painting the Portrait of Beatrice Cenci, 34
Rawdon, Ralph
  "Venerate the Plough," 123-124
Reed, Anna C., 48
Regnier, [Claude?], 31
Remington, Albert G., 23
Revoil, Pierre-Henri
  Giotto Discovered by Cimabue, 52
Reynolds, Sir Joshua, 11, 14, 23
Richards, T. Addison
  The Romance of American Landscape, 77
Richardson, Jonathan, 16
"Rising Sun Chair," 163, 164
Ritchie, Alexander H.
  Lady Washington's Reception, 167
  Washington and His Generals, 168
Robinson, C. N.
  Shade of Washington, 200
Rogers, George, 191

SELECTED BIBLIOGRAPHY

Abbott, Richard H., "The Agricultural Press Views the Yeoman: 1819-1859," Agricultural History, 42, January, 1968, 35-48.

Adams, Randolph G., "The Historical Illustrations in Weems's Washington," The Colophon, Part 8, New York, 1931, n.p.

Addison, Agnes, "The Legend of West's Death of Wolfe," College Art Journal, 5, November, 1945, 23-25.

Address of Hon. John W. Houston, on the Purchase of Mount Vernon, by the Ladies of the United States, delivered Before the Ladies of Milford, Del., on the Evening of February 22, 1856, Wilmington, Del., 1856.

An Address on the Life and Character of George Washington, Delivered on the 4th of July, 1857, at Chambersburg, by Hon. George W. Brewer, Chambersburg, Pa., 1874.

Aesop, Junior, in America: Being a series of Fables written especially for the People of the United States of North America, New York, 1834.

An Album of American Battle Art 1755-1918, Washington, D.C., 1947.

The American Academy of Fine Arts and American Art-Union, Edited by Mary Bartlett Cowdrey, 2 vols., New York, 1953.

"American Art," Gleason's Pictorial Drawing-Room Companion, 6, May 13, 1854, 301.

"American Art; the need and nature of Its History," The Illustrated Magazine of Art, 3, 1854, 262-263.

"American Artists," House Reports, 35 Cong., 2 Sess., 1, No. 198, March 3, 1859, 1-21.

American Life in the 1840s, Edited by Carl Bode, Garden City, N.Y., 1967.

"American Literature," The Green Mountain Gem, 7, 1849, 84-85.

American Narrative Painting, Exhibition catalogue, Los Angeles County Museum of Art, October 1-November 14, 1974.

"American Painters, Their Errors as Regards Nationality," Cosmopolitan Art Journal, 1, June 1857, 116-119.

"The American School of Art," The American Whig Review, 16, August, 1852, 138-148.

Americana, Sotheby, Parke, Bernet Sale Catalogue No. 3834, January 29-31, 1976.

Anderson, Anne, "George Washington, The Making of a Hero," M.A. Thesis, University of Delaware, 1972.

An Appeal for the Preservation of the Home and Grave of Washington, Philadelphia, 1855.

"Arlington and Mount Vernon, 1856, As Described in a Letter of Augusta Blanche Herard," Introduction and notes Clayton Torrence, The Virginia Magazine of History and Biography, 57, April, 1949, 140-175.

Arnason, H. H., The Sculptures of Houdon, New York, 1975.

"Art and Artists," The Home Journal, January 25, 1851, 3.

"Art and Artists," The Home Journal, March 22, 1851, 3.

"Art and Artists," The Home Journal, April 5, 1851, 3.

"Art and Artists," The Home Journal, August 16, 1851, 3.

"Art and Artists in America," Bulletin of the American Art-Union, November 1851, 130-132.

"Art and Artists in America," Bulletin of the American Art-Union, December, 1851, 149.

"Art at Home," Cosmopolitan Art Journal, 1, July, 1856, 15-16.

"Art at the National Capital," The International Review, 1, April, 1874, 327-345.

"Art at Washington," New-York Daily Times, 20, May 19, 1860, 5.

"Art-Desecration of the Capitol," Cosmopolitan Art Journal, 2, March-June, 1858, 134-136.

Art Division Files, The New York Public Library, New York.

"Art in the Capitol," New-York Times, 23, March 18, 1874, 4.

"The Art Commission," The Century, 1, June 4, 1859, 188.

"Art Matters in Washington," Evening Star, 17, March 30, 1861, 3.

"Art Notes--The Art Gallery of the Sanitary Fair," New-York Times, 13, April 11, 1864, 2.

"Art Union, and the Apollo Association," The New World, 5, October 1, 1842, 223.

"The Artist's Studio--John G. Chapman," The New-York Mirror, 12, March 21, 1835, 301-302.

B., D. W., "From Our Washington Correspondent," Independent, 12, October 11, 1860, 1.

Baily, Thomas, "The Mythmakers of American History," The Journal of American History, 55, June 1968, 5.21.

Baker Collection of Washingtoniana, The Historical Society of Pennsylvania, Philadelphia.

Baker, W. S., American Engravers and Their Works, Philadelphia, 1875.

_____, Bibliotheca Washingtoniana--A Descriptive List of Biographies and Bibliographical Sketches of George Washington, Philadelphia, 1889.

_____, Character Portraits of Washington as Delineated by Historians, Orators and Divines Selected and Arranged in Chronological Order with Biographical Notes and References, Philadelphia, 1887.

_____, The Engraved Portraits of Washington with Notices of the Originals and Brief Biographical Sketches of the Painters, Philadelphia, 1880.

Bancroft, George, The History of the United States from the Discovery of the American Continent, 10 vols., Boston, 1834-1875.

Barber, John W. and Elizabeth G., Historical Poetical and Political American Scenes, New Haven, 1852.

Barck, Dorothy C., "Proposed Memorials to Washington in New York City, 1802-1847," The New-York Historical Society Quarterly Bulletin, 15, October, 1931, 79-90.

Barker, Virgil, American Painting, New York, 1950.

_____, "Colloquial History Painting," Art in America, 42, May, 1954, 118-125, 156.

"Baron Renfrew in the United States," The Albion, 38, October 6, 1860, 475.

Bartlett, Irving H., The American Mind in the Mid-Nineteenth Century, New York, 1967.

"Battle of the Monongahela," Baltimore Monument, 2, November 11, 1837, 48.

"The Benevolence of Washington," Eclectic Magazine, 34, January, 1855, 143.

Benson, E., "Historical Art in the United States," Appleton's Journal of Literature, Science and Art, 1, April 10, 1869, 45-46.

Bercovitch, Sacvan, The Puritan Origins of the American Self, New Haven and London, 1975.

Bethune, George W. The Prospects of Art in the United States. An Address before the Artists' Fund Society of Philadelphia, at the opening of their Exhibition, May, 1840, Philadelphia, 1840.

Bevan, Mrs. William F., "Biography of T. P. Rossiter and A Checklist of His Paintings," Unpublished paper, March, 1957, Archives of American Art, Washington, D.C.

Bicentennial Inventory of American Paintings, National Collection of Fine Arts, The Smithsonian Institution, Washington, D.C.

"The Birth-Place of Washington," The Columbian Magazine, 3, February, 1845, 92.

Bloch, E. Maurice, George Caleb Bingham, 2 vols., Berkeley, 1967.

Bode, Carl, The Anatomy of American Popular Culture 1840-1861, Berkeley and Los Angeles, 1959.

Bolton, Theodore, "The Book Illustrations of Felix Octavious Darley," Proceedings of the American Antiquaries Society, 61, part 1, April, 1951, 137-182.

Boorstin, Daniel J., The National Experience, New York, 1965.

Branch, Douglas, The Sentimental Years, 1836-1860, New York and London, 1934.

Brant, Irving, James Madison: Father of the Constitution, 1787-1800, Indianapolis and New York, 1950.

Brent, John Carroll, "The Arts as Connected to the Smithsonian Institution," The Anglo American, 9, September 4, 1847, 461-462.

_____, "The Polite Arts, Useful and Practical," The Anglo American, 9, May 1, 1847, 35-36; May 8, 1847, 58-59.

"Brooklyn Art Association," The Aldine, 7, 1874, 48.

Bryan, William Alfred, George Washington in Literature 1775-1865, New York, 1952.

Bulletin of the American Art-Union, New York, 1848-1851.

Burroughs, Charles, An Oration on the Moral Grandeur of George Washington, delivered on the Centennial Anniversary of his Birth Day, February 22, 1832, at the request of the Citizens of Portsmouth, N.H., Portsmouth, N.H., 1832.

Callow, James T., Kindred Spirits, Knickerbocker Writers and American Artists, 1807-1855, Chapel Hill, N.C., 1967.

Cantor, Jay, "Prints and the American Art-Union," Prints in and of America to 1850, Edited by John D. Morse, Charlottesville, Va., 1970, 297-326.

Carlson, Robert A., The Quest for Conformity: Americanization Through Education, New York, 1975.

Carey, William, To the President and Members of the Artists' Fund Society of Philadelphia, Philadelphia, 1838.

Catalogue of the Entire Collection of Paintings, Studies and Sketches of Mr. T. P. Rossiter, Cold Spring on Hudson, Leavitt, Strebeigh and Co., New York, 1868.

Catalogue of Paintings of Colonel Trumbull, New Haven, 1864.

"Catalogue of Premiums," Supplement to the Cosmopolitan Art Journal, 3, December, 1859, 254.

Catalogue of Rossiter's Collection of Pictures and Sketches, to be sold at Auction by Thomas J. Miller, on Tuesday Evening December 29, 1859, at 7 O'clock at the National Academy of Design, Tenth Street, near Broadway, New York, 1859.

Catalogue of the Thirty-Ninth Annual Exhibition of the Pennsylvania Academy of the Fine Arts, Philadelphia, 1862.

Catalogue of Works by the late Henry Inman, New York, 1846.

Cecil, E., The Life of George Washington for Children, Boston, 1859.

Centennial Celebration of the Inauguration of George Washinton as First President of the United States at the Metropolitan Opera House, exhibition catalogue, New York, April 17-May 8, 1889.

"The Character of Washington," The North American Review, 83, July, 1856, 1-30.

"Charles the First Taking Leave of his Children," Godey's Lady's Book, 30, May, 1845, 196.

"City Items," New-York Daily Tribune, 21, October 12, 1861, 7.

Cobb, Josephine, "The Washington Art Association: An Exhibition Record, 1856-1860," Records of the Columbian Historical Society of Washington, D.C., 1963-1965, Edited by Francis Coleman Rosenberger, Washington, D.C., 1966, 122-160.

Cobb, Lyman, Cobb's New Sequel to the Juvenile Readers, or, Fourth Reading Book, Containing a Selection of Interesting, Historical, Moral, and Instructive Reading Lessons in Prose and Poetry, from Highly Esteemed American and English Writers, New York, 1853.

Combe, George, Notes on the United States of America during a Phrenological Visit in 1838-9-40, 2 vols., Philadelphia, 1841.

Commager, Henry Steele, "The Search for a Usable Past," American Heritage, 16, February, 1965, 4-9, 90-96.

Companion to the Historical Paintings, of the ever memorable Battle of Bunker's Hill, By the Americans, and regular British Forces, June 17th, 1775, Boston, 1807.

Compilation of Works of Art and Other Objects in the United States Capitol, Washington, D.C., 1965.

Conkling, Margaret, Memoirs of the Mother and Wife of Washington, Auburn, N.Y., 1850.

Cooper, James Fenimore, The Spy: A Tale of the Neutral Ground, New York, 1861.

_____, The Spy, foreward by Curtis Dahl, New York, 1946.

[Cooper, Susan L.], Mount Vernon: A Letter to the Children of America, New York, 1859.

Cornwallis, Kinahan, Royalty in the New World, London, 1860.

"Courtship and Marriage of Washington," The Rover, 3, 1844, 321-322.

Craven, Wayne, American Painting, 1857-1869, Newark, Del., 1962.

Cresswell, Donald H., The American Revolution in Drawings and Prints, A Checklist of 1765-1790 Graphics in the Library of Congress, Washington, D.C., 1974.

Criswell, Robert, Jr., "Mount Vernon," Godey's Lady's Book, 39, October, 1849, 247-248.

"Criticisms of Art by A Resident of Washington [Letter to the Editor]," The Century, 1, June 18, 1859, 205.

Cropsey, J. F., "Up Among the Clouds," The Crayon, 2, August 8, 1855, 79-80.

Cummings, Thomas S., Historic Annals of the National Academy of Design, Philadelphia, 1865.

Cumulative Record of Exhibition Catalogues, The Pennsylvania Academy of the Fine Arts, 1807-1870, Edited by Anna Wells Rutledge, Philadelphia, 1955.

Cunliffe, Marcus, George Washington, Man and Monument, Boston, 1958.

Curti, Merle, The Roots of American Loyalty, New York, 1946.

Curtis, George Ticknor, Life of James Buchanan, 2, New York, 1883.

Custis, G. W. Parke, Recollections and Private Memoirs of Washington, Washington, D.C., 1859.

Dangerfield, George, The Awakening of American Nationalism 1815-1828, New York, 1965.

Davis, Vincent, "Of War and Warriors (American Style)," Naval War College Review, 25, November-December, 1972, 20-31.

Dawson, Henry B., Battles of the United States by Sea and Land, 2 vols., New York, 1860.

DeCordova, R. J., The Prince's Visit: A Humorous Description of the Tour of His Royal Highness, The Prince of Wales, Through the United States of America, in 1860, New York, 1861.

Description of Mr. Huntington's Picture of Lady Washington's Reception Day, Engraved by A. H. Ritchie, New York, n.d.

"Desecration of the Statue of Washington at Richmond, Virginia," Harper's Weekley, 5, May 18, 1861, 311.

"Development of Nationality in American Art," Bulletin of the American Art-Union, December, 1851, 137-139.

The Diary of George Templeton Strong, Edited by Allan Nevins and Milton Halsey, 4 vols., New York, 1952.

The Diary of Philip Hone 1828-1851, Edited by Allan Nevins, 2 vols., New York, 1927.

"A Dinner At Mount Vernon--From the Unpublished Journal of Joshua Brooks (1773-1859)," Edited by R. W. G. Vail, The New-York Historical Society Quarterly, 31, April, 1947, 72-85.

The Discourses of Sir Joshua Reynolds, P.R.A., London, 1924.

Doane, George Washington, One World; One Washington: The Oration, in the City Hall, Burlington, on Washington's Birth-Day, 1859, Burlington, N.J., 1859.

"Domestic Art Gossip," Cosmopolitan Art Journal, 3, September, 1859, 183-184.

Dowe, William, "George Washington," Graham's Magazine, 43, July, 1853, 33-40.

Duncan, Carol, The Pursuit of Pleasure: The Rococo Revival in French Romantic Art, New York and London, 1976.

E., D., "Correspondence," The Crayon, 1, February 7, 1855, 88.

"The Early Days of Washington," The Gift: A Christmas and New Year's Present, Philadelphia, 1844, 139-140.

Edgerton, Samuel Y., Jr., "The Murder of Jane McCrea: The Tragedy of An American Tableau D'Historie," The Art Bulletin, 47, December, 1965, 481-492.

"Editorial Notes--Fine Arts," Putnam's Magazine, 2, November, 1853, 574-576.

"Editorial Notices--Fine Arts," Putnam's Monthly, 4, November, 1854, 568.

"Editor's Book Table," Godey's Lady's Book, 27, November, 1843, 238-240.

"Editor's Table," Godey's Lady's Book, 34, April, 1847, 220-221.

"Editor's Table," The Ladies' Repository, 17, December, 1857, 763.

"Editor's Table," The Ladies' Repository, 22, July, 1862, 447.

Eisen, Gustavus A., Portraits of Washington, 3 vols., New York, 1932.

Eitner, Lorenz, "The Open Window and the Storm-Tossed Boat: An Essay in the Iconography of Romanticism," The Art Bulletin, 37, December, 1955, 281-290.

Ellet, E. F., "Firesides and Facts of the Revolution," Godey's Lady's Book, 56, February, 1858, 121-124.

Ellis, G. E., Commemoration of Washington, A Discourse, on the New Holiday, preached in Harvard Church, Charlestown, on Sunday, February 22, 1857, Charlestown, 1857.

Ellsworth, Lucius F., "The Philadelphia Society for the Promotion of Agriculture and Agricultural Reform, 1785-1793," Agricultural History, 42, July, 1968, 189-199.

Elson, Ruth Miller, Guardians of Tradition, American Schoolbooks of the Nineteenth Century, Lincoln, Neb., 1964.

Emerson, B. D., The First Class Reader: A Selection for Exercises in Reading, from Standard British and American Authors in Prose and Verse, Claremont, N.H., 1845.

Entertaining Anecdotes of Washington, New Edition, Boston, 1846.

"The Epochs and Events of American History, As Suited to the Purposes of Art in Fiction," The Southern and Western Monthly Magazine and Review, 1, 1845, 109-127, 182-191, 257-261, 385-392; 2, 1845, 10-16, 87-94, 145-154.

Evans, Grose, Benjamin West and the Taste of His Times, Carbondale, Ill., 1959.

Everett, William, The Prince of Wales at the Tomb of Washington, Cambridge, Mass., 1861.

"Exhibition of the Academy of Design," New-York Semi-Weekly Tribune, 15, April 17, 1859, 2-3.

Exhibition of Leutze's Great National Picture of Washington Crossing the Delaware, Stuyvesant Institute of the City of New York, New York, [1851?].

"Exhibition of Pictures at the Sanitary Fair," New-York Daily Tribune, 24, April 16, 1864, 12.

"The Explanation of the Frontispiece," The Philadelphia Magazine and Review, or Monthly Repository of Information and Amusement, 1, January, 1799, v-vi.

Explanation of the Painting, by James Burns of Washington Crowned by Three Angels, Emblematic of Equality, Fraternity and Liberty, with a halo formed of the hues of the Rainbow surrounded by eminent Patriots of other Countries, New York, 1850.

F., "Sketches of American History," The Youth's Companion, 29, March 20, 1856, 192.

Fairman, Charles E., Art and Artists of the Capitol of the United States of America, Washington, D.C., 1927.

Fanshaw, D., "The Exhibition of the National Academy of Design," The United States Review and Literary Gazette, 2, July, 1827, 241-263.

Fehl, Philipp P., "Thomas Sully's Washington's Passage of the Delaware: The History of a Commission," The Art Bulletin, 55, December, 1973, 548-599.

"Fine Arts," The Albion, 9, November 30, 1850, 573.

"Fine Arts," The Albion, 12, October 8, 1853, 489.

"Fine Arts," The Albion, 13, November 11, 1854, 537.

"Fine Arts," The Albion, 13, November 18, 1854, 549.

"Fine Arts," The Albion, 15, May 17, 1856, 237.

"Fine Arts," The Albion, 37, October 1, 1857, 477.

"Fine Arts," The Albion, 36, December 18, 1858, 609.

"The Fine Arts," The American Repertory of Arts, Sciences, and Manufacturers, 2, January, 1841, 433-436.

"Fine Arts," Baltimore Monument, 2, June 2, 1838, 278-279.

"The Fine Arts," Gleason's Pictorial Drawing-Room Companion, 5, August 27, 1853, 141.

"Fine Arts," The Home Journal, November 3, 1860, 2.

"The Fine Arts," The Knickerbocker, 5, June, 1835, 550-556.

"The Fine Arts," The Literary World, 1, March 27, 1847, 182-183.

"The Fine Arts," The Literary World, 2, December 25, 1847, 510.

"The Fine Arts," The Literary World, 2, January 8, 1848, 559.

"The Fine Arts," The Literary World, 3, March 11, 1848, 106-107.

"The Fine Arts," The Literary World, 6, February 9, 1850, 132-133.

"The Fine Arts," The Literary World, 6, May 4, 1850, 447-449.

"The Fine Arts," New-York Daily Tribune, 25, October 21, 1865, 9.

"Fine Arts," New-York Times, 13, October 14, 1864, 5.

"The Fine Arts--The Apollo Association," Arcturus, 2, November, 1841, 373-374.

"The Fine Arts--Apollo Association, The New-York Mirror, 19, December 18, 1841, 407.

"The Fine Arts--The Art Union Pictures," The Literary World, 2, October 23, 1847, 227-278.

"The Fine Arts--Exhibition at the National Academy," The Literary World, 1, April 24, 1847, 279-280.

"The Fine Arts--Exhibition of the National Academy," New-York Daily Tribune, 12, June 7, 1852, 5.

"Fine Arts--An International Picture," The Home Journal, November 3, 1860, 2.

"Fine Arts--Lessing's Martyrdom of Huss," The Albion, 9, December 7, 1850, 585.

"Fine Arts--Leutze's Washington Crossing the Delaware," The Literary World, 9, October 18, 1851, 311.

"The Fine Arts--National Academy Exhibition," The Literary World, 3, June 3, 1848, 350-351.

"Fine Arts--National Academy of Design," The Critic: A Weekly Review of Literature, Fine Arts, and the Drama, 2, May 23, 1829, 46-47.

"Fine Arts--A National Engraving," The Albion, 14, August 11, 1855, 381.

"The Fine Arts--The Pennsylvania Academy of the Fine Arts," The Broadway Journal, 1, February 22, 1845, 121-122.

"Fine Arts--Rossiter and Mignot's 'Home of Washington After the War',"
    The Albion, 37, November 26, 1859, 573.

"Fine Arts--Mr. Rothermel's 'Republican Court in the Time of Lincoln',"
    New-York Daily Tribune, 26, March 12, 1867, 2.

"Fine Arts--Washington Crossing the Delaware: By Leutze," The Albion,
    10, November 1, 1851, 525.

"The Fine Arts--The Washington Exhibition," The Albion, 12, March 12,
    1853, 129.

"The Fine Arts--The Washington Pictures," The Century, 1, February 26,
    1859, 3.

"Fine Arts--Washington's Inaugural Address," The Albion, 8, May 5,
    1849, 213.

"Fine Arts--Works of Art Now on Exhibition," The Nation, 1, October 12,
    1865, 472-474.

First Annual Exhibition of the Yale School of the Fine Arts, New Haven,
    1867.

Fisher, Sydney G., "The Legendary and Mythmaking Process in Histories of
    the American Revolution," Proceedings of the American Philosophical
    Society, 51, 1912.

Fishwick, Marshall, American Heroes, Myth and Reality, Washington, D.C.,
    1954.

_____, The Hero, American Style, New York, 1969.

_____, Virginians on Olympus, Richmond, Va., 1951.

Flagg, Jared B., The Life and Letters of Washington Allston, New York,
    1892.

Flexner, James Thomas, George Washington and the New Nation, 1783-1793,
    Boston, 1970.

_____, George Washington: Anguish and Farewell (1793-1799), Boston,
    1972.

_____, George Washington in the American Revolution, 1775-1783,
    Boston, 1968.

_____, George Washington, The Forge of Experience (1732-1775),
    Boston, 1965.

_____, That Wilder Image, Boston, 1962.

_____, Washington, The Indispensible Man, Boston, 1974.

Fort, Susan Ilene, "High Art and the American Experience: The Career of Thomas Pritchard Rossiter," M.A. Thesis, Queens College, New York, 1975.

Fox, Frederic, "Pater Patriae as Pater Familias," American Heritage, 14, April, 1963, 32-37, 100-102.

Frankenstein, Alfred, William Sidney Mount, New York, 1975.

Freeman, Douglas Freeman, George Washington, A Biography, 7 vols., New York, 1948-1951.

Friedlaender, Walter, "Napoleon as 'Roi Thaumaturge'," Journal of the Warburg and Courtauld Institutes, 4, 1940-1941, 139-141.

Friedman, Lawrence J., Inventors of the Promised Land, New York, 1975.

Frost, John, The Pictorial History of the United States of America, from the Discovery by the Northmen in the Tenth Century to the Present Time, 4 vols., Philadelphia, 1843.

_____, The Pictorial Life of George Washington, New York, 1857.

_____, Remarkable Events in the History of America, From the Earliest Times to the Year 1848, 2 vols., Philadelphia, 1848.

Garland, Claude M., Washington and His Portraits, Chicago, 1931.

"Gen. Washington," The Monument, 1, July 29, 1837, 344.

"George Washington," The Amaranth, Boston, 1851, 274-276.

George Washington Bicentennial Historical Loan Exhibition of Portraits of George Washington and His Associates, Also a Collection of Washingtoniana, Exhibition Catalogue, Corcoran Gallery of Art, Washington, D.C., March 5-November 24, 1932.

George Washington Scrapbooks, Prints Division, The New York Public Library, New York.

Gerdts, William H., Jr., "Rembrandt Lockwood, An Artist of Newark," Proceedings of the New Jersey Historical Society, 76, October, 1958, 265-279.

[Godman, John D.], Ode Suggested by Rembrandt Peale's National Portrait of Washington, Philadelphia, 1824.

Goldberg, Alfred, "School Histories of the Middle Period," Historio-graphy and Urbanization, Edited by Eric F. Goldman, Baltimore, 1941, 171-188.

Goodrich, Lloyd, "The Painting of American History: 1775 to 1900," American Quarterly, 3, Winter, 1951, 283-294.

[Goodrich, Samuel G.], The Life of George Washington, Philadelphia, 1836.

"Gov. Wise's Oration at Lexington, Va., 4th July, 1856," The Southern Literary Messenger, 23, July, 1856, 1-19.

"The Great Sanitary Fair," Philadelphia Inquirer, June 20, 1864, 2.

"Greenough the Sculptor, and His Last Production," Bulletin of the American Art-Union, September, 1851, 96-97.

Grindhammer, Lucille Wrubel, "Art and the Public: The Democratization of the Fine Arts in the United States, 1830-1860," Amerikastudien/America Studies, 41, Stuttgart, 1975.

Griswold, Rufus W., The Republican Court, or, American Society in the Days of Washington, New Work, 1855.

Groce, George and David Wallace, The New-York Historical Society's Dictionary of Artists in America, 1514-1860, New Haven, 1957.

Groseclose, Barbara S., "Emanuel Leutze, 1816-1868: A German-American History Painter," Ph.D. Dissertation, University of Wisconsin, 1973.

_____, "Washington Crossing the Delaware: The Political Context," The American Art Journal, 7, November, 1975, 70-78.

Grubar, Francis S., William Ranney, Painter of the Early West, Exhibition catalogue, Corcoran Gallery of Art, Washington, D.C., October 4-November 11, 1962.

Grund, Francis J., The Americans, in their Moral, Social, and Political Relations, Boston, 1837.

H., "Revolutionary Recollections, The New-York Mirror, 7, January 23, 1830, 227.

H--., Mary W. B., "My First Visit to Washington," Southern and Western Magazine and Review, 2, December, 1845, 405-408.

Hamilton, Sinclair, Early American Book Illustrators and Wood Engravers, Princeton, 1958, Supplement, 1968.

348

Hamilton, Thomas, Men and Manners in America, New Edition, Edinburgh and London, 1843.

The Hampton L. Carson Collection of Engraved Portraits of Gen. George Washington, Compiled by Stan. V. Heckels, Philadelphia, 1904.

"A Hard Subject to Paint," Godey's Lady's Book, 30, February, 1845, 60.

Harding, Walter, "American History in the Novel, 1585-1900: The Period of Expansion, 1815-1861," The Midwest Journal, 8, Spring-Fall, 1956, 393-406.

Harley, Robert L., "George Washington Lived Here--Some Early Prints of Mount Vernon, Part I," Antiques, 47, February, 1945, 103-105; Part II, March, 1945, 166-167.

Harrington, Rev. Henry F., "Anecdotes of Washington," Godey's Lady's Book, 38, June, 1849, 427-429.

Harris, Neil, The Artist In American Society, The Formative Years 1790-1860, New York, 1966.

_____, "The Persistence of Portraiture," Perspectives in American History, 1, 1967, 380-389.

Hart, Charles Henry, The Engraved Portraits of Washington, New York, 1904.

Haskell, Francis, "The Manufacture of the Past in Nineteenth-Century Painting," Past and Present, 53, November, 1971, 109-119.

_____, "The Old Masters in Nineteenth Century French Painting," The Art Quarterly, 34, Spring, 1971, 55-85.

Hay, Robert F., "The American Revolution Twice Recalled: Lafayette's Visit and the Election of 1824," The Indiana Magazine of History, 69, April, 1973, 43-62.

_____, "George Washington: American Moses," American Quarterly, 21, Winter, 1969, 780-791.

_____, "The Glorious Departure of the American Patriarchs: Contemporary Reactions to the Deaths of Jefferson and Adams," Journal of Southern History, 35, November, 1969, 543-555.

_____, "Providence and the American Past," The Indiana Magazine of History, 15, June, 1969, 79-101.

Headley, J. T., "George Washington," Graham's Magazine, 45, November, 1854, 413-424.

_____, The Illustrated Life of Washington, New York, 1859.

_____, Washington and His Generals, 2 vols., New York, 1851.

[Heady, Morrison], The Farmer Boy, and How He Became Commander-In-Chief, by Uncle Juvinell, Edited by William M. Thayer, Boston, 1864.

Highly Important Eighteenth and Nineteenth Century American Paintings, Sotheby, Parke, Bernet Sale Catalogue No. 3561, October 25, 1973.

"Hints to Art Union Critics," The American Review: A Whig Journal of Politics, Literature, Art and Science, 4, December, 1846, 599-610.

"Historical Paintings," The Congressional Globe, 32 Cong., 1 Sess., 24, part 2, Washington, D.C., 1852, 1004-1005.

History of the George Washington Bicentennial Celebration, 5 vols., Washington, D.C., 1932.

Hofland, Thomas R., "The Fine Arts in the United States, with a sketch of their present and past History in Europe," The Knickerbocker, 14, July, 1839, 39-52.

"The Home of Washington," The Ladies' Repository, 14, March, 1854, 138.

Homes of American Statesmen, Hartford, 1855.

H[omespun]., H[enry]., Jr., "Original," The Plough Boy, 1, June 5, 1819, 1-2.

Howat, John K., "Washington Crossing the Delaware," The Metropolitan Museum of Art Bulletin, 26, March, 1968, 289-299.

Hughes, Rupert, George Washington, 3 vols., New York, 1926-1930.

Hunt, Leigh, "Put up a Picture in Your Room," The New-York Mirror, 20, August 13, 1842, 262.

Huntington, D., "Sketches of the Great Masters--Rembrandt," The Crayon, 1, January 17, 1855, 41.

Hutton, Ann Hawkes, Portrait of Patriotism, "Washington Crossing the Delaware," Philadelphia, 1959.

I[nman]., J[ohn]., "Washington's Death Bed," The Columbian Magazine, 5, May, 1846, 236-237.

[Inman, John], "Washington," The Columbian Magazine, 2, July, 1844, 23.

_____, "Washington Crossing the Allegheny," The Columbian Magazine, 2, November, 1844, 233.

Irving, Washington, The Life of George Washington, 5 vols., New York, 1855-1859.

"Irving's Life of Washington," The North American Review, 86, April, 1858, 330-358.

"Irving's Life of Washington," Putnam's Monthly, 6, July, 1855, 1-7.

Jaffe, Irma B., John Trumbull, Patriot-Artist of the American Revolution, Boston, 1975.

[Jarves, James Jackson], "Art and Artists of America," The Christian Examiner, 75, July, 1863, 114-127.

Jarves, James Jackson, The Art-Idea: Sculpture, Painting, and Architecture in America, 2nd Edition, New York, 1865.

Judson, L. Carroll, The Sages and Heroes of the American Revolution, Philadelphia, 1851; Port Washington, N.Y., 1970 Reprint.

Kammen, Michael, People of Paradox, New York, 1972.

Kaufmann, Ruth, "Henry IV and President Carter: The Loving Father as a Political Image," Arts Magazine, 51, March, 1977, 114-119.

Kelt, Joseph F., "Adolescence and Youth in Nineteenth-Century America," The Journal of Interdisciplinary History, 2, Autumn, 1971, 283-298.

Kennedy, E., "Mount Vernon--A Pilgrimage," The Southern Literary Messenger, 17, January, 1852, 53-57.

Kennedy, W. S., "Conditions of the Development of National Art," Cosmopolitan Art Journal, 3, September, 1859, 150-152.

Key to and Description of (by English, German, French and Spanish) "The Last Judgement"; A Scriptural Painting, by Rembrandt Lockwood, Newark, N.J., 1854.

Keyes, Donald, "A Working Checklist of the Non-Portrait Paintings by Tompkins Harrison Matteson (1813-1884)," Unpublished paper, n.d.

Kiefer, Monica, American Children Through Their Books 1700-1835, Philadelphia, 1948.

Kinnaird, Clark, George Washington, The Pictorial Biography, New York, 1967.

The Kirby Collection of Historical Paintings Located at Lafayette College, Easton, Pa., 1963.

Kirkland, Mrs. C. M., Memoirs of Washington, New York, 1857.

Knapp, Samuel L., Lectures on American Literature, with Remarks on Some Passages of American History, New York, 1829.

Lacour-Gayet, Robert, Everyday Life in the United States before the Civil War 1830-1860, Translated by Mary Ilford, New York, 1969.

"Lady Washington's Reception-Day," Harper's Weekly, 19, February 17, 1875, 178.

Lancaster, Bruce, The American Heritage Book of the Revolution, New York, 1958.

"The Landing of Columbus," The New-York Mirror, 14, January 7, 1837, 218.

Lane, David G., "A Son's Tribute," American Heritage, 17, February, 1966, 16-21, 85-87.

Lanman, Charles, "Correspondence--Our National Pictures," The Crayon, 1, February 28, 1855, 136-137.

_____, "On the Requisites for the Formation of a National School of Historical Painting," The Southern Literary Messenger, 14, December, 1848, 727-730.

_____, "Our Landscape Painters," The Southern Literary Messenger, 16, May, 1850, 272-280.

"The Last Day of the Fair," Philadelphia Inquirer, June 25, 1864, 2.

Lawall, David B., "American Painters as Book Illustrators, 1810-1870," The Princeton University Library Chronicle, 20, Autumn, 1958, 18-28.

Leslie, Frank, "Report of the Fine Arts," Reports of the United States Commissioners to the Paris Universal Exposition, 1867, Edited by William P. Blake, 1, Washington, D.C., 1870.

Lester, C. Edwards, The Artists of America: A Series of Biographical Sketches of American A-tists with Portraits and Designs on Steel, New York, 1846.

"Leutze's Washington at the Battle of Monmouth," The Crayon, 1, January 10, 1855, 22.

"Leutze's Washington," The Crayon, 1, January 31, 1855, 67-68.

Levey, Michael, Painting at Court, New York, 1971.

Levin, David, History as Romantic Art, New York, 1967.

Lewis, E. Anna, "Art and Artists of America," Graham's Magazine, 45, August, 1854, 140-144; October, 1854, 318-322.

"Lines on the Statue of Washington in the Capitol," The Southern Literary Messenger, 2, March, 1836, 253.

Lippard, George, Washington and His Generals: Or, Legends of the Revolution, Philadelphia, 1847.

_____, Washington and His Men: A New Series of Legends of the Revolution, New York, 1850.

"Literary Notices," Godey's Lady's Book, 54, June, 1857, 563.

Locquin, Jean, La peintre d'historie en France de 1747 à 1785, Paris, 1912.

Lossing, Benson J., Life of Washington, 3 vols., New York, 1860.

_____, Martha Washington, New York, 1861.

_____, Mount Vernon and Its Associations, Historical, Biographical, and Pictorial, New York, 1859.

_____, The Pictorial Field-Book of the Revolution, 2 vols., New York, 1860.

_____, Washington and the American Republic, 3 vols., New York, 1870.

Lovejoy, David S., "American Painting in Early 19th-Century Gift Books," The Art Quarterly, 7, Winter, 1955, 345-361.

Ludlow, Miss, A General View of the Fine Arts, New York, 1851.

Lynch, Anne C., "Washington Crossing the Alleghany," The Gift, Philadelphia, 1845, 277-278.

M. and M. Karolik Collection of American Paintings 1815 to 1865, Boston, 1949.

McCarty, William, Songs, Odes and Other Poems, on National Subjects, 3 vols., Philadelphia, 1842.

McCormick, Richard P., "Washington as A Hero," Reports and Abstracts of Proceedings of the Annual Meeting of the Washington Association of New Jersey, February 22, 1969, 17-28.

McCoubrey, John W., American Art 1700-1960: Sources and Documents, Englewood Cliffs, N.J., 1965.

McGroaty, William Buckner, "The Death of Washington," The Virginia Magazine of History and Biography, 54, April, 1946, 152-156.

McGuire, E. C., Religious Opinions and Character of Washington, New York, 1836.

[McHenry, James], The Wilderness; or, Braddock's Times, New Edition, Pittsburgh, 1848.

McRae, Sherwin, Washington: His Person as Represented by the Artists, Richmond, Va., 1873.

Marks, Arthur S., "Emanuel Leutze's Washington Crossing the Delaware," Talk presented at the Temple University Symposium "Aspects of Art in the Nineteenth Century," Philadelphia, April 2, 1974.

Marlor, Clark S., A History of the Brooklyn Art Association with an Index of Exhibitions, New York, 1970.

Marshall, John, The Life of George Washington, 5 vols., 1804-1807.

Matthiessen, F. O., American Renaissance: Art and Expression in the Age of Emerson and Whitman, New York, 1941.

Mayo, Bernard, Myths and Men: Patrick Henry, George Washington, Thomas Jefferson, Athens, Ga., 1959.

The Memory of Washington: An Oration by the Rev. Noah Hunt Schenck, A.M. Rector of Emmanuel Church, Delivered in Baltimore on the Evening of February 22, 1861, Baltimore, 1861.

Men and Times of the Revolution, Edited by Winslow C. Watson, London, 1856.

"Mere Mention: George Washington at Home," The Home Journal, November 26, 1859, 2.

"Mere Mention: The Home of Washington," The Home Journal, January 21, 1860, 2.

Midcentury America--Life in the 1850s, Edited by Carl Bode, Carbondale and Edwardsville, Ill., 1972.

Miller, Lillian B., "Painting, Sculpture, and the National Character, 1815-1860," Journal of American History, 53, March, 1967, 696-717.

_____, "Patronage, Patriotism, and Taste in Mid-Nineteenth Century America," Magazine of Art, 45, November, 1952, 322-328.

_____, Patrons and Patriotism, Chicago, 1966.

Minutes of the Philadelphia Society for the Promotion of Agriculture from Its Institution in February, 1785 to March, 1810, Philadelphia, 1854.

Mitchell, Charles, "Benjamin West's 'Death of General Wolfe' and the Popular History Piece," Journal of the Warburg and Courtauld Institutes, 7, 1944, 20-33.

"Modern French Painters." The North American Review, 74, January, 1852, 121-147.

Moore, Thomas, The Works of Byron: With His Letters and Journals, and His Life, 10, London, 1832.

Morgan, John Hill and Mantle Fielding, The Life Portraits of Washington and their Replicas, Philadelphia, 1931.

Morin, John Scott, An Oration Delivered Before the Washington Benevolent Society of Pennsylvania, Philadelphia, 1815.

Mott, Frank Luther, A History of American Magazines: 1741-1850, New York, 1930.

_____, A History of American Magazines: 1865-1880, Iowa City, 1928.

Mott, Kay, "Forgotten Painter," Philadelphia Inquirer Magazine, May 5, 1957, 12-13.

"Mount Vernon," The Columbian Magazine, 4, September, 1845, 139.

"Mount Vernon," The Columbian Magazine, 10, February, 1849, 87-88.

"Mount Vernon," Gleason's Pictorial Drawing-Room Companion, 5, October 29, 1853, 273.

Murdock, Myrtle Cheney, Constantino Brumidi, Michelangelo of the United States Capitol, Washington, D.C., 1950.

"National Academy Exhibition," Brother Jonathan, 5, May 6, 1843, 8.

"The National Academy of Design," The New-York Mirror, 14, June 17, 1837, 407.

"National Academy of Design," The Expositor, 1, May 18, 1839, 261-262.

"National Academy of Design," The New Mirror, 1, May 13, 1843, 94.

"The National Academy of Design Exhibition," The New-York Mirror, 19, May 22, 1841, 167.

The National Academy of Design Exhibition Records, Edited by Mary Bartlett Cowdrey, 2 vols., New York, 1943.

The National Academy of Design Exhibition Record 1861-1900, Edited by Maria Naylor, 2 vols., New York, 1973.

"A National Historical Museum and Portrait Gallery in New-York," New-York Times, 15, March 30, 1860, 5.

"National Paintings," The Opera Glass, 1, October 6, 1828, 33; October 13, 1828, 41; October 20, 1828, 49; November 3, 1828, 58.

"The National Portrait Gallery of Distinguished Americans," The New York Review, 4, April, 1839, 266.

"Nationality in Art," Cosmopolitan Art Journal, 1, March, 1857, 75-77.

Neal, John, Randolph, 2 vols., Philadelphia, 1823.

Neil, J. Meredith, Toward a National Taste, America's Quest for Aesthetic Independence, Honolulu, 1975.

Nevins, Allan, "The Emergence of Modern America, 1865-1875," The Historians' History of the United States, Edited by Andrew S. Berky and James P. Shenton, 2, New York, 1966, 806-815.

Nochlin, Linda, Realism, Harmondsworth, England, 1971.

Nourse, James D., Remarks on the Past and its Legacies to American Society, Louisville, 1847.

Novak, Barbara, "American Landscape: The Nationalist Garden and the Holy Book," Art in America, 60, February, 1972, 46-57.

Nye, Russel Blaine, Society and Culture in America, 1830-1860, New York, 1974.

_____, This Almost Chosen People, Essays in the History of American Ideas, East Lansing, Mich., 1966.

Observations on American Art, Selections from the Writings of John Neal (1793-1876), Edited by Harold Dickson, State College, Pa., 1943.

O'Connor, John, Jr., "Reviving a Forgotten Artist," The Carnegie Magazine, 11, September, 1938, 115-118.

One Hundred Early American Paintings, Exhibition catalogue, Ehrich
      Galleries, New York, 1918.

Orians, G. Harrison, "The Rise of Romanticism: 1805-1855," Transitions
      in American Literary History, Edited by Harry Hayden Clark, Durham,
      N.C., 1953, 163-244.

"Our Artists--No. II," Godey's Lady's Book, 33, September, 1846, 117-
      120.

"Our Artists and Their Critics," The New Path, 2, May, 1864, 3-7.

"Original Portraits of Washington," Putnam's Monthly, 6, October, 1855,
      336-349.

"Paintings for the Rotundo," Debates in Congress, 23 Cong., 2 Sess.,
      2, part 1, December 15, 1834, 791-795.

Palmer, Robert M., Washington and the Union, Harrisburg, 1861.

Paulding, James K., A Life of Washington, 2 vols., New York, 1836.

"Paulding's Washington," The Southern Literary Messenger, 2, May, 1836,
      396-399.

Pericles, Jonathan, "Letters on the Fine Arts--No. 14; Historical Art,"
      The New-Yorker, 10, November 21, 1840, 158-159.

Peter Frederick Rothermel's "The Republican Court in the Days of
      Lincoln," New York, n.d., Broadside Collection, The Library of
      Congress, Washington, D.C.

Peters, Harry T., America on Stone, Garden City, N.Y., 1931.

_____, Currier and Ives, Printmakers to the American People, 2,
      New York, 1931.

Phillips, William, "American History in the Novel, 1585-1900: The
      Colonial Period, 1585-1775," The Midwest Journal, 8, Spring-Fall,
      1956, 376-384.

Pierce, Bessie L., Civic Attitudes in American School Textbooks,
      Chicago, 1930.

Poore, Ben: Perley, "Waifs from Washington," Gleason's Pictorial
      Drawing-Room Companion, 4, February 12, 1853, 103.

_____, "Waifs from Washington," Gleason's Pictorial Drawing-Room
      Companion, 4, February 14, 1853, 123.

Popular Culture and Industrialism, 1865-1890, Edited by Henry Nash Smith, New York, 1967.

Praz, Mario, Conversation Pieces, University Park, 1971.

Prentiss, George L., Lesson of Encouragement from the Times of Washington, New York, 1863.

"The Prescription; or, the Beneficience of Washington," Godey's Lady's Book, 33, November, 1846, 193-194.

"The Present Condition of Historical Literature," The New-Yorker, 9, August 22, 1840, 365.

Priest, Joseph, A History of the Early Adventure of Washington among the Indians of the West, Albany, 1841.

"The Prince and the President," New York Herald, October 5, 1860, 6.

"The Prince in Boston," New York Times, 10, October 19, 1860, 4.

"The Prince of Wales," New York Herald, October 6, 1860, 10.

"The Prince of Wales at the Tomb of Washington," Harper's Weekly, 4, October 13, 1860, 642.

"The Prince's Visit to the United States," Times [London], October 23, 1860, 7.

"Progress of the Prince," Daily National Intelligencer, 48, October 20, 1860, 3.

Quimby, Ian M.G., "The Doolittle Engravings of the Battle of Lexington and Concord," Winterthur Portfolio, 4, 1968, 83-108.

Raglan, Lord, The Hero, London, 1936.

Raichle, Donald Roderic, "The Image of the Constitution in American History, A Study in Historical Writing From David Ramsey to John Fiske 1789-1888," Ph.D. Dissertation, Columbia University, 1956.

Ratcliff, Carter, "Americana," Art in America, January-February, 1977, 71-73.

Recollections and Private Memoirs of Washington, By His Adopted Son, George Washington Parke Custis, with a Memoir of the Author by His Daughter, Edited by Benson J. Lossing, Philadelphia, 1861.

Reed, Anna C., The Life of George Washington, Philadelphia, 1842.

Reed, Henry, "Address before the Art-Union of Philadelphia, May 7, 1849," Transactions of the Art-Union of Philadelphia. For the Year 1849, Philadelphia, 1849, 41-71.

Remington, Albert G., "The Influence of Art," Sartain's Magazine, 9, December, 1851, 473-476.

"Report of the U.S. Art Commissioners," The Crayon, 7, April, 1860, 106-109.

"Review of Modern Painters. By a Graduate of Oxford," The North American Review, 66, January, 1848, 110-145.

"Review of New Books," Graham's Magazine, 22, June, 1843, 367.

"A Revolutionary Patriot," The National Magazine, 12, June, 1858, 532-538.

Ricciotti, Dominic, "Popular Art in 'Godey's Lady's Book': An Image of the American Woman 1830-1860," Historical New Hampshire, 27, 1972, 3-26.

Richards, T. Addison, The Romance of American Landscape, New York, 1854.

Rogers, George, George Washington Crowned by "Equality, Fraternity and Liberty." A Democratic Poem, New York, 1849.

"The Romance of the Colonies," The Nassau Literary Magazine, 9, October, 1849, 37-43.

Romanticism in America, Edited by George Boas, Baltimore, 1940.

Rosenblum, Robert, Transformations in Late Eighteenth Century Art, Princeton, 1967.

Rossiter, T. P., A Description of the Picture of the Home of Washington After the War. Painted by T. P. Rossiter and L. R. Mignot. With Historical Sketches of the Personages Introduced, New York, 1859.

_____, "Mount Vernon, Past and Present," The Crayon, 5, September, 1858, 243-253.

_____, "Plan for a National School of Art," The Crayon, 5, October, 1858, 299.

"Rossiter Art Sale," New-York Tribune, 32, February 7, 1873, 5.

Rowland, Benjamin, Jr., "Popular Romanticism: Art and the Gift Books, 1825-1865," The Art Quarterly, 20, Winter, 1957, 364-381.

Rudisill, Richard, Mirror Image, The Influence of the Daguerreotype on American Society, Albuquerque, 1971.

Rush, Richard, Washington in Domestic Life, Philadelphia, 1857.

Rutledge, Anna Wells, Artists in the Life of Charleston through Colony and State from Restoration to Reconstruction, Philadelphia, 1949.

Sanford, Charles L., The Quest for Paradise: Europe and the American Moral Imagination, Urbana, Ill., 1961.

Saum, Lewis O., "Death in the Popular Mind of Pre-Civil War America," Death in America, Edited by David E. Stannard, Philadelphia, 1975, 30-48.

Savoie, Adelaide H., "A Biographical Sketch of Thomas P. Rossiter," Unpublished paper for the Department of Art, The George Washington University, January, 1968, The National Collection of Fine Arts, Washington, D.C.

Schorsch, Anite, Mourning Becomes America, Exhibition catalogue, Pennsylvania Historical and Museum Commission, Harrisburg, 1976.

Schroeder, John Frederick, Life and Times of Washington, 2 vols., New York, 1857-1861.

Sears, Robert, Pictorial History of the United States, New York, 1846.

_____, A New and Popular Pictorial Description of the United States, New York, 1848.

Shinn, Earl [Edward Strahan], The Art Treasures of America, being the Choicest Works of Art in the Public and Private Collections of North America, Philadelphia, 1879.

The Signing of the Constitution. Sept. 17, 1787. A Study Sketch, Painted by Thomas P. Rossiter, N.A. Washington, D.C., 1867, Etting Collection, The Historical Society of Pennsylvania, Philadelphia.

Simoni, John P., "Art Critics and Criticism in Nineteenth-Century America," Ph.D. Dissertation, Ohio State University, 1953.

Sketch of Washington and His Family to Accompany An Engraving, by William Sartain, from a Painting by Schussele, Philadelphia, 1865.

"Sketchings--Art of the Capitol, Washington," The Crayon, 5, October, 1858, 295-296.

"Sketchings--Domestic Art Gossip," The Crayon, 4, April, 1857, 121-124.

"Sketchings--Domestic Art Gossip," The Crayon, 6, May, 1859, 158-161.

"Sketchings--Domestic Art Gossip," The Crayon, 6, July, 1859, 220-221.

"Sketchings--Domestic Art Gossip," The Crayon, 6, October, 1859, 318-321.

"Sketchings--Domestic Art Gossip," The Crayon, 8, July, 1861, 151.

Slavin, Barbara J., "Thompkins Harrison Matteson: Illustrator of Mid-Nineteenth Century America," M.A. Thesis, State University of New York College at Oneonta, 1969.

Smith, "The World of Art," The New World, 1, November 2, 1839, n.p.

Smith, Henry Nash, Virgin Land, New York, 1950.

Smith, Seba, "Examples of Female Heroism," Godey's Lady's Book, 27, December, 1843, 267-269.

Somkin, Fred, The Unquiet Eagle: Memory and Desire in the Idea of American Freedom, 1815-1860, Ithaca, N.Y., 1967.

Sparks, Jared, The Life of George Washington, Boston, 1843.

_____, The Writings of George Washington, Boston, 1837.

Spencer, Benjamin, The Quest for Nationality: An American Literary Campaign, Syracuse, N.Y., 1957.

Spencer, J. A., History of the United States, 3 vols., New York, 1858.

"The Spirit of the Morning Press," Evening Star, 16, October 23, 1860, 2.

Stauffer, David McNealy, American Engravers Upon Copper and Steel, 2 vols., New York, 1907, Supplement by Mantle Fielding, 1917.

Stehle, Raymond L., "The Düsseldorf Gallery of New York," The New-York Historical Society Quarterly, 58, October, 1974, 305-314.

_____, "Washington Crossing the Delaware," Pennsylvania History, 31, July, 1964, 269-294.

Stober, Laura, "Daniel Huntington's History Paintings: A Survey," Unpublished paper for the Department of Art History, The Graduate Center, The City University of New York, 1975.

Stone, Horatio, Inaugural Address, Delivered February 24, 1857, and An Address on National Art, before the Washington Art Association, February 10, 1858, Washington, D.C., 1858.

Strauss, Betty Isla, "The Memorial Iconography of George Washington," M.A. Thesis, University of Delaware, 1966.

Le Style Troubadour, Exhibition catalogue, Musée de Ain Brou, Ville de Boug-en-Bresse, 1971.

Sussman, Warren I., "History and the American Intellectual: Uses of a Usable Past," The American Experience, Edited by Hennig Cohen, Boston, 1968, 84-105.

Tarr, Augustus DeKalb, The American Reader of Prose and Poetry, Philadelphia, 1860.

Thompkins H. Matteson 1813-1884, Exhibition catalogue, Sherburne Art Society, Sherburne, N.Y., 1949.

Tillim, Sidney, "Notes on Narrative and History Painting," Artforum, 15, May, 1977, 41-43.

Todd, Ruthven, "Benjamin West vs. the History Picture," Magazine of Art, 41, December, 1948, 301-305.

Tomes, Robert, Battles of America by Sea and Land, 3 vols., New York, 1861.

Transactions of the American Art-Union, New York, 1844-1850.

Transactions of the Apollo Association, New York, 1839-1843.

The Trenton Battle Monument Eakins Bronzes, Edited by Zoltan Buki and Suzanne Corlette, Trenton, 1973.

"The Trumbull Gallery and its Founder," The New-Yorker, 10, October 17, 1840, 76.

Trussell, John B. B., Jr., Epic on the Schuylkill, The Valley Forge Encampment, 1777-1778, Harrisburg, 1974.

Tuckerman, Henry T., Book of the Artists, New York, 1867.

_____, Essays, Biographical and Critical, Boston, 1857.

"Twenty-Sixth Exhibition of the National Academy of Design," Bulletin of the American Art-Union, May, 1851, 21-23.

Tyack, David, "Forming the National Character: Paradox in the Educational Thought of the Revolutionary Generation," Harvard Educational Review, 36, 1966, 29-41.

Tyson, J. R., Address Delivered before the Washington Art Association, Philadelphia, 1858.

The Union of States: An Oration before the Order of United Americans, at the Academy of Music, New York, Feb. 22, 1855, on the Occasion of the Celebration of the One Hundred & Twenty-Third Anniversary of the Birthday of Washington, by the Hon. Thomas R. Whitney, New York, 1855.

The United States Capitol, An Annotated Bibliography, Edited by John R. Kerwood, Norman, Okla., 1973.

The Valuable Collection of Engravings, Etchings, Paintings, Antique Furniture, Armor, Bronzes, Rich Brocades, Draperies, Costumes, Etc., A Valuable Library, the Studio, Furniture Stock of Artists' Materials, Etc., Etc. Belonging to the late Thomas Prichard Rossiter, Esq., George A. Leavitt and Co., Auctioneers, Clinton Hall, New York, February 5-8, 1873.

Van Alstyne, Richard W., "American Nationalism and Its Mythology," Queen's Quarterly, 65, Autumn, 1958, 423-436.

Van Tassel, David D., "Benson J. Lossing: Pen and Pencil Historian," American Quarterly, 6, Spring, 1954, 32-44.

_____, Recording America's Past, Chicago, 1960.

Verplanck, Gulian C., Discourses and Addresses in Subjects of American History, Arts and Literature, New York, 1833.

"The Vignette," The New-York Mirror, 10, July 7, 1832, 1.

"Visits to the Painters by An Amateur," Godey's Lady's Book, 29, December, 1844, 277-278.

W., "Development of Nationality in American Art," Bulletin of American Art-Union, December, 1851, 137-139.

"Washington," American Magazine of Useful and Entertaining Knowledge, 2, March, 1836, 265-266.

"Washington," Evening Post, 59, October 6, 1860, 2.

"Washington and His Generals," The American Review: A Whig Journal of Politics, Literature, Art and Science, 5, May, 1847, 517-534.

Washington and the Principles of the Revolution--An Oration delivered before the Municipal Authorities of Boston at the Celebration of the Seventy-Fourth Anniversary of the Declaration of American Independence, July 4, 1850, by Edwin P. Whipple, Boston, 1850.

Washington and the Revolutionary Campaigns. Painted by Mr. John M'Nevin, New York, 1859.

Washington at the Battle of Monmouth. A National Historical Painting, by E. Leutze, New York, 1854.

"Washington at Monmouth," American Heritage, 16, June, 1965, 14-15.

"Washington Crossing the Allegheny," The Columbian Magazine, 2, November, 1844, 233.

"Washington Delivering his Inaugural Address," The Literary World, 4, May 5, 1849, 400.

"Washington Delivering his Inaugural Address," The Literary World, 4, May 19, 1849, 435.

"Washington in Domestic Life. From Original Letters and Manuscripts. by Richard Rush. Philadelphia, 1857," The Historical Magazine, 1, June, 1857, 191.

Washington Eulogies: A Checklist of Eulogies and Funeral Orations on the Death of George Washington, December, 1799-February, 1800, Compiled by Margaret Bingham Stillwell, New York, 1916.

Washington Receiving his Mother's Last Blessing. Painted by W. H. Powell, engraved by Henry Cousins, New York, 1864.

"The Washington Tableaux," Daily Journal [Wilmington, N.C.], 10, October 1, 1860, 2-3.

"Washington Taking Farewell of His Mother," The Illustrated Magazine of Art, 4, 1854, 73-74.

"Washington's Early Days," Putnam's Monthly, 3, January, 1854, 1-10; February, 1854, 123-134.

"Washington's First Interview with Mrs. Custis," Godey's Lady's Book, 32, April, 1846, 145-146.

"Washington's Marriage," The Ladies' Repository, 9, January, 1849, 4-5.

"Washington's Marriage in 1759," Alexandrian Gazette, 49, September 30, 1848, 2.

W[aterston]., R[obert]. C., American Art and Art Unions, Cambridge, Mass., 1850.

Wector, Dixon, The Hero in America, New York, 1941.

Weems, Mason Locke, The Life of George Washington, Edited by Marcus Cunliffe, Cambridge, Mass., 1962.

[Weld, Horatio Hastings], Life of George Washington, Philadelphia, 1845.

Wellford, Beverly, Jr., "Address Delivered Before the Ladies' Mount Vernon Association, July 4, 1855," The Southern Literary Messenger, 21, September, 1855, 562-566.

White, R. G., "Something about our Painters," The American Review: A Whig Journal of Politics, Literature, Art and Science, 4, August, 1846, 180-187.

"The Wilderness," The North American Review, 19, July, 1824, 209-223.

Williams, Hermann Warner, Jr., Mirror to the American Past, Greenwich, Conn., 1973.

Willson, Marcius, Juvenile American History, for Primary Schools, Revised edition, New York, 1847.

Wind, Edgar, "Penny, West, and the 'Death of Wolfe'," Journal of the Warburg and Courtauld Institutes, 10, 1947, 159-162.

_____, "The Revolution of History Painting," Journal of Warburg Institute, 2, October, 1938, 116-127.

Wineberger, J. A., Tomb of Washington at Mount Vernon, embracing a full and accurate description of Mount Vernon, as well as of the birthplace, genealogy, character, marriage, and last illness of Washington, together with incidents pertaining to the burial of Washington, Washington, D.C., 1858.

Wishy, Bernard, The Child and the Republic, Philadelphia, 1968.

Woodness, James, "American History in the Novel, 1585-1900: The Revolution and Early National Periods, 1775-1815," The Midwest Journal, 8, Spring-Fall, 1956, 385-392.

Woodward, William E., George Washington, The Image and the Man, New York, 1926.

Worcester, Samuel, A Fourth Book of Lessons for Reading, Boston, 1842.

The Works of Daniel Webster, 16th edition, 1, Boston, 1872.

The Works of James Buchanan, Edited by John Bassett Moore, 2, Philadelphia and London, 1910.

The Works of Jonathan Richardson, Supplement to Walpole's Anecdotes of Painters and Sculptors, London, 1792.

A Wounded Soldier, "Recollections of the Fair in New York.-No. 2," Our Daily Fare, June 10, 1864, 18.

[Wylie, T. W. J.],Washington. A Discourse Preached Feb. 23, 1862 in the First Reformed Presbyterian Church, Philadelphia, by the Pastor, Philadelphia, 1862.

Ziff, Norman, "Paul Delaroche: A Study in Nineteenth-Century French History Painting," Ph.D. Dissertation, New York University, 1974.

Manuscript Material

American Art-Union Papers and Clipping Book, The New-York Historical Society, New York.

Archives of the Pennsylvania Academy of the Fine Arts, Philadelphia.

Custis Family Papers, The Library of Congress, Washington, D.C.

The Diary of Joseph Sill, The Historical Society of Pennsylvania, Philadelphia.

Etting Collection, The Historical Society of Pennsylvania, Philadelphia.

Dreer Collection of American Artists, The Historical Society of Pennsylvania, Philadelphia.

Jackson Collection, The Historical Society of Pennsylvania, Philadelphia.

Society Collection, The Historical Society of Pennsylvania, Philadelphia.

Thomas P. Rossiter Files, Independence National Historical Park, Philadelphia.

Verplanck Papers, The New-York Historical Society, New York.

Addendum:

Bacon, Rev. Henry, "Ideas from Pictures," Gleason's Pictorial Drawing-Room Companion, 4, July 9, 1853, 23.